Law in Antebellum Society:
Legal Change
and Economic Expansion

BORZOI BOOKS IN LAW AND AMERICAN SOCIETY

Law in Antebellum Society: Legal Change and Economic Expansion

Jamil Zainaldin

ALFRED A. KNOPF   NEW YORK

This book was originally developed as part of an American Bar Association program on law and humanities with major funding from the National Endowment for the Humanities and additional support from the Exxon Education Foundation and Pew Memorial Trust. The ABA established this program to help foster improved understanding among undergraduates of the role of law in society through the creation of a series of volumes in law and humanities. The ABA selected a special advisory committee of scholars, lawyers, and jurists (Commission on Undergraduate Education in Law and the Humanities) to identify appropriate topics and select writers. This book is a revised version of the volume first published by the ABA. However, the writer, and not the American Bar Association, individual members and committees of the Commission, the National Endowment for the Humanities, Exxon Education Foundation, or Pew Memorial Trust, bears sole responsibility for the content, analysis, and conclusion contained herein.

THIS IS A BORZOI BOOK
PUBLISHED BY ALFRED A. KNOPF, INC.

First Edition

9 8 7 6 5 4 3 2 1

Copyright © 1983 by Alfred A. Knopf, Inc.

LIBRARY OF CONGRESS CATALOGING IN PUBLICATION DATA

Zainaldin, Jamil S., 1948–
    Law in antebellum society.

    (Borzoi books in law and American society)
    Bibliography: p.
    Includes index.
    1. Law—United States—History and criticism.
    . Title. II. Series.
KF366.Z34 1983   349.73'09   83–51
                        347.3009

ISBN 0-394-33196-6 (Paperbound)   394-33580-5 (Casebound)

Manufactured in the United States of America

TO THE STUDENTS OF HISTORY C-14,
NORTHWESTERN UNIVERSITY, 1976-1978

Preface

This book attempts to convey some of the excitement and richness of nineteenth-century American legal history. There is no attempt to provide an overview or survey of the field; that has already been done (see the bibliographical essay). Rather, *Law in Antebellum Society* elaborates on a few important themes that have guided the work of historians and others writing in the field of law and society. Reflecting the strengths of the now considerable body of published research, its focus is on legal change and economic expansion during the first half of the nineteenth century. My premise is that law matters—that any study of the history of society must account for how people use law to shape events and control the directions of social change. For law is power, and like all instruments of power it is self-consciously used to promote or defend objectives that are essentially political in nature. My goal, then, is to show that law is anything but inanimate. It is a living embodiment of human struggle and conflict, and often of noble aspiration. Law is at the center of much of our society's life: its politics, its economics, its social and familial life, and, perhaps most important, its values.

My indebtedness to the prodigious research and insights of many historians should be evident in the book. But I would like to acknowledge, in particular, the contribution of the following individuals: Richard E. Ellis, R. Kent Newmyer, Leonard W. Levy, J. Willard Hurst, Lawrence M. Friedman, Bernard Schwartz, Harry N. Scheiber, Oscar Handlin and the late Mary Flug Handlin, Stuart Bruchey, Douglass North, Morton J. Horwitz, William Nelson, Maxwell Bloomfield, the late Alfred Kelly, Winfred Harbison, and my mentor and my friend, Stanley N. Katz.

I would also like to thank the members of the history panel of the National Commission on Undergraduate Education in Law and the Humanities, including Gerald Fetner, Stephen Botein, John L. Thomas, Jonathan Lurie, and George Dargo, who gave support and guidance, and the National Endowment for the Humanities for a grant to undertake the writing. Herman Belz, Harry Scheiber, Stephen Presser, Paul Finkelman, Douglas Jones, Rayman Solomon, Thomas Bender, and William Cooper, Jr., read the essay and offered many valuable suggestions for improving it.

The cases examined in document sections 2, 3, and 4 also appear in revised form in Stephen B. Presser and Jamil S. Zainaldin, *Law and American History: Cases and Materials* (1980). I would like to express my appreciation to West Publishing Company for their cooperation.

I have learned that the best test of an idea's worth is the ability to communicate it and endow it with some meaning for people. And if this book should prove of any worth, I would like to dedicate it to my undergraduate students of History C-14, Northwestern University, 1976–1978.

I alone am responsible for any errors of fact, interpretation, or omission that may appear in this book.

JAMIL ZAINALDIN

Contents

Essay

Documents

Law in Antebellum Society:
Legal Change
and Economic Expansion

Essay

Introduction

During the first half of the nineteenth century, America was a boundless society. Energy, vitality, impatience with restrictions, a measured scorn for old ways, and an embellishment of the new were features of the American character that most impressed European visitors and observers. Alexis de Tocqueville captured this spirit in his classic *Democracy in America*, portraying a society impelled by visions of freedom and limitless opportunity; a nation cut loose from the traditional moorings of family, community, church, and aristocracy. Tocqueville also saw a troubling side. In freedom was a potential for anarchy, in equalitarianism, a vulnerability to demagogic dictatorship, in the urge for improvement and material acquisition, an underside of greed. To Tocqueville and others, the enslavement and inhuman exploitation of one race by another was a dark specter of hidden contradictions.

The contrasts between antebellum America and our own time are sharp, for we must learn to live with a shrinking economic pie, limitations on opportunity, and an uncertain future. Antebellum Americans looking back on life in prerevolutionary America must also have been struck by a sense of a world apart. Richard Hofstadter, building on the new social history in *America at 1750: A Social Portrait* (1971), described a society that was becoming settled, almost rigid in its economy, demography, and class structure. The colonies of the eighteenth century were commercially developed, but they were also mindful of the limits that geography, social values, international politics, and trade restrictions placed on their physical and economic growth. They had become the outgrown children of empire, restless yet chained.

1

Historians have long debated the causes and consequences of the American Revolution. Certainly the Revolution burst the legal and constitutional bonds of dependence on England. More deeply, the experience of revolution infected Americans with a new self-consciousness. To be sure, this new self-consciousness preceded 1776. Americans for some time had been aware of the derivative nature of their society and of the anomaly of their status in the empire. But it had been an awareness fraught with ambivalence about the future. As Bernard Bailyn has brilliantly shown, this changed in the revolutionary era. The political and intellectual justifications of revolution gave rise to a uniquely American logic—and confidence—about the purpose of government and the ends of society.[1]

The Revolution did not end with the peace of 1783. Once launched, the heady prospect of remaking society anew took on a momentum of its own. The implications of 1776—who should rule and to what end—were played out, first, in the debates over the ratification of the federal Constitution and, later, in the sharp ideological clashes between the Federalists and the Republicans at both the state and national levels. It was not until about 1815 that some of the most fundamental questions raised by the Revolution seemed to be settled. A new consensus and a new generation of leaders had begun to emerge that found a meaning for the Revolution and set a course for the future. This consensus included a commitment to republican forms of government and the value of individual liberty. In the process, political ideology had become inseparable from matters of economy. The true glory of the republic, it was commonly believed, lay in its vast productive potential, in the development of its physical resources, and in the ingenuity of a people set free—a vision lyrically captured in the nation's poetry, where metaphors of movement, freedom, and action abound. Walt Whitman, in *Leaves of Grass* (1855), imagined the United States as essentially "poetical," and of its people he wrote:

> In the history of the earth hitherto the largest and most stirring appear tame and orderly to their ampler largeness and stir. Here at last is something in the doings of man that corresponds with the broadcast doings of the day and night. Here is not merely a nation but a teeming nation of nations. Here is action untied from strings necessarily blind to particulars and details magnificently moving in vast masses. . . . Here are the roughs and beards and space and ruggedness and nonchalance that the soul loves.[2]

[1] Bernard Bailyn, *The Ideological Origins of the American Revolution* (1967).
[2] *Leaves of Grass* (1968 ed.), pp. 709–710.

Until recent years, historians had not fully grasped the ways in which law was part of this process. The reluctance of historians to engage in the historical study of law stems from the vastness and the seemingly mysterious nature of law itself. There are the institutions of law: the courts of the separate states and of the federal government, state and national legislatures, executive branch agencies, and the state and national constitutions. And there is the substance of law: the decisions of the U.S. Supreme Court, the common law of the states (the decisions of courts based on prior judicial determinations), and the substance of legislation at the national and state levels. Then all these must be set in motion through time: the complex action and interactions of law must be explained and linked to developments in the society if we are to gain a perspective on the role of law. Not surprisingly, the task of writing legal history seemed better suited to lawyers, the trained technicians of law, than to historians. The development of law described from within the terse microstudy of the evolution of legal doctrine necessarily produced a truncated history of law. In a brilliant essay on the "common-law tradition" in American legal-historical scholarship, Robert Gordon has shown that lawyers brought to their research and writing the pedagogical and intellectual concerns unique to their profession. Their histories mirrored their law: they were complex, not easily accessible to the mind untrained in law, and divorced from any social context. Law was pictured as "evolving" according to its own internal logic.[3]

Today, the picture has vastly improved. Historians, and historically minded lawyers, are now literally rewriting America's legal history. Lawrence M. Friedman's *A History of American Law* (1973) was the first general and readable survey of law in American history, and his work is distinguished by what it has to say about law *and* society. This book attempts to convey to the reader some of the spirit of this new—and the best of the older—work. Its focus is on law, public policy, and economic expansion in the first half of the nineteenth century, an era in the history of law that Morton Horwitz has called "transformational." "Law" is meant to include the activities of legislatures and courts; and the "policy" of law

---

[3] Robert Gordon, "J. Willard Hurst and the Common Law Tradition in American Legal Historiography," *Law & Society Review,* 10 (1975), 9. See also Morton J. Horwitz, "The Conservative Tradition in the Writing of American Legal History," *American Journal of Legal History,* 17, (1973), 275. There are important exceptions, of course. J. Willard Hurst, professor emeritus of the University of Wisconsin Law School, and Richard B. Morris, professor emeritus of the department of history of Columbia University, are examples of a legal educator and a historian whose works are of towering importance in legal history.

refers to the definite course or method of action, selected from among competing alternatives, that embraces a general goal.

The starting point of that era is the judicial reform that occurred in the states during the period from 1790 to 1815. A key feature of antebellum law was its open-endedness, its rough character, and its capacity for being molded by legislators and judges to fulfill broad social and economic goals. But before there could be a creative manipulation and expansion of law, the conception of law as a valid instrument of public policy would first have to be established. Courts and legislatures have always made policy. What was new in the nineteenth century was the dominance of considerations of the "public good" and "public welfare" in so much of the nation's judicial and legislative decision making. Moreover, the formulation of policy to encompass a wide range of social and economic behavior was seen as an appropriate function for legal agencies. Chapter 1 attempts to explain how and why this occurred in the early years of the republic, setting the stage for the subsequent chapters that examine how courts and legislatures used their new power.

The early leadership role of the national government in the physical and economic expansion of the nation is the subject of Chapter 2. In the opening decades of the century, individual states lacked the financial and constitutional bases needed to fulfill what increasingly was being described as the nation's God-given destiny to spread out across the continent. The federal government, acting on the very terms of the Constitution, responded by embarking on ambitious internal improvement projects, by disposing of public lands, by granting (through the Supreme Court) privileges and protection to private property owners and entrepreneurial capital. There were limits, however, to what the federal government could do. Moreover, after 1820, the very idea of national stewardship became discredited, mired in the bog of sectionalism and a victim of the aggressive economic individualism that its policies had helped establish.

As the prospects of national stewardship dimmed, and with the gradual development of the states' internal economies, state governments became involved in society and in the economy as never before, as described in Chapter 3. Like their colonial predecessors, state governments had always been active. But now they were motivated by a new commonwealth theory of state power that placed positive responsibilities and obligations on legislatures. By regulating economic behavior, by building an infrastructure, by protecting the free market, and by encouraging capital accumulation through the creation of new corporate forms, the state legislatures "liberated" popular energy, helping people to do what they could not accomplish on their own. The long-term implications of antebellum public policy for social and economic inequality and for corporate nonaccountability to the public interest, are the subject of the chapter's conclusion.

State courts and the transformation of the common law are the subject of Chapter 4. The ends of antebellum common law reinforced those of state legislation. Judges created new rules of law in areas of contract, torts, private property, and domestic relations that gave maximum effect to the assertion of individual will. They enlarged the possibilities of private action in the economy by redefining personal rights. Like the legislatures, a new theory of decision making supported an expansive policy-making role for courts. Creative lawmaking was justified as an extension of the popular will. By the eve of the Civil War, the courts had moved into a position of unprecedented power, fully rivaling state legislative power in allocating rights among individuals and between individuals and the state. The extent to which courts were "neutral," as they claimed, producing egalitarian results and the corrosive impact that antebellum common law would have on centralized state power and planning in the post-Civil War industrial era are discussed at the end of the chapter.

The special focus of this volume on economic and physical expansion means that some issues that are of critical importance in American legal history—civil liberties, the rise of the penitentiary, issues of church and state, the history of the legal profession, and the law of slavery—are not treated. A guide to further reading appears in the bibliographic essay.

ONE

The State Legal Systems

Early Constitutions and the Common Law

Compared to modern third-world revolutionary movements, the American Revolution appears distinctive in its emphasis on law and constitutionalism. The great events leading up to 1776 read like a series of legal disputes. In the colonies, each new act of Parliament called forth a train of opposition in the form of learned discourses on legal rights and constitutional theory. Patriots were equally at home in the complexities of the English common law, culling ancient treatises and precedent books for decisional authority in support of colonial liberties. It was in typical colonial fashion that the lawyer James Otis, in the celebrated *Writs of Assistance* case (1761), used a 1610 English court decision, *Bonham's* case, to reach the conclusion that a statute of Parliament "against the Constitution is Void."[1]

The American Revolution, then, was a legal as well as a social or political phenomenon. To Edmund Burke, England's great political thinker, this came as no great surprise. "In no country, perhaps in the world," he had earlier said, "is the law so general a study. The profes-

[1] On the opposition pamphlet literature, see Bernard Bailyn, *Ideological Origins of the American Revolution* (1967), and Bernard Bailyn (ed.), *Pamphlets of the American Revolution, 1750–1776* (1965–). Background to the *Writs of Assistance* case appears in M. H. Smith, *The Writs of Assistance Case* (1978), and Stephen B. Presser and Jamil S. Zainaldin, *Law and American History: Cases and Materials* (1980), pp. 33, 61–89.

sion itself is numerous and powerful, and in most provinces takes the lead." Nor was the discussion of law and liberty limited to circles of lawyers. "All who read, and most do, endeavor to obtain some smattering of that science."[2] Burke may have been thinking of Sir William Blackstone's *Commentaries on the Laws of England* (1765-1767), which, astoundingly, sold almost as many copies in America as in England.[3]

While patriots were quick to use the sources of English constitutional thought and common law as a bulwark in the defense of liberty, consensus faded when they began the task of constructing governments for the new states.[4] To some extent, the ideology of the Revolution supplied a rich resource of ideas. Constitutions appeared in each of the states guaranteeing "fundamental rights" and delineating the powers of the separate executive, legislative, and judicial branches of government. That these constitutions were written, like the earlier colonial charters, and subject to legislative approval or popular ratification, was itself an important departure from the experience in England. Certainly there was much in the new state constitutions that was bold and innovative.[5] A no less important task though was the reorganization of the legal system.

Most of the states simply enacted legislation that perpetuated, with slight modifications in form, their antecedent colonial judical systems.[6] But there were still numerous important questions that remained to be answered. What portion of the English common law should be retained, decisions of judges (as distinct from legislation) which had the force of law "common to the realm"? What statutes enacted by the colonial legislatures still applied? Would English legislation have force in the states? Perhaps most important, what authority and role should be ascribed to courts? Should courts and judges be protected from the pressures of public opinion, or should they remain ever attentive to the people's will?

[2] Quoted in Francis R. Aumann, *The Changing American Legal System: Some Selected Phases* (1969 ed.), pp. 29-30.

[3] A "commentary" is a treatise that purports to summarize and present legal rules and maxims in an area of law. A commentary by a distinguished jurist or legal scholar may be cited by courts as evidence of what the law is; but a commentary is not of itself a binding authority of law. Blackstone's commentaries were extraordinarily influential in England and in America in the late eighteenth and early nineteenth centuries. They were superseded in America by James Kent's commentaries.

[4] Elisha P. Douglass, *Rebels and Democrats: The Struggle for Equal Political Rights and Majority Rule During the American Revolution* (1955).

[5] Gordon S. Wood, *The Creation of the American Republic: 1776-1787* (1969), pp. 125-256, and sections of J. Willard Hurst, *The Growth of American Law: The Law Makers* (1950).

[6] Benjamin F. Wright, "The Early History of Written Constitutions in America," in *Essays in History and Political Theory in Honor of Charles H. McIlwaine* (1936), pp. 344-371.

Should judges be appointed or elected, and should they serve for fixed terms or for life? What power should the jury have in determining what did, or did not, constitute the law of a state? To what extent should the legal system be dependent on the existence of trained lawyers? These were wrenching questions, for they touched on the most basic issue of who should rule in society. It was perhaps for this reason that these questions remained unanswered for so long.

The push to resolve these issues had begun in some states by 1790, and it gained momentum with Thomas Jefferson's election to the presidency in 1800. Following an extremely divisive and politically virulent era of Federalist rule at the national level, in the first decade of the nineteenth century, the future of the republic seemed more assured. It was now possible to look back and wonder if existing American law and legal institutions did not owe too much to England. As one reformer had asked, were the state judiciaries and the common law really nothing more than an "engine of oppression," a "badge and momento of our dependence"? Jefferson himself signaled an opening in the discussion about the means and ends of law, and in particular the validity of vast portions of America's common law, when he shifted his ground and derided the "doctrine that we brought with us from England the Common Law rights." In truth, "we brought with us the rights of men."[7]

Much of the debate over legal and judicial reform in the new republic took place in the popular press, in the state legislatures, and in the constitutional conventions called to revise the now aging frameworks of government in the older states. By 1815 most of the reform was completed. At stake, as Richard E. Ellis has so well shown, were opposing visions of government and society, the outcome of which was bound to influence the course of legal change and economic expansion in America.[8]

Judicial Reform, 1800–1815

Three political groups participated in the state and national discussions of reform. At one extreme were the radical Republicans, an offshoot of the

[7] Jefferson to John Tyler, June 17, 1812, in Tyler, *Letters and Times of the Tylers*, vol. 1 (1884), p. 265; quoted in Bernard Schwartz, *The Law in America: A History* (1974), p. 11.
[8] The analysis in the following section of the text is based on Richard E. Ellis, *The Jeffersonian Crisis: Courts and Politics in the Young Republic* (1971), especially pts. 2 and 3. See also Aumann, *Changing American Legal System*, pp. 67–94, and Fletcher M. Green, *Constitutional Development in the South Atlantic States, 1766–1860* (1930). The texts of the state constitutions can be found in Francis N. Thorpe (ed.), *The Federal and State Constitutions . . .* (1909).

new Jeffersonian Republican party. The radicals were agrarian-minded and antielitist; they tended to be active in evangelical reform movements and were deeply suspicious of a rational form in religion. The radicals were strongest in the rural regions of the country, in the settlements removed from urban centers and networks of transportation. Their ranks were composed predominantly of farmers with little or no formal education, and they were only marginally, if at all, involved in the market economy. Radicals were vocal in all states, but they were most visible in Pennsylvania, Kentucky, and Virginia.

As a political group, radicals were opposed to unnecessary government structures, preferring instead to keep power as localized and decentralized as possible. Because power was viewed as inherently corrupting, government was seen as an evil necessity at best. A Kentucky pamphleteer captured the essence of the radicals' fears when he said that "The business of government is a cheat. For what do you think men are to understand by governing a country? Is it not to get good salaries and keep common people in subjection? . . . government is nothing but playing rogue by authority of law."[9]

The radicals' fear of concentrated power and "governors" influenced their attitudes toward the existing courts and the legal profession. They envisioned a judicial system that would be under the direct control of the people. They worked, therefore, for the frequent election and rotation of judges; for the abolition of appellate courts,[10] which symbolized a distant and arbitrary check on popular rule, and for the creation of a vast and affordable trial court system that would make justice available to all.

Their sharpest ire was reserved for the common law and the lawyers who depended on it for their living. Lawyers were viciously and variously described as "parasites," "leeches," "swindlers," "sharpers," and "plunderers." They preyed on the ignorance of the people, stirred up law suits, and fattened their fees by confusing the legal issues and delaying court proceedings. The adversarial process, a basic ingredient of the common-law system,[11] was roundly criticized as pitting neighbor against neighbor, and permitting cases to turn upon clever arguments. It fanned the flames of hostility and resentment by placing the value of conflict

---

[9] *Kentucky Gazette,* October 15, 1791; quoted in Ellis, *Jeffersonian Crisis,* p. 124.

[10] An appellate court possesses the power to review the proceedings of another court, usually a lower one.

[11] The adversarial process is the trial or appellate judicial action in which there are two opposing parties, plaintiff and defendant (the plaintiff is the party initiating the case against the defendant), who are usually represented by attorneys. Each party is given a full opportunity to present and establish its contentions or arguments before a judge, a judge and jury, or a panel of judges.

above the value of conciliation and arbitration. At the root of the legal system's problems was the common law, denigrated as a "relic of feudal tyranny" and a "hodge-podge of mystery." Because the common law consisted of a seemingly endless number of precedents stemming back hundreds of years, it was seen as susceptible to manipulation by lawyers and judges to justify practically any legal proposition. "If one asserts that *white* is *black*, he gravely comes forward with his *authority*, and if his antagonist says that *black* is *white*, he produces with like gravity an authority equally 'learned in the law.'" [12]

The radicals' remedy most often was to replace the common law with a simple code of laws drawn up by the legislature, and the adversarial process with a procedure that allowed each person to present his own case before a panel of men known in the community. There was confidence in the ability of laymen to settle controversies, because they would be "directed by reason, equity and a few simple and plain laws.[13] Lawyers would no longer be needed because the law would be clear for all to see.

In all, the radicals were deeply democratic, and they wished to mold law and institutions in their own self-image: it would be local and agrarian in orientation, wedded to the ebb and flow of daily communal life, utterly responsive to the will of the majority, and based on "common sense and common honesty between man and men."[14]

At the opposite end of the political spectrum were the Federalists. The Federalist party was strongest in the established population centers, the coastal regions, and the river valleys with an involvement in the market economy. With the defeat of President John Adams in the election of 1800, they were thrown on the defensive. The more extreme members of the party had predicted that the worst excesses of the French Revolution would now be repeated in America. Such a serious misreading of American politics was symptomatic of the Federalists' problems as a party. They were extreme in thought and action, and as James Morton Smith has so convincingly argued, won few friends while in power because of their vindictive policies toward political enemies.[15] They had disdained the mixing, the handshaking, and the small compromises that successful election campaigns increasingly demanded. They adopted an attitude of

---

[12] "Decius," *Independent Chronicle* (Boston), January 30, 1804; quoted in Ellis, *Jeffersonian Crisis,* p. 203.
[13] "Decius," *Independent Chronicle* (Boston), January 31, 1804; quoted in ibid.
[14] Judge John Dudley's charge to the jury, Documents, pp. 83–84.
[15] James Morton Smith, *Freedom's Fetters: The Alien and Sedition Laws and American Civil Liberties* (1956).

"preaching wisdom to the untutored masses,"[16] believing in the right of the wise and the rich to rule. As a party they were marked for extinction, and a sense of urgency now impelled them into the arenas of legal reform. Here was an opportunity, perhaps their last, to reshape the nation's institutions of law and government.

The primary function of law, in the Federalist view, was the protection of life, liberty, and property—an aim indistinguishable from that of restraining the natural rapaciousness of the people. But more than anything, it was the concern for protecting property that brought consistency to Federalist theory. As John Adams had said, "The moment the idea is admitted into society that property is not as sacred as the laws of God. . . anarchy and tyranny commence."[17] Averting the tyranny as viewed by the Federalists dictated that power be placed in the branches of government furthest removed from majority will—in the presidency, in the United States Senate, in the upper houses of the state legislatures, and in the nonelective courts. The Federalists were staunch advocates of an independent judiciary. Judgeships must be appointive, with life tenure, if courts were to be cushioned from the passing whims of the electorate.

If the radicals saw the common law as perpetuating inequality and oppression for the benefit of the propertied classes, the Federalists saw it as the "diadem of civilization," and they bitterly fought any attempt to restrict its domain in America. In their view, it was the ancient origins of the common law that made it superior to legislation, for it embodied the "collected wisdom of the ages, combining the principles of original justice with the infinite variety of human concerns."[18] They had no quarrel with the radicals' claim that the common law was mysterious; but to the Federalists, it was a mystery that could be likened to majesty. Those who reviled the common law were dismissed as ignorant:

> the enemies of the common law do not attack it as a system[,] but they single out some detached branch of it, declare it absurd or intelligible, without understanding it. Those who understand it best entertain the highest opinion of its excellence. . . No other persons are competent judges of it. As well might a circle of a thousand miles diameter be described by the man, whose eye could only see a single inch, as the common law be characterized by those who have not devoted years to its study.[19]

---

[16] John C. Miller, *The Federalist Era* (1960), pp. 276–277, and David Hackett Fischer, *The Revolution of American Conservatism* (1965), pp. 91–110.

[17] Donovan (ed.), *The John Adams Papers* (1964), p. 184.

[18] *New England Palladium* (Boston), April 12, 1806; quoted in Ellis, *Jeffersonian Crisis*, p. 206.

[19] Case of the Philadelphia Cordwainers, Documents, p. 125.

Only a mind trained in the intricacies of law could perceive and appreciate the logical interconnections in so vast a system of principles.

Because the common law was the special domain of lawyers, their continued existence in the new republic was seen as an absolute necessity. Lawyers were the spokesmen of law, trained interpreters, legal tribunes, and it was to be expected that they should monopolize all legal discourse. It followed that the Federalists sought a judiciary recruited from among the most experienced and skilled of the legal profession. On the judge fell the weighty responsibility of discovering the law of a case, and to him the jury looked for guidance. Without a judiciary staffed by "wise and independent" judges, "the best devised constitutions are no more than paper walls, and the most wholesome laws dead letters."[20] It was law as idea, law as protector of society's most sacred values and traditions.

Of course, even the best of judges might commit occasional errors of interpretation. An elaborate system of appellate courts, in the Federalist plan, would serve as a corrective to trial court misjudgments, protecting the rights of all while preserving the purity, consistency, and reason of law. Appellate courts, moreover, should be endowed with the authority to review the constitutionality of legislation. The security of property could never be sacrificed to bare legislative majorities.

Like the radical attack on legalism, the Federalist proposals flowed from fundamental political premises. At the heart of the legal system was to be a common law dedicated to protecting "liberty," property, and the social order, and enforced within a multitiered court system presided over by the most learned and respected members of the legal profession.[21]

At the political center stood the moderate wing of the Jeffersonian Republican party. Their constituency overlapped that of both radicals and Federalists, centering in the more commercially developed regions of the country. The strength of the moderates, however, rested less in numbers than in political style. They possessed a flexibility of viewpoint that permitted the building of coalitions among ostensibly disparate groups; they were disciplined and well organized, and had developed an astuteness born of solid political experience. Like the radicals, the Republican moderates viewed agriculture as the foundation of society; but they valued as well the nation's commercial potential. They differed from the

---

[20] *The Palladium* (Frankfort, Kentucky), February 3, 1801; quoted in Ellis, *Jeffersonian Crisis*, p. 153.
[21] On the priority of protecting social order through strict adherence to common law, see Stephen B. Presser, "A Tale of Two Judges: Richard Peters, Samuel Chase, and the Broken Promise of Federalist Jurisprudence," *Northwestern Law Review*, 73 (1978), 48.

Federalists in three important respects. They wished to burst the bonds of America's economic and cultural dependence on England; they were unalterably committed to a modern style of democratic electioneering and a republican form of government; and they fought for the preservation of states' rights, in order to avoid the domination of commercial development by a national elite. Yet they remained cautious of majority rule. Whether in a monarchial or a republican form of government, unbridled power inevitably led to tyranny.

Poised between the radicals on their left and the Federalists on their right, moderate Jeffersonian Republicans were suspicious of "propertied" and "popular" interests alike, and so resisted any proposals that would result in either an extreme concentration or an extreme decentralization of power. What the moderates most believed in was the value of law itself, "a government of laws and not men." Law was the very foundation of liberty and order in any society, for "that which is not regulated by law must depend on the arbitrary will of the rulers, which would put an end to the civil society."[22] Their belief in the value of certain and known laws, and in the validity of legal processes generally, made them allies of the common-law tradition. They viewed the jury as an institution indispensible to the protection of liberty from power's grasping reach; they admired the common law as a repository of wise rules and protections, but they also recognized that it contained some feudal aspects that must be purged. An independent judiciary was seen as vital to the operation of the system of checks and balances, and crucial as well to the elaboration of a system of jurisprudence capable of responding to changing social and economic needs. Finally, they wanted an inexpensive and accessible system of courts: "a cheap, ready and plain manner of obtaining remedies from wrongs, and of compelling the execution of contracts, by fixed, established rules, [so as to] form the strongest lines of a good government."[23]

The Outcome of Reform:
Toward an Expansive System of Law

The radical attack on legalism, the conservative defense of traditions, the

---

[22] "Government of Law," *The Reportory* (Boston), March 22, 1804; quoted in Ellis, *Jeffersonian Crisis*, pp. 204–205.

[23] Massachusetts Governor Sullivan in his inaugural address; quoted in ibid., p. 221.

moderate proposals for judicial reform—all three coalesced in the elections, assembly halls, and constitutional conventions in the second decade of the century. Every state that had existed at the time of the Revolution—with the exception of two—had revised its constitution by 1815, and many of them had supplemented judicial and legal reforms with legislation. The other two states modified their legal systems by means of statutes. The new states entering the Union were no less drawn into the storm centers of debate. Ultimately, it was the moderates who proved victorious. The various judicial systems that came into existence bore the imprint of a great compromise, but it was one that pleased Federalists more than radicals. Only Kentucky, a new state, registered a victory for radicalism.

There were shades of difference from state to state in the form and content of the new legal systems, reflecting the local mix of issues and coalitions. Pennsylvania, Vermont, and Georgia produced the most striking reform measures; Massachusetts, through legislation, produced the most conservative. But more apparent were the underlying similarities in the state reforms. For the first time, it was possible to speak of an "American legal system."

Virtually all the states acknowledged the need for an expanded and cheap trial court system that would make legal forums for the orderly settlement of disputes available to all towns and counties. The typical state created fifteen or more trial court districts. Each trial court possessed an original criminal or civil jurisdiction and was to be staffed by three or more judges. Most states expected that these judges would have some legal training or professional experience. These trial courts eclipsed the old justice-of-the-peace courts, dear to radicals, which were town-based and run by laymen. Directly above trial courts were intermediate courts of appeal, sitting in specified locations at different times of the year to review petitions of error or complaint from trial court proceedings. At the apex of the court system was a "supreme" appellate court. All states allotted funds for court reporting, whereby appellate court decisions and some trial court proceedings were collected, arranged chronologically, indexed, and published in book form and disseminated.

These reforms meant that the administration of justice would be somewhat decentralized yet organized in a hierarchical form. Presumably, there would be more certainty, uniformity, and predictability in legal decision making, with more control over the direction of legal development placed in the hands of legal technicians.

Compromise, too, was evident in the treatment of common law. No state abolished the common law, although most did recognize that the values implicit in vast parts of Anglo-American common law, especially land law, criminal law, and domestic relations, were hostile to republican sentiments. Reflecting the prejudices of one caustic critic, who wrote that "I do not like this everlasting copying of British publications, this everlasting waiting for the word of the fugelman beyond the sea,"[24] a few states went so far as to ban any citation of English cases in their courts. The general trend, however, was to leave to judges and legislators the responsibility of determining what constituted the common law of each state. Common law and legislation thus became the definitive foundation of American law.

Most states took steps to ensure the existence of an independent judiciary, although here there were hedges. Appointment of judges for life tenure during "good behavior" was the rule. Errant judges could be removed through impeachment proceedings on grounds stipulated in statutes. All states made appointment contingent on the approval of the legislature, and a few states provided for the election of judges in the upper house of the state's assembly.

The adversarial mode of proceeding and trial by jury survived, as did the principle of judicial review—though it remained so controversial that it was rarely invoked. Some streamlining of judicial procedure was seen as necessary, especially regarding the rules of evidence and the arcane pleading forms associated with the older "forms of action."[25] For the most part, these changes were to be accomplished by piecemeal legislation or by judges themselves. The existence of the legal profession and the limited autonomy of the professional bar were indirectly ensured, for the efficient operation of the entire judicial system depended on the technical expertise of counsvl and judges.

The triumph of the moderate Republican point of view, nevertheless, was something more than a political compromise. It was a turning point. It represented a victory for a particular vision of the future that would have wide-ranging consequences for future social, economic, and legal development.

---

[24] Quoted in *American Jurist*, 1 (1839), iii.

[25] "Forms of action" were technical pleading formulas that ascribed an appropriate "form of action" for each type of civil-law dispute. The plantiff had to "fit" his or her allegations into the prescribed and proper form of action. Each form of action had its own prescribed mode of pleading and procedure. Under English common law, forms of action became so complex and cumbersome that they threatened to subvert the whole purpose of the trial, to ascertain the truth of a claim and to do justice to the injured. Thus, a case could be thrown out if a wrong action was used or if there was a technical error in pleading and procedure.

The emergent framework of the state law was the product, first, of a clash over ideology. The Federalists and radicals held opposing views concerning the nature and purpose of society. These differences were deep and irreconcilable; they stemmed back to the American Revolution and kept American politics in a state of turmoil until at least 1815. According to Richard Ellis, "the main and fundamental line of division during these years [1775–1815] was between a provincial, anti-intellectual, agrarian democracy on the one hand and a highly rationalized, elite-directed commercial society on the other."[26] The moderates' great achievement was to break the grip that this conflict had held over public life and to write the terms of a new settlement into the institutions of law.

State legal systems incorporated both elite and democratic features, but in such a unique blend as to make them compatible with overarching republican values. An obvious tension—and a productive one, which prevented law from becoming the permanent domain of any single interest group or economic class—was built into the heart of the system. While the judiciary had won independence, its decisions could never run for long against the grain of popular will. Moreover, lawyers had to upgrade their image as competent and apolitical servants of the court, or they risked losing their professional autonomy.

Second, the new legal systems were the product of an economic and social resolution. The rationalization of the legal system (evident in the hierarchy of courts managed by legal professionals, in reforms in judicial procedure, in the publication of appellate decisions, and in the proliferation of published legal commentaries and periodicals) helped to produce a somewhat more uniform, efficient interstate legal culture. There would be more predictability, rationality, and certainty in law—not only within but among the states. In turn, the "frequent migrations and active commerce among the different states, and the consequent intermixture of the interests and affairs of the subjects of distinct jurisdictions" was seen as making the "ordering" of law a critical precondition for continental expansion and commercial development.[27]

Law, then, would be both fixed yet malleable, capable of accommodating the changing needs of society and the requirements of the business community. This meant that law had become a vehicle, a mechanism for use by shifting political parties, interest groups, legislators, and judges, for effecting social change. Conflicts over policy would be resolved not

---

[26] Ellis, *Jeffersonian Crisis*, p. 261.
[27] *American Jurist*, 1 (1839), iii.

only through the political process but through the legal process as well. And by the middle of the century, as an article in the *North American Review* so well attests, the legal process took on a new order of importance in the nation. "Through the whole country, not a bargain is made, nor an institution founded, nor a death occurs, but that this powerful and almost unseen agent controls the expectations of the actors or the spectators, and decides what shall be the consequences of the act. . . . Whoever suffers a wrong, or claims a right, whatever be its nature or extent, looks to the judiciary for redress or support."[28]

Tocqueville, of course, fully appreciated the centrality of law to American ambitions. With some wonder he observed that "scarcely any political question arises in the United States that is not resolved, sooner or later, into a judicial question."[29] In light of the outcome of judicial reforms in the new republic, it is not so amazing at all.

---

[28] "The Independence of the Judiciary," *North American Review* (1843), p. 403.
[29] Alexis de Tocqueville, *Democracy in America,* vol. 1, ed. Phillips Bradley (1945 ed.), p. 290.

TWO

National Stewardship

Centralization

The history of federalism and national power in the economic expansion of the new nation played out a struggle "over the basic question of the extent to which power ought to be centralized in our federal system."[1] To the early Federalists, centralized power responded to more than purely economic needs. Theodore Sedgwick, a staunch Federalist who helped obtain passage of the short-lived Judiciary Act of 1801, which expanded the federal court system, saw a necessity "to spread out the judicial so as to render the justice of the nation acceptable to the people . . . and to overawe the licentious, and to punish the guilty."[2] With the decline of the Federalist party, advocates of centralized power linked national authority more directly with matters of economy.

At the outset, the need for national leadership in developing the republic's economic infrastructure was strong. The individual states lacked the financial and constitutional bases required to fulfill what increasingly was being described as a providential destiny to spread out across the continent. At first, the national government was responsive to this need,

---

[1] Harry N. Scheiber, "Federalism and the American Economic Order, 1789-1910," *Law and Society Review*, 10 (1975), 57. See also William H. Riker, *Federalism: Origin, Operation, Significance* (1964).
[2] Theodore Sedgwick to Rufus King, Nov. 15, 1799, quoted in Kathryn Turner, "Federalist Policy and the Judiciary Act of 1801," *William and Mary Quarterly*, 22 (3d ser.), note 49 at 9; Scheiber, "Federalism and the American Economic Order," p. 74.

in obedience to the terms of the Constitution itself, which gave the national government certain exclusive powers to formulate financial and internal improvement policies and to dispose of public lands, and through the U.S. Supreme Court, which granted constitutional protection to property and contractual rights and interstate commerce. The overall trend until the Civil War, nevertheless, was in the direction of decentralization. In part because of the success of federal policies and the problem of sectional conflict, state and local governments in time moved into a position of dominance in lawmaking and the formulation of public policy.

═══════════════   ═══════════════

Internal Improvements

Certainly one of the most remarkable developments in antebellum society was the spectacular increase in population and the surge westward. Between 1820 and 1860, America's population increased by almost 35 percent each decade. By contrast, the rate of population increase in Europe over the same period rarely climbed above 15 percent. Much of this increase was absorbed by the newly opened Western states and territories. Tocqueville's observation of the American's "strange unrest" typified the Europeans' amazement at the geographic rootlessness of the population:

> In the United States a man builds a house in which to spend his old age, and he sells it before the roof is on; he plants a garden and lets it just as the trees are coming into bearing; he brings a field into tillage and leaves other men to gather the crops; he embraces a profession and gives it up; he settles in a place, which he soon afterwards leaves to carry his changeable longings elsewhere . . . and if at the end of a year of unremitting labor he finds he has a few days' vacation, his eager curiosity whirls him over the vast extent of the United States, and he will travel fifteen hundred miles in a few days to shake off his happiness. Death at length overtakes him, but it is before he is weary of his bootless chase of that complete felicity which forever escapes him.[3]

As Americans moved West, they formed dispersed and somewhat remote settlements. And with the rapid commercialization of agriculture, there emerged a strong lobby for improved waterways, canals, and turnpikes "to enable them to transport their products to market and to have manufactured and other needed goods imported at reasonable prices."[4]

[3] Tocqueville, *Democracy in America*, vol. 2, pp. 144–145.
[4] Alfred H. Kelly and Winfred A. Harbison, *The American Constitution: Its Origins and Development* (1976 ed.), p. 242.

However, the new trans-Appalachian region was too thinly populated to make "internal improvements" appealing to private developers. There was a clear need for large multistate developments, which were beyond the capacities of individual states. As a result, Americans, especially those in the West, turned to the national government for assistance.

The issue of internal improvements first arose in Congress in 1806. President Thomas Jefferson recommended to Congress that surplus federal revenue from the national bank, land sales, and the tariff be applied to education, roads, rivers, canals, and "such other objects of public importance as it may be thought proper. . . "[5] Jefferson envisioned something more than a transportation program. He sought to further the nation's economic development by easing the restraints on territorial expansion, the free movement of population, and domestic trade. That year, Congress passed "An Act to Regulate the Laying Out and Making of a Road from Cumberlånd, in the State of Maryland," which eventually became the National Road, running all the way to the Mississippi River. Nothing more was done until after the War of 1812, which underscored the importance of an adequate network of highways to the nation's national defense. Then, President James Madison, in his annual messages of 1815 and 1816, issued an ambitious call for a comprehensive federal program of road and canal construction.

John C. Calhoun and Henry Clay garnered support in Congress, and in December 1816 they helped produce a "Bonus Bill" that would set aside more than $1 million in a permanent fund for internal improvement. Significantly, the bill tied federally sponsored development to a vigorous and proud nationalist vision that came of age in the decade after 1812 and became known as the "American System." "No country, enjoying freedom, ever occupied anything like as great an extent of country as this Republic," Calhoun said. "We are great, and rapidly . . . growing. . . . We are under the most imperious obligation to counteract every tendency to disunion." Clay emphasized the practical elements in the bill. Individual states, he believed, lacked the money and internal political support necessary to initiate improvements of great magnitude. Therefore, the states "must be patronized, efficaciously patronized, by the general government, or they never could be accomplished."[6] The bill passed the House and Senate, though support was qualified by a growing tide of sectional conflict. Madison, however, vetoed the bill because it did not conform with his strict constructionist view of the Constitution.

---

[5] Quoted in ibid., p. 243.
[6] Quoted in ibid., p. 244.

The state of the federal treasury, depleted by the Panic of 1819, prompted Presidents James Monroe and John Quincy Adams to renew the call for federal leadership in internal improvements. But now the issue had become lost in the politics of sectionalism and the resurgence of powerful sentiments in favor of states' rights. The shift from centralized to decentralized policies of development met with near universal approval, for by the 1820s the Western states, the ones that had the greatest need for federally directed programs, were in a position to begin undertaking their own internal improvement projects with federal financial assistance. The radical shift in federal leadership came in 1831, when President Andrew Jackson vetoed the modest Maysville Road Bill, and with it died any lingering hopes for a substantial federal involvement in internal improvement and transportation policy. Jackson's decision accorded with a new mood in the country that favored the enlargement of personal liberty, individual initiative, and state power, over national government stewardship. His veto halted the drift toward centralization and economic nationalism that had followed the War of 1812. Not until the middle of the century did a national transportation network emerge, linking the great internal markets (by land, waterway, and rail) and fueling commerce and migration, and then it was under the aegis of private and quasi-public corporations.[7]

The Constitution and the Market Economy

The declining federal sponsorship of internal improvement and economic development left vast policymaking discretion in the hands of state governments and quasi-public developers. But in other ways, the national government was instrumental in creating a legal-economic environment that ensured the success of state and private enterprise.

Up to the Civil War, the economic growth of the United States depended on the existence of a national market that encompassed a regionally specialized economy. Regional specialization in turn relied on the availability of credit to underwrite financially risky manufacturing ventures in the urban Northeast and the development of land in the agrarian South,

[7] Ibid., pp. 247–248; see also: Curtis P. Nettels, *The Emergence of a National Market Economy, 1775–1815* (1962), chap. 2; George Rogers Taylor, *Ohio Canal Era: A Case Study of Government and the Economy, 1820–1861* (1969), chap. 9; Harry N. Scheiber, *The Transportation Revolution, 1815–1860*; Robert A. Lively, "The American System: A Review Article," *Business History Review*, 29(1955), 81; Carter Goodrich, *Government Promotion of American Canals and Railroads, 1800–1890* (1960).

Southwest, and the Old Northwest. Most important was the confidence of the investor, at home and abroad. Before there could be anything like sustained growth, capitalists had to be convinced, first, that law would guarantee the security of their property and, second, that capital invested, discounting risks, stood a reasonable chance of turning a profit.[8]

Not least important to the development of a favorable investment atmosphere was the federal Constitution itself. Under the U.S. Constitution, the national government had assumed state debts incurred during the years of the Revolution and of the Confederation, and it possessed the power to levy taxes to retire them. By so doing, the government raised the confidence of investors in the repayment of loans; the creation of a stable capital market at a time when American financial resources were scarce acted as a lure for foreign investment and stimulated entrepreneurial and speculative activities. The Constitution additionally gave the national government the exclusive power over the coining and supply of money and the regulation of its value. Congress acted on this power in 1791 by establishing the United States Bank. One early result of the Bank, in the words of Douglass North, was that it helped produce "a uniform, centrally controlled monetary system" that added substantially to market capital.[9] The government's exclusive power to conduct foreign affairs also included the authority to impose tariffs on imports. The tariff gave Congress a means of shielding the country's "infant industries" from European competition. And for the first two decades of the century, Congress pursued mildly protectionist policies.

The Land and Its Native Inhabitants

America's richest resource, certainly her most abundant, was land. Since the colonial period, land had been an article of commerce. Significantly, through the Constitution the national government held title to the public domain—and from the beginning Congress decided that these lands ought to be privately owned. At first there was little to dispose of, but with the Louisiana Purchase of 1803, the national reserve grew vast and rich.

[8] Stuart Bruchey, *The Roots of American Economic Growth* (1965), and Stuart Bruchey, *Growth of the Modern American Economy* (1975).
[9] Douglass C. North, *Growth and Welfare in the American Past: A New Economic History* (1966), p. 55; and see Nettels, *The Emergence of a National Market Economy,* pp. 109-129.

Subsequent acquisitions, culminating in the Gadsden Purchase of 1853, settled the modern continental boundaries of the United States.

The history of federal land policy, as Paul W. Gates has shown, is a study in controversy between the industrial Northeast and the slave South, between urban and agrarian interests, and between speculator and settler. There are, however, two salient themes that illustrate the disposition of land. The evolution of policy favored the squatter, or settler—those who tilled, used, and exploited the land. Second, the disposal of land followed demographic and market trends. The great westward population movements in 1816–1818, the 1830s, the 1850s, and the late 1860s, flowed in rhythm with rising agricultural prices, a growing demand for goods, produce, and labor, and the waves of immigration. The federal responsibility for the disposition of the public domain, then, coupled with a preference for private ownership and land improvement, made national expansion a somewhat ordered process consistent with a high rate of growth.[10]

The land that the Americans settled, of course, had already been occupied. Approximately 125,000 Indians still lived east of the Mississippi River in 1820, occupying prime farm lands that white men wanted. The country's efforts at managing the "Indian problem," largely a problem of how to acquire rights to their land, was aggravated by a series of increasingly contradictory federal policies that evolved from colonial and post-revolutionary era precedents. According to David Brion Davis, federal policies toward the Indians rested on several conflicting premises.

First, the federal government, in its earliest years, acknowledged that the Indians possessed qualified rights to their land that white settlers were bound to recognize. This premise produced the early Indian treaties, where individual tribes ceded portions of their land to the states or the federal government or exchanged their land for settlements in the West.

A second premise was that Indian occupancy must, in some measure, make allowances for what Jefferson called the "expectancy" of settlement by whites. This did not mean that Indian land claims were to be extinguished entirely. Jefferson had hoped that the Indians could be civilized, thereby freeing up more land for use by whites. In a letter to Benjamin Hawkins in 1803, Jefferson stated that he considered[11]

---

[10] North, *Growth and Welfare in the American Past,* pp. 122–136; Lawrence M. Friedman, *A History of American Law* (1973), pp. 202–205; and Richard A. Easterlin, *Population, Labor Force, and Labor Swings in Economic Growth: The American Experience* (1968). See generally, Paul W. Gates, *History of Public Land Law Development* (1968).

[11] Thomas Jefferson to Benjamin Hawkins, Feb. 18, 1803, in P. L. Ford (ed.), *The Writings of Thomas Jefferson* (1892–1899), vol. 8, pp. 213–214.

the business of hunting as already . . . insufficient to furnish clothing and sub-
sistence to the Indians. The promotion of agriculture, therefore, and household
manufacture, are essential in their preservation, and I am disposed to aid and
encourage it. This will enable them to live on much smaller portions of
land . . . while they are learning to do better on less land, our increasing
numbers will be calling for more land, and thus a coincidence of interests will
be produced between those who have such necessaries to spare, and want
lands.

Under this premise, dealing with the Indians was to be accomplished by
legal means through agencies of the national government; the national
government, in turn, became the legal protector of the Indians' treaty
rights.

A third premise of Indian policy was based on the belief that the
Indians, in their "savage" state, could not live peaceably with
"civilized" white society. Andrew Jackson, in a letter to President James
Monroe in 1817, presented the threat—and the implicit solution to the Indian problem—in stark terms: "The hunter or savage state requires a
greater extent of territory to sustain it, than is compatible with the progress and just claims of civilized life, and must yield to it."[12]

Indian policy, clearly, was built on conflicting foundations—and it was
sporadically, at best, enforced. White settlers continuously encroached on
Indian tribal lands guaranteed by treaties; violence inevitably erupted,
followed by the illegal occuption of Indian land by settlers. "Unfortunately," according to Davis, "no federal administration had the will or
military power to protect Indian rights while supervising the equitable
acquisition of land by whites. In a government increasingly attuned to the
voice of the people, the Indians had no voice of their own."[13]

The development of a consistent national policy further was undermined
by the theory of states' rights, reaching its zenith under Jackson's administration. Jackson railed against "the farce of treating with Indian tribes"
on a case-by-case basis. Put simply, Jackson believed that the Indians
were bound by the laws of the states in which they lived. If they believed
themselves to be unfairly treated, or if they preferred to be governed by
their own laws and customs, they could relocate beyond the Mississippi.

---

[12] Andrew Jackson to James Monroe, March 4, 1817, in John S. Bassett (ed.), *Cor-
respondence of Andrew Jackson* (1927), vol. 2, p. 279.
[13] David Brion Davis, "Expanding the American Republic," in Bernard Bailyn *et al.*, *The
Great Republic* (1977), p. 437.

The challenge of states' rights theory to national policy came to a head in Georgia. In a treaty with the federal government in 1802, the Cherokee were recognized as an "independent nation." They subsequently adopted their own constitution and, in many respects, met Jefferson's test of civility: they evolved their own alphabet, undertook extensive agricultural development, and made use of technology. Georgian settlers ignored the 1802 treaty and encroached on Cherokee land. In 1828, Georgia declared the Cherokee constitution null and void. In 1829, gold was discovered on Cherokee land, and the Cherokee Nation sought injunctive relief against Georgia in the U.S. Supreme Court. The case was to be a test both of the 1828 Georgia statute and the validity of the Cherokee constitution. However, in an opinion for the Court, Chief Justice John Marshall denied relief on the grounds that the Cherokee Nation lacked standing to sue in the federal courts. The Cherokee comprised a "domestic dependent," and not a foreign state as stipulated in the Constitution (*Cherokee Nation v. Georgia*, 1831).[14]

In 1830, Georgia enacted another law that challenged federal jurisdiction over Cherokee land. That law required white residents living in Cherokee territory to take an oath of allegiance to the state. Samuel A. Worcester, a New England missionary, refused to obey the law and was convicted in a state court. In *Worcester v. Georgia* (1832), Marshall obliquely recognized the legal autonomy of the Cherokee Nation.[15] The federal government, under the 1802 treaty, had exclusive jurisdiction over the land of the Cherokee Nation, which the Georgia law unconstitutionally violated. Georgia refused to recognize the decision, however, and President Jackson is reported to have said, "John Marshall has made his decision, now let him enforce it."[16]

The effect of Jackson's nonaction—to prompt hostile encroachment on Indian tribal land by other Southern states—became, in practice, the new policy of Western Indian removal. First articulated by President John Quincy Adams in 1825, the policy of evacuating the Indians from the East was implemented by Congress in 1830, when it appropriated funds to enable the federal government to purchase Indian land east of the Mississippi, to pay for the Indians' transportation to lands in the West, and to provide them with agricultural implements, seed, and clothing. In ninety-four separate treaties concluded under Jackson's two terms, the Creeks, Choctaw, and Chickasaw evacuated the Old Southwest, on a "Trail of

[14] 30 U.S. (5 Pet.) 1.
[15] 31 U.S. (6 Pet.) 515.
[16] Richard B. Morris (ed.), *Encyclopedia of American History* (1953), p. 171.

Tears," to the territory of Oklahoma. In 1835, the Cherokee Nation relinquished its land titles in exchange for $5 million, transportation costs, and land in the Indian Territory. Indians living north of the Ohio River fared little better. The Sac and Fox Indians of Illinois and the Wisconsin Territory were defeated in the Black Hawk War of 1832. And in Florida, the Second Seminole War broke out in 1835. By 1844, the land east of the Mississippi had been cleared of Indians, though pockets of settlement remained in Maine, Pennsylvania, New York, Michigan, Wisconsin, North Carolina, Alabama, and Mississippi.

The removal of eastern tribes into regions west of the Mississippi was a temporary conclusion at best. The flood of migrants into the far West repeated the earlier pattern of encroachment, hostile Indian reaction, and bloody confrontation. Texas, when annexed as a state in 1845, took the extraordinary step of denying all Indian land claims. The Apaches and other tribes were told to leave the state or face destruction. Gradually, Congress moved toward a policy of placing Indians on federally protected enclaves. With the Indian Appropriations Act of 1851, the Western tribes were gathered in agricultural "reservations." Demoralized, ravaged by disease and hunger, uprooted and resettled on new and often forbidding land, and unfairly treated by the federal government which had promised full compensation and protection, the native inhabitants of America lived on the brink of extinction. "The shock-word genocide," Lawrence M. Friedman has written, "so loosely and so often used, comes embarrassingly close to describing the white man's treatment of the Indian."[17]

The Marshall Court

Alexander Hamilton, in The Federalist Papers, described the judiciary under the proposed constitution as the "least dangerous branch" of government. Hamilton sought to allay fears that a national, nonelective judiciary would impose its will with impunity on a reluctant republican society. What Hamilton could not have foreseen was that during the first third of the century the U.S. Supreme Court would evolve into a coequal branch of government with the Congress and the executive—indeed, that

[17] Lawrence M. Friedman, *A History of American Law* (1973), p. 443. See generally: Francis Prucha, *American Indian Policy in the Formative Years* (1962); Ronald Satz, *American Indian Policy in the Jacksonian Era* (1975); Bernard Sheehan, *Seeds of Destruction* (1973); Robert A. Trennert, *Alternative to Extinction: Federal Indian Policy and the Beginnings of the Reservation System, 1846-51* (1975).

the Supreme Court would move into a position of defining and settling the boundaries of national authority. And it was Chief Justice John Marshall, more than anyone else, who helped move the Court into a powerful superintending position.

Prior to the appointment of Marshall as chief justice in 1801, the federal system of government, to use James Madison's phrase, was still "a novelty and a compound."[18] In particular, there were numerous clauses in the Constitution that had enormous implications for the distribution of power between the federal and state governments, but they lacked precise meaning, such as the commerce clause, the supremacy clause, the contract clause, and the necessary and proper clause. Under the leadership of Marshall (1801–1835), the Court interpreted the Constitution in dozens of decisions that extended fundamental legal protection to private property rights, national power, and the interstate market economy—part of a process that Harry N. Scheiber describes as "centralization."[19]

In *Dartmouth College v. Woodward* (1819), for example, the Court ruled that state legislatures could not interfere with a prior legislative grant of corporate power and privilege. Its decision was based on an interpretation of Article I, Section 10 of the Constitution, prohibiting the "impairment of the obligation of contract." The state of New Hampshire, in effect, had attempted a public takeover of Dartmouth College by adding several persons appointed by the governor to the board of trustees. Marshall, in his opinion for the Court, acknowledged the state's argument that "the framers of the Constitution did not intend to restrain the states in the regulation of their civil institutions adopted for internal improvement." But Marshall emphasized the fact that Dartmouth College was a "private eleemosynary institution." Although he cited no authorities, he deduced that the charter granted by King George III (the "contract" between the government and the corporation) survived the revolution and New Hampshire's statehood to become a contract that was still binding on the legislature. The great significance of the decision is that it appeared to limit the states in regulating corporations they had chartered.[20]

In *McCulloch v. Maryland* (1819), expounding on the meaning of the necessary and proper clause, Marshall defended the second Bank of the

---

[18] James Madison to N.P. Trist (Dec. 1831), *Records of the Federal Convention of 1787*, vol. III, p. 517 (Max Farrand, ed., 1937 revision), quoted in Scheiber, "Federalism and the American Economic Order," p. 57.

[19] Scheiber, "Federalism and the American Economic Order," pp. 72–78.

[20] 17 U.S. (4 Wheat.) 518. See Francis N. Stites, *Private Interest and Public Gain: The Dartmouth College Case, 1819* (1972).

United States, and in the process he delivered his most comprehensive exposition on the power of the federal government. The U.S. Bank and its branches had become the object of considerable, and in some measure justified, criticism for doing so little to help avert the Panic of 1819. A few states turned on the Bank's branches and attempted to legislate them out of existence. In the *McCulloch* case, two questions were before the Court. Did Congress have the power to incorporate the Bank? Second, could the state of Maryland tax the bank notes of the Baltimore branch of the Bank?

Nowhere in the Constitution, Marshall granted, could the words "bank" and "incorporation" be found. But Marshall observed that "it is a *constitution* we are expounding." The power to create the Bank was clearly implied, he believed, since it was "necessary and proper" to the government's execution of the enumerated authority to "lay and collect taxes; to borrow money; to regulate commerce; to declare and conduct war; and to raise and support armies and navies." To the second question, relying on the supremacy clause, Marshall answered that the national government *must* be able to exempt itself from state taxation, for implicit in the power to tax is a power to destroy. "The government of the Union, though limited in its powers, is supreme within its sphere of action . . . It is the government of all, its powers are delegated by all; it represents all, and acts for all."[21]

The centralizing thrust of Marshall's jurisprudence reappears in the Court's construction of the commerce clause. *Gibbons v. Ogden* (1824), the "steamboat monopoly" case, "gave federal protection to an interstate common market."

Robert Fulton and Robert Livingston, developers of the commercial steamboat, obtained a charter from the New York legislature, which granted them a monopoly over the operation and navigation of steamboats in New York waters. Under the authority of the charter, Aaron Ogden was given a monopoly over the Hudson River trade between New York and New Jersey. When Thomas Gibbons, a rival operator, then engaged in steamboat operations across the Hudson River between the two states, he was sued by Ogden for violating the New York monopoly franchise. Marshall, in his opinion for the Court, voided the New York charter, because it restrained interstate commerce. Counsel for the New York monopoly had argued that the congressional power to regulate interstate commerce should be narrowly construed as "traffic," the mercantile ex-

---

[21] 17 U.S. (4 Wheat.) 316.

change of goods. Marshall acknowledged that the "completely internal commerce of a state" was reserved to the state. But "commerce" as it was used in the Constitution, according to Marshall, applied to "every species of commercial intercourse." Interstate commerce would be crippled if it were made to observe "the external boundary-line of each state." More correctly, Marshall asserted, it "comprehends navigation within the limits of every state in the Union." And finally, Congress's power alone to regulate this commerce "is complete in itself, may be exercised to its utmost extent, and acknowledges no limitations other than are prescribed in the constitution."[22]

The process of centralization, or the Marshall Court's "nationalism," was furthered through the establishment of the doctrine of judicial review. Here, the Court's power of review became intertwined with questions of state power to interfere with vested property rights.

Five years before Marshall's appointment, in *Hylton v. U.S.* (1796), the Supreme Court had implied that it possessed the power to rule federal statutes unconstitutional.[23] In *Marbury v. Madison* (1803), Marshall established the Court's power of judicial review. In the case, the Court declared Section 13 of the Judiciary Act of 1789 unconstitutional and therefore void, since the Constitution did not specifically delegate to Congress the power to alter the Supreme Court's original jurisdiction.[24] *Fletcher v. Peck* (1810) extended the power of judicial review to include state legislation. The case originated in an act of the Georgia legislature in 1795, which granted large tracts of land to speculative land companies. Later, the legislature rescinded the statute on the grounds of fraud and corruption. The Court ruled that the rescinding legislation impaired the obligation of contracts, and thus abridged the vested rights of the land companies, and so was invalid.[25] The Supreme Court's authority to review certain state court decisions was established in *Martin v. Hunter's Lessee* (1816). Again, a state legislature had abridged vested rights in property, this time through Virginia's confiscation of the Fairfax land grants and its legislation barring noncitizens from inheriting land. Earlier, the Court had invalidated the legislation. An angry Virginia appellate court refused to accept the Court's decision, ruling that Section 25 of the

[22] 22 U.S. (9 Wheat.) 1. See Maurice Baxter, *Gibbons v. Ogden: The Steamboat Monopoly* (1972).

[23] 3 U.S. (3 Dallas) 171.

[24] 5 U.S. (1 Cranch) 137; see D. O. Dewey, *Marshall Versus Jefferson: The Political Background of Marbury v. Madison* (1970).

[25] 10 U.S. (6 Cranch) 87; see C. P. McGrath, *Yazoo: Law and Politics in the New Republic: Fletcher v. Peck* (1966).

Judiciary Act (upon which federal jurisdiction was based) was an unconstitutional infringement on the sovereign rights of the states. When the case came before the Supreme Court a second time, Justice Joseph Story affirmed that the Constitution's grant of concurrent jurisdiction in certain cases did not deprive the Supreme Court of its ultimate authority to review state court decisions.[26] Marshall reaffirmed the *Martin* decision in *Cohens v. Virginia* (1821), basing his ruling on the doctrine of national supremacy.[27]

Among the greatest challenges to property and contractual rights that the Supreme Court faced were the state statutes, common by the 1820s, that helped relieve debtors of some or all of their obligations. The Court's most important decision in this area, *Sturges v. Crowninshield* (1819), invalidated a New York State bankruptcy statute as an impairment of the obligation of contract, because the statute relieved insolvent debtors of contractual obligations entered into before the passage of the act.[28] In *Green v. Biddle* (1823), the Court applied the contract clause to contracts between two states. It invalidated a Kentucky statute that abridged land titles originally based on an agreement between Kentucky and Virginia at the time of Kentucky's organization as a state.[29]

The Marshall Court's jurisprudence realized several objectives. First, it gave meaning to the theory of federalism, assuring the supremacy of the national government and establishing the jurisdiction of federal courts over such issues as commerce, corporate charters, and contracts emanating from within the states. Second, the Court advanced important national economic interests, which "included the giant speculative land companies that sought federal protection from state actions adversely affecting them, the rising commercial elements that needed maximum uniformity of law to conduct multistate transactions on a secure legal basis, and . . . large-scale investors and banking firms whose business horizons stretched out across state lines."[30] In all, the Court, as a policymaking institution, advertised the judicial process to future developers, speculators, and businessmen who were anxious to avoid the hostile interventionism of grassroots democracy.[31]

---

[26] 14 U.S. (1 Wheat.) 304.
[27] 19 U.S. (6 Wheat.) 264.
[28] 17 U.S. (4 Wheat.) 122.
[29] 21 U.S. (8 Wheat.) 1.
[30] Scheiber, "Federalism and the American Economic Order," p. 73.
[31] R. Kent Newmyer, *The Supreme Court Under Marshall and Taney* (1968), pp. 56–81.

Toward Decentralization and the Taney Court

While the terms of the federal Constitution, the congressional exercise of enumerated and implied powers in such areas as banking and the tariff, and the jurisprudence of the Marshall Court cast government in a centralized, protective, and promotional role, the overall thrust from the 1820's until the Civil War was in the direction of decentralization.

Congress, for one, left dormant many powers given to it under the Constitution. The areas of lawmaking left entirely to the states were not insignificant: conditions of labor and labor relations, civil rights, education, domestic relations, business organization, and the law of credit and debt. The role of the federal government in areas where it had established an early leadership diminished with time. The National Road, planned with great fanfare under Jefferson's administration, became under Jackson's administration the property of the states through which it coursed. Congress's management of the public domain emphasized denationalization at the outset. In the same spirit, later amendments to the federal law gave ever greater powers to the states in the development and sale of the public lands within their territorial boundaries. The United States Bank, salutary while it lasted, was the subject of endless litigation in state and federal courts. Jackson sealed its fate when he refused to renew its charter. The tariff, like other improvements, fell prey to sectionalism. With the exception of the Civil War tariffs, it was not until the close of the century that Congress again became active in the regulation of foreign trade.

There is a considerable scholarly dispute over the extent to which the Supreme Court, under the new leadership of Chief Justice Roger Taney (1836–1864), moved away from the nationalism of the Marshall Court. However, there is general agreement that the Court did tip the balance in favor of a theory of federalism that left expansive powers to state governments.[32] Yet here, too, there were early reservations about the desirability of extreme national centralization of authority.

In *Gibbons*, for example, Marshall, while striking down the chartered

---

[32] Robert J. Harris, "Chief Justice Taney: Prophet of Reform and Reaction," in *American Constitutional Law: Historical Essays,* ed. Leonard Levy (1966), p. 93; Alpheus T. Mason, *The States' Rights Debate* (2d ed., 1972), 192; Carl Brent Swisher, *The Taney Period, 1836–1864* (1974); Scheiber, "Federalism and the American Economic Order," p. 76.

monopoly as a violation of the commerce clause, simultaneously opened
the door to inspection, quarantine, and other regulatory laws enacted
under the police power of states. He said they were "a portion of that immense mass of legislation which embraces everything within the territory
of a state, not surrendered to the general government; all of which can be
most advantageously exercised by the states themselves."[33] And in
Willson v. Blackbird Creek Marsh Company (1829), Marshall affirmed
the validity of a state law that affected interstate commerce (developing
the theory of the "dormant commerce power") in an area where Congress
had not acted.[34] In *Ogden v. Saunders* (1827), Marshall, for the first time,
was in the minority in the interpretation of a constitutional provision.
Justice Johnson, for the majority, upheld a New York bankruptcy law,
ruling that it did not violate the contract clause by relieving insolvent debtors of their obligations entered into *after* the act's passage. Johnson anticipated the police powers of states that Chief Justice Taney later would
elaborate on, stating that "all the contracts of men receive a relative, and
not a positive interpretation: for the rights of all must be held and enjoyed
in subserviency to the good of the whole."[35]

The shift in jurisprudence, though, became pronounced in the earliest
of the Taney Court's decisions. In *Briscoe v. Bank of Kentucky* (1837),
the Court upheld the authority of state-owned banks to issue notes and,
more broadly, the authority of the states to regulate internal banking and
currency.[36] The nature and extent of change became fully evident in
another important decision of the same year, the *Charles River Bridge*
case (see Documents, pp. 197–210). Rejecting a charge that a
Massachusetts statute violated the contract clause when it created a new,
prospectively toll-free public bridge that directly competed with a
chartered, privately owned toll bridge, Taney offered the fullest development yet of the states' police power. Taney refused "by legal intendments
and mere technical reasoning, [to] take away from [the states] any portion
of that power over their own internal police and improvement, which is so
necessary to their well being and prosperity."[37] The Court further nar-
rowed the applicability of the contract clause to state infringements on
vested property rights in the *West River Bridge* case (1848). The Vermont
legislature seized a privately chartered bridge, making it part of a public

---

[33] 22 U.S. (9 Wheat.) 1.
[34] 27 U.S. (2 Pet.) 245.
[35] 25 U.S. (12 Wheat.) 212.
[36] 36 U.S. (11 Pet.) 257
[37] See Stanley N. Kutler, *Privilege and Creative Destruction: The Charles River Bridge Case*
(1971).

highway. Taney held that the legislature was acting within its police power authority: "This power, denominated the eminent domain of the State, is as its name imports, paramount to all private rights vested under the government, and these last are, by necessary implication, held in subordination to this power, and must yield in every instance to its proper exercise."[38] The Taney Court also eroded centralized power in such important areas as taxation and eminent domain—indeed, as Alfred Kelly and Winfred Harbison have argued, to such a degree that the supremacy of the national government seemed threatened.

It would be a mistake to argue that the Taney Court entirely reversed Marshall's centralizing jurisprudence. The Supreme Court continued the process of consolidating its *own* power and reach, as is nowhere more evident than in the *Dred Scott* case. Nevertheless, "a new spirit was . . . apparent." The Court affirmed doctrines of state sovereignty and legitimized "certain state powers and functions which Marshall might well have argued intruded upon federal authority."[39]

The gradual devolution of practical power and decision-making authority from the central government to the states can be attributed to several developments. Politically, Democratic administrations held sway in national life after 1829, and Democrats subscribed to a philosophy of limited national government. The antebellum intellectual climate likewise favored individual initiative and state mercantilism over national stewardship. Egalitarianism, ascendant in Jackson's day, elevated the active individual to a plane of cultural symbol. Conflicting sectional, state, and occupational interests, the products of growth and wealth, further sapped the vigor of national government. The inability of the political system to arrive at agreement over wide areas of national life (aggravated by persistent tensions over slavery) made decentralization politically wise, if not necessary. Finally, the success of the national government's early promotional role, and the real benefits of the constitutional system in fostering a national market economy, had the ironic effect of undercutting the national government's leadership position. As the pool of capital swelled, as private banks proliferated and flourished, as manufacturing and commercial agriculture developed, the opportunity for personal advancement seemed limitless. Nascent entrepreneurs and small businessmen, eager to make their way in the world, came to resent pockets of privilege sanctioned under the old law. Freedom to compete, unhindered by government, was becoming the new ideal.

[38] 47 U.S. (6 How.) 507.
[39] Kelly and Harbison, *American Constitution,* p. 322.

THREE

The Commonwealth of the States

Commonwealth Theory and the New Public Policy

Chief Justice Lemuel Shaw of Massachusetts described the first half of the nineteenth century, which his own life spanned, as one of "prodigious activity and energy in every department of life."[1] It is an apt description as well of the state governments. Like their colonial predecessors, state governments had always been deeply involved in their own internal economies. But as the prospects for national stewardship dimmed, the responsibilities and activities of state governments burgeoned as never before. The states enacted laws regulating manufacturing, banking, insurance, and transportation. They created public schools, hospitals, libraries, and modern penal institutions. They regulated occupational licensing, public health, crime, bankruptcy, corporations, and the inspection of commodities. The new state laws unlocked the productive potential of society and promoted what J. Willard Hurst has called the "release of energy."[2] It was law that harnessed the resources of society to the national urge for expansion.

Fueling legislative activism was a uniquely American vision of the state as a "commonwealth." The "commonwealth idea," Leonard W. Levy has written, "was essentially a quasi-mercantilist concept of the state

---

[1] Lemuel Shaw, "Profession of Law in the United States," Documents, p. 100.
[2] J. Willard Hurst, *Law and the Conditions of Freedom in the Nineteenth-Century United States* (1967), p. 1.

within a democratic framework." In Europe, "where the state was not responsible to the people and was the product of remote historical forces, mercantilism served the ruling classes who controlled the state."[3] In America, the state became intensely real and immediate, forged in the heat of a republican revolution. The state was the people, their "Common Wealth," and through its agencies gave effect to the popular will.

Regulation, Promotion, and Criminal Prosecution

It has always been a function of government to regulate or oversee the dealings of merchants and artisans in the interest of the community. Colonial assembly laws were swollen with such provisions.[4] In the nineteenth century, though, regulatory measures took on added import.

Every state legislature regulated weights and measures, provided standard measures for commodities, laid down rules for packaging, and provided for inspection to ensure that laws were followed. The remarkably detailed regulation of the nailmaking industry in Massachusetts was typical. In a series of statutes, the General Court (the legislature of the state) set exacting standards for the number, size, and weight of iron nails to be packed in casks, dictated the make and shape of casks, called for the branding of each cask to indicate the town of origin and the maker, created a rating system among nails, and prohibited the export of nails of the "second sort."[5] New York State directed that salt be packed "in barrels, casks or boxes," and that it be "free from dirt, filth and stones, and from admixtures of lime . . . and fully drained from pickle."[6]

None of the states could afford to pay the costs associated with a massive inspection and enforcement system. Lawmakers gradually evolved a system that was inexpensive, practical, and simple. The governor appointed inspectors, usually well-known and respected members of a community, such as lawyers or skilled artisans, and permitted them to extract nominal fees for their services. Fines for violations went to the inspectors and flowed back into the treasury of the state. So lucrative was the business that individuals often lobbied for the office.

[3] Levy, *Law of the Commonwealth,* p. 305; and see Oscar Handlin and Mary F. Handlin, *Commonwealth: A Study of the Role of Government in the American Economy: Massachusetts, 1774–1861* (1947), p. 31.
[4] See, for example, Richard B. Morris, *Government and Labor in Early America* (1946).
[5] Cited in Handlin and Handlin, *Commonwealth,* pp. 66–67.
[6] Revised Statutes of New York (1829), vol. 1, pt. 1, title 10, chap. 9, sec. 103; quoted in Friedman, *A History of American Law,* p. 161.

Tied as they were to local patronage and the fee system for enforcement, regulatory laws such as those concerning nailmaking or the packing
of salt were doomed in practice to a certain amount of inefficiency, corruption, and evasion. In essence, lawmakers left to the citizen the burden
of carrying out what the statutes decreed. There was little else that could
be done. America lacked a tradition of administration. Even if states could
have drawn on such a tradition, few were willing to tax the people to support a bureaucracy or a class of civil servants. Yet the economic utility of
regulation, as the Handlins and Louis Hartz have shown, seems never to
have been doubted. Inspection in principle enhanced the prestige of goods
manufactured within a state. And because regulations were tailored to
marketability standards and the demand for exports, they contributed to
the distribution and sale of a state's products.[7]

States were also active in supporting the infrastructure of their
economies. The state set moral boundaries on the kinds of trades and occupations people could pursue. Legislatures prohibited "gaming,"
"gambling," and "pimping." Licenses were required for peddlers, auc-
tioneers, hawkers, and tavernkeepers. The power to license practitioners
of professions, such as medical doctors, was delegated to local organizations. Laws also existed for the protection of consumers. States regulated
the packing of beef, flour, pork, fish, and other foodstuffs to prevent
adulteration. States established exacting standards for labeling to prevent
fraud and deception. In Massachusetts, "pure spermaceti oil" could be
sold only under the names "sperm, spermaceti, lamp, summer, fall,
winter and second winter oils," with fines prescribed for adulteration or
false labeling.[8] Quarantine laws also were common. Ships entering New
York City harbor were instructed to anchor near "the marine hospital on
Staten-Island." Ships placed under quarantine could be cleared only after
certain procedures had been complied with, such as fumigation "with

---

[7] Handlin and Handlin, *Commonwealth*, pp. 51–86. See also Milton Heath, *Constructive Liberalism: The Role of the State in Economic Development in Georgia to 1860* (1954); Alfred G.
Smith, *Economic Readjustment of an Old Cotton State: South Carolina, 1820–1860* (1958); James
N. Primm, *Economic Policy in the Development of a Western State: Missouri, 1820–1860* (1954);
and John W. Cadman, *The Corporation in New Jersey: Business and Politics, 1791–1875* (1949).
A recent study by Charles McCurdy points out the importance of regulation in a Far Western state
in the 1850s: "Stephen J. Field and Public Land Law Development in California, 1850–1866: A
Case Study of Judicial Resource Allocation in the Nineteenth Century," *Law and Society Review*,
10 (1975).
[8] *Massachusetts Laws*, 1833, chap. 215; quoted in Friedman, *A History of American Law*,
pp. 161–162.

mineral acid gas."[9] While prohibitions placed on certain trades, licensing, and public health codes were crude by modern standards, the larger goal was the preservation of the prevailing moral and economic health of the state.

The promotional thrust of antebellum law is no less apparent in the criminal system. All of the prohibitions on classic crimes, such as murder, rape, and theft, continued in existence after the Revolution. But in the first half of the nineteenth century, new laws appeared that brought the protection of property to the forefront. Patterns in the prosecution of crime, studied in detail by William E. Nelson, seem to bear this out.[10]

The great majority of criminal prosecutions in colonial Massachusetts pertained to moral and religious offenses. The priority of policing crimes of sin was evident in the General Court's admonition to the people of the colony in 1776 to "lead sober, Religious and peaceable Lives, avoiding all Blasphemies, contempt of the holy Scriptures, and of the Lord's day and all other Crimes and Misdemeanors, All Debauchery, Prophaneness, Corruption, Venality, all riotous and tumultuous Proceedings, and all Immoralities whatsoever."[11] By 1800, the purposes behind criminal prosecution had begun to change—to ensuring "the peace and safety of society" and to ridding the people of the "depradations" of "notorious offenders" and the "tax levied on the community by . . . privateering of" thieves.[12] Criminal prosecutions increasingly were for offenses of theft, trespass, larceny, and embezzlement. Nelson concludes that the legal system, by striking out with special fervor at those who threatened the security of property, announced that property had replaced morality as the foundation of society.

---

[9] *Revised Statutes of New York* (1929), vol. 1, p. 425 ff; quoted in Friedman, *A History of American Law,* p. 162.

[10] William E. Nelson, *Americanization of the Common Law: The Impact of Legal Change in Massachusetts Society, 1760–1830* (1975), pp. 117–121; and William E. Nelson, "Emerging Notions of Modern Criminal Law in the Revolutionary Era: An Historical Perspective," *New York University Law Review,* 42 (1967), 450. See also Lawrence M. Friedman, "Notes Toward a History of Criminal Justice," in *American Law and the Constitutional Order,* ed. Lawrence M. Friedman and Harry N. Scheiber (1978), pp. 13–26; and Michael Stephen Hindus, *Prison and Plantation* (1980).

[11] Proclamation of the General Court, 23 January 1776, in *The Popular Sources of Political Authority: Documents on the Massachusetts Convention of 1780,* ed. Oscar Handlin and Mary F. Handlin (1966), p. 68.

[12] Gamaliel Bradford, *State Prisons and the Penitentiary System Vindicated* (1821), p. 5; Gamaliel Bradford, *Description and Historical Sketch of the Massachusetts State Prison* (1816); Bradford, *State Prisons,* p. 12; quoted in Nelson, *Americanization of the Common Law,* p. 118.

The agencies of enforcement evolved in harmony with these new concerns. Cities and towns traditionally relied on the night watch and constabulary to maintain public order. The customary method of tracking down and capturing a criminal was the "hue and cry." As cities grew, so did the opportunities for plunder, while the growing anonymity of city life eroded the communal and moral underpinnings of self-restraint. The more urbanized and developed states, in the 1840s and after, founded professional police departments to quell public disturbances and more systematically prosecute crime.[13] "Asylums" for the rehabilitation of criminals, in reality prisons that for the first time permitted the long-term incarceration of offenders, were simultaneously established.[14] After 1850, detective bureaus were created that promised to ferret out clever criminals who resorted to stealth and cunning.[15] Making property owners secure in their possessions, then, freed them to use property in legitimate ways. And like the changing substance and emphasis of criminal law, the professionalization of enforcement and the institutionalization of punishment testify to the importance of a stable social and business environment in the new order of things.

The linkage between criminal law and the economy was sometimes more subtle. Nineteenth-century statute books bulged with laws that had little taint of criminality: selling spoiled strawberries, inhibiting the flow of fish in streams, placing epsom salt containers near grazing herds, shooting prairie hens. Some of the laws, such as those prohibiting the selling of spoiled strawberries, did touch on issues of ethical business practice. These laws may also have served a discrete business interest in an era when monitoring agencies and boards were nonexistent. Inhibiting the flow of fish, for example, interfered with the common-law water rights of upstream or downstream landowners. But the expense of litigation tended to preclude questionable infringements being attacked by landowners in civil law courts. Making such "offenses" criminal, on the other hand, spread the costs of enforcement to the entire community and allowed the state to prosecute a rainbow of activities that touched on economy and the public interest. With the advent of administrative agencies later in the century, most of these laws disappeared.[16]

[13] Irving Johnson, *Policing the Urban Underworld* (1979).
[14] David J. Rothman, *The Discovery of the Asylum: Social Order and Disorder in the New Republic* (1971), and Walter David Lewis, *From Newgate to Dannemora: The Rise of the Penitentiary in New York, 1796–1848* (1965).
[15] Wilbert R. Miller, *Cops and Bobbies: Police Authority in New York and London, 1830–1870* (1977).
[16] Friedman, *A History of American Law*, pp. 257–258, 508–510.

Debt

In an era when the institution of the market seemed to sweep all before it, the persistence of ancient laws of credit and debt must have seemed grossly anomalous. There had always been a social stigma attached to insolvency. A "bankrupt" suggested moral degeneracy more than unlucky impoverishment. Cotton Mather in 1716, seeking an explanation for the "Grand Cause of Peoples running into Debt," blamed it on the pridefulness of people who could "not bear the Humiliations of a Low and a Mean Condition in the World," especially if they had "sometimes Lived in more of Splendor."[17] Not surprisingly, the law of debt bore down with crushing force on the insolvent. Colonial American laws, following the English practice, directed the imprisonment of defaulted debtors. There was as well a practical side to the moral perception of debt. In theory, debts were negotiated in good conscience with a promise to pay. These promises sometimes were sealed by contract, and so carried with them the heavy freight of personal obligation. That a person behind bars was hardly in a position to make good on a debt was overshadowed by the violation of a promise.[18]

Efforts to change the law of credit and debt after the Revolution took several forms, from gradual amelioration of prison terms to declarations of insolvency. The most dramatic of the early changes occurred at the national level. The U.S. Constitution gave Congress the power to "establish uniform laws on the Subject of Bankruptcy throughout the United States."[19] Congress first acted to relieve debtors in 1800, following the commercial failures in Adams's administration. This first bankruptcy law, however, benefited merchants. It merely permitted creditors to initiate proceedings against tradesmen. Denounced as "partial, immoral . . . impolitic . . . anti-Republican," it was repealed in 1803.[20] Congress enacted a second general bankruptcy act in 1841, in the wake of the Panic

[17] Cotton Mather, *Fair Dealing Between Debtor and Creditor* (1716), p. 13; quoted in Nelson, *Americanization of the Common Law,* p. 45.
[18] See Peter J. Coleman, *Debtors and Creditors in America: Insolvency, Imprisonment for Debt, and Bankruptcy, 1607-1900* (1974), an exhaustive study of these aspects of the law. See also Nelson, *Americanization of the Common Law,* pp. 41–45 and 147–154, for the complexity and intricacy of debt law in one state, Massachusetts.
[19] Art. I, Sec. 8.
[20] Quoted in Charles Warren, *Bankruptcy in United States History* (1935), p. 21; Friedman, *A History of American Law,* p.238.

of 1837. Daniel Webster spoke in favor of the bill, noting that it "extends its provisions, not only to those who, either in fact or in contemplation of law, are traders, but to all persons who declare themselves insolvent, or unable to pay their debts and meet their engagements."[21] The 1841 law was repealed within a few years of its enactment (1846).

States attempted to enact their own bankruptcy laws, and not always under the very exacting standards set down in *Crowninshield*. The demand for debtor relief laws in the states ran deep. Commercial failures had revealed the degree to which personal fortune in America had become linked with the impersonal mechanisms of national and international markets. An economic downturn injured "every class of society . . . all must inhale it and none . . . escape it."[22] People were in danger of being "pressed to the earth forever, by a load of hopeless debt."[23] If the law could be called on to "wipe the debtor's slate clean," it could also be used to erect a more equitable credit system, one more attuned to the economic realities of free-market capitalism. This is precisely what the states attempted to do.

Many states filled the void left by repeal of the federal laws by initiating changes in the local law of credit and debt. The patterns of reform varied among the states, reflecting differences in power bases and the dominance of commercial, manufacturing, or agrarian interests. Most states gradually eliminated imprisonment for debt. Insolvency laws, debtor relief laws, stay laws, and moratoria on mortgages waxed and waned with fluctuations in the business cycle. While these actions did not abolish all debts, they at least recognized the legitimacy of such amelioratives as installment payments and allowed for the more equitable division of assets. Perhaps most important, cushioning people from the adverse effects of sudden market changes became viewed as a duty of the state. Justice Dixon of Wisconsin, in an 1858 opinion sustaining a statute that extended the time period before foreclosures could occur, wrote that

> such changes are in general exceedingly unwise and unjust, yet if from sudden and unlooked-for reverses or misfortune, or any other cause, the existing remedies become so stringent in all or a particular class of actions that great

[21] Daniel Webster, Speech, May 18, 1840, in *Speeches and Orations of Daniel Webster*, ed. Edwin P. Whipple (1879), p. 471; reprinted in Charles M. Haar (ed.), *The Golden Age of American Law* (1965), p. 374.

[22] Henry Clay, Speech, 1824; quoted in Warren, *Bankruptcy in United States History*, p. 38.

[23] Daniel Webster, in Haar, *Golden Age of American Law*, p. 378.

and extensive sacrifices of property will ensue, without benefit to the creditor or relief to the debtor, a relaxation of the remedies becomes a positive duty which the State owes to its citizens.[24]

The development of the law of debt was more random than planned. Credit relief laws "abounded in the states and were astonishing in their variety,"[25] and many were of dubious constitutionality. Like all antebellum regulatory measures, they were poorly administered, and vocal opposition continued to accompany reforms. Nevertheless, the cumulative effect of the laws was to protect both creditors and debtors. They liberated "human capital" for reentry into the economy. For insolvent persons, "many of them meritorious and respectable," had "capacities both for action and enjoyment."[26] And to some extent they protected developers engaged in high-risk ventures, while ensuring that creditors might one day collect. At the heart of the laws was a desire, as J. Willard Hurst has written, to "afford the debtor a breathing spell in which he might regather his strength," and to "reasonably . . . preserve the general course of dealings."[27]

Technology, Information, and Education

There are limits to what investment and the free play of market forces can accomplish. As economic historians Douglass C. North and Stuart Bruchey have shown, sustained growth also required continual technological expansion, which in turn relied on investment in society's human capital.[28] Technology was the cutting edge of economic growth. Successive waves of technological advancement constantly opened up new frontiers of development. Canals such as the Erie, in Chancellor Kent's words "a great public object, calculated to intimidate by its novelty, its expense, and its magnitude,"[29] for a time replaced the contiguous roads

[24] *Von Baumbach v. Babe,* 9 Wis. 510 (1859); quoted in Hurst, *Law and the Conditions of Freedom,* p. 27.
[25] Harry N. Scheiber, "Federalism and the American Economic Order," *Law and Society Review,* 10 (1975), p. 75.
[26] Daniel Webster, in Haar, *Golden Age of American Law,* p. 378.
[27] Hurst, *Law and the Conditions of Freedom,* pp. 26–27.
[28] Bruchey, *Roots of American Economic Growth,* pp. 178–207. And see Nathan Rosenberg, *Technology and American Economic Growth* (1972).
[29] *Rogers v. Bradshaw* (1823), 6 New York Common Law Reports [20 Johns. 735] (Sup. Ct. of N.Y.).

and turnpikes as a cheap and efficient system of transport; steamships replaced manpowered vessels and allowed upriver navigation of the great internal waterways; the steam locomotive knitted vast inland regions into a commercial and communications network, while the eventual application of steam technology in factories obviated the dependence on water power. America was becoming a "land of wonders, in which everything is in constant motion and every change seems an improvement."[30]

Americans were keen on technology. As a people, Tocqueville wrote, they were "addicted" to the "purely practical part of science" and possessed a "clear, free, original, and inventive power of mind."[31] At least in part, American ingenuity was the product of experience. What engineers and workers learned through trial and error on one project or undertaking they refined and extended to another. Motivation was also important. The desire to save labor, expand output, and increase the efficiency of machines to compensate for the shortage of skilled labor, led to hundreds of lesser inventions by a multitude of workers in shops, mills, and factories. Technological expansion was no overnight revolution but a series of piecemeal modifications, a steady accretion of little details.

A major spur to American innovation came in the 1840s and after, as state and local governments began chartering and promoting professional scientific societies, founded public libraries, and subsidized lyceums. Of incalculable importance was the creation of free elementary schools and, after the Civil War, of high schools, land grant colleges, and vocational institutes, fostering the accumulation and diffusion of information that was so vital to the development and spread of technology. "The most remarkable characteristic of Americans," wrote one European traveler to America in 1837, "is the uncommon degree of intelligence which pervades all classes. I do not here speak of the higher branches of learning which, in the language of Europe, constitute scholarship; but of the great mass of useful knowledge calculated to benefit and improve the conditions of mankind."[32] Nobody, though, defined the nature and purpose of education in America so well as did Horace Mann. The creation of a formalized, free, public educational system was foremost among the state's

---

[30] Tocqueville, *Democracy in America*, vol. 1, p. 443. And see Don E. Fehrenbacher, *The Era of Expansion: 1800–1848* (1969), pp. 53–76, and Elting E. Morison, *From Know How to No Where: The Development of American Technology* (1974), pp. 37–64, on engineering and the Erie canal. On transportation, see Louis C. Hunter, *Steamboats on the Western Rivers* (1949); Edward C. Kirkland, *Men, Transportation, and Cities*, 2 vols. (1948).

[31] Tocqueville, *Democracy in America*, vol. 2, p. 43.

[32] Francis J. Grund, *The Americans, in Their Moral, Social, and Political Relations* (1837), pp. 26–27; quoted in Alice Felt Tyler, *Freedom's Ferment* (1962 ed.), p. 234.

legislative responsibilities, he believed, for the "true business of the school room" was "identical with the great interests of society."[33] Education expanded knowledge, promoted organized habits of thought, improved the quality and dependability of the work force, enriched entrepreneurial talents, and sustained popular ambitions for self-improvement.

Corporations: From Quasi-Public to Private

Corporations, so ubiquitous in modern America, are of distant origin. In eighteenth-century England and America they functioned very much like arms of government, usually serving some specific public end. The use of a "charter" of incorporation, bestowed by a legislature on a body of persons united to accomplish some purpose, was in essence a legal grant of privilege. Corporations did not die with the officers or stockholders; and they could impose levies, condemn property, and in some instances raise capital through the sale of stock. In the colonial era, the most common corporations were towns, church parishes, or charities. In the years after the Revolution, the corporate charter gradually emerged as a convenient vehicle through which the state could promote internal improvements that were otherwise too risky or expensive for private undertaking. Before examining this new kind of corporation, something should be said about the circumstances that called it into being.

Roads formed a vital transportation and communications link in all of the states, yet numerous obstacles stood in the way of their construction. The great turnpikes crossed byways and rivers, passed through towns, and coursed over private and public property. Laying out and building a major thoroughfare necessarily involved innumerable infringements on property rights. Understandably, towns were reluctant to carry out such projects, as quarrels would inevitably erupt over which town would benefit the most and therefore which should shoulder the costs. In an era of capital scarcity, the young states themselves were incapable of financing construction. Nor were there incentives for private development, since condemning and paying for land, and settling disputes with aggrieved property owners, threatened to offset long-run profits. Gristmills, too, although valuable to

---

[33] *Report of the Massachusetts Board of Education,* 1848, in *Life and Works of Horace Mann,* ed. Mary Mann, (1868), reprinted in Daniel J. Boorstin (ed.), *An American Primer,* vol. 1 (1966), p. 343.

farmers and consumers alike, caused a good deal of damage to contiguous lands. Damming a stream flooded neighboring meadowland, interfered with the flow of fish, and obstructed the course of water. Mills, like roads, infringed on the property rights of others, and they were expensive to build and maintain. It made little sense to invest in a milling operation without a grant of monopoly and some immunity from civil damage suits.

The corporate form of organization, in the words of Lawrence M. Friedman, offered an "efficient way to structure and finance" precisely such precarious but useful business ventures.[34] By means of special charters, lawmakers delegated eminent domain powers to builders of roads, allowed them to raise capital by levying taxes on stockholders, and permitted them to cross byways and rivers. As an inducement, lawmakers also granted builders the right to collect tolls on the finished road for a period of years. In the case of mills, legislators often granted monopoly rights to operators, legalized the flooding of neighboring lands, and protected operators from possibly ruinous damage suits by creating *ad hoc* commissions, which set a reasonable rate of annual compensation for injured neighbors. An early and especially appealing feature of the corporate charter was the protection of the officers "from the onerous and appalling liabilities" of the corporation.[35] The limitation on liability for corporate debts lowered the threshold of personal risk and invited public investment.

In return for limited grants of immunity, monopoly, and privilege to corporate bodies, the state retained the authority to structure individual charters in the public's interest. That roads and bridges after a period of years of usage would pass into public hands, and that tolls would then be eliminated, was a common provision. State governments stipulated that corporation officers must submit annual accounting reports; and lawmakers reserved the power to amend, renew, alter, or withdraw the charter. Lawmakers also placed strict limits on what corporations could and could not do. "All corporate acts which the legislature has not authorized remain prohibited," and officials and courts were to con-

---

[34] Friedman, *A History of American Law*, p. 167; and see generally Handlin and Handlin, *Commonwealth;* Louis B. Hartz, *Economic Policy and Democratic Thought, Pennsylvania, 1776–1860* (1948); and E. M. Dodd, *American Business Corporations Until 1860* (1954); John W. Cadman, *The Corporation in New Jersey, Business and Politics,* 1791–1875 (1949); Peter J. Coleman, *The Transformation of Rhode Island, 1790–1860* (1963).

[35] "Corporations," *American Jurist,* 4 (October 1830), 298; reprinted in Haar, *Golden Age of American Law,* p. 339. On mills and legislation, see Horwitz, *The Transformation of American Law,* pp. 47–53.

strue their charters with a "narrow, jealous eye."[36] Further, states regulated the internal management of corporate bodies: the coercive powers of officers, stockholders' meetings, voting, stock prices, and stock issuance. States might even direct how funds were to be invested. The charters of commercial banks, for example, at times directed that the banks invest in the capital stock of the state's canal, bridge, or turnpike companies.

Governments did more than direct. They aided corporate enterprise directly by buying large shares of stock—thus winning the right to place public officials on corporate boards. The people of Georgia owned that state's railroads; the government of Massachusetts did most of its early banking through the private Massachusetts State Bank; Pennsylvania owned in whole or in part canal companies, bridge companies, and later, railroads. While charters of incorporation in the new Republic resonated with tones of monopoly and privilege, the state nonetheless attempted to mold corporate venture to a public purpose. That private investors stood to profit was acknowledged; that the fruits of privileged corporate enterprise would enrich the commonwealth was assumed.[37]

The most common corporate bodies before 1820 included improvement companies, banking institutions, and insurance houses. In the period after 1820, a change in the nature and purpose of the corporation began to take place. It was during this time that the modern private business corporation gradually emerged out of the old quasi-public charter. The climax to this development came after the Civil War, but the outlines were clear long before then.

One source of change was technological. Corporate monopolies and franchises established early in the century threatened to strangle new competing enterprises. Should a turnpike franchise be allowed to bar the building of a canal or railroad along the same route? Should a bridge company collecting tolls bar the construction of a larger bridge in the vicinity that would provide free passage? Could a grist mill stand in the way of sawmills or of paper, textile, logging, and powder mills—mills that raised

[36] Victor Morawetz, *The Law of Private Corporations* (1886 ed.), vol. 2, p. 617; "narrow, jealous eye," quoting Friedman, *A History of American Law*, p. 453. On the role of corporations in the business and politics of two states, see, John W. Cadman, *The Corporation in New Jersey*, and Peter J. Coleman, *The Transformation of Rhode Island*.

[37] See, for example, Hartz, *Economic Policy and Democratic Thought* (Pennsylvania); Handlin and Handlin, *Commonwealth* (Massachusetts); Heath, *Constructive Liberalism* (Georgia); Smith, *Economic Readjustment of an Old Cotton State* (South Carolina); Primm, *Economic Policy in the Development of a Western State* (Missouri).

higher dams, absorbed a greater flow of the river, and altered the water-courses? Each new improvement signified some economic and technological advance; each promised to introduce a new service, furnish a cheaper way of making or doing things, lubricate the channels of commerce. Chief Justice Roger B. Taney posed the issue in his opinion in the *Charles River Bridge* case as one of progress versus stagnation, of new versus old:

> If this Court should establish the principles now contended for [the monopoly rights of chartered corporations], what is to become of the numerous rail roads established on the same line of travel with turnpike companies . . . ? We shall be thrown back to the improvements of the last century, and obliged to stand still, until the claims of the old turnpike corporations shall be satisfied; and [shall they] consent to permit these states to avail themselves of the lights of modern science, and to partake of the benefit of those improvements which are now adding to the wealth and prosperity, and the convenience and comfort, of every other part of the civilized world?[38]

A second source of antagonism toward the privileged corporation was related to rising expectations. The corporate charter, it was noted, was an extremely effective business device; the limitation on liability was especially appealing. The availability of charters, though, was limited. Legislators were accustomed to writing charters on a case-by-case basis, and then only for certain kinds of undertakings or ventures. The growth of the economy prompted a demand by new interests, often under the banner of equality, for freer access to the corporate form.

The attack on privileged enterprise received sustenance from political quarters as well. In the 1830s and after, the opponents of quasi-mercantilist policies accused government of having entered into an alliance with "purse proud men who now almost monopolize certain branches of business."[39] Government, went the charge, had tied the economic future of the country to a set of business interests that had prevailed in an earlier day. Now, the state was called on to open "a wide, unlimited field for competition" by making "a general law of partnerships" available to humble men.[40] Such policies would ensure economic and social progress because, it was believed, a truly free and competitive market rewarded innovation, efficiency, and productivity.

---

[38] Documents, pp. 197–210; and see Kutler, *Privilege and Creative Destruction*, and Horwitz, *Transformation of American Law*, pp. 130–139.
[39] William Leggett, *New York Evening Post*, December 30, 1834; in Theodore Sedgewick, Jr., *A Collection of the Political Writings of William Leggett* (1840), p. 144.
[40] John W. Vethake, *The Doctrine of Anti-Monopoly*, Documents, pp. 189–197.

There was also a party dimension behind the movement to "open wide" business activities and access to corporate forms. Jacksonian politicians attacked corporations as "having no souls or consciences" and possessed of a powerful "accumulating character."[41] But the models most often held up for vilification were entrenched monopolies, such as the Bank of the United States. Small business interests became natural allies of antimonopolism. Private banking interests, for example, had no qualms at all about criticizing the national bank as a foreign influence in the market, a concentrator of power and money that choked private entrepreneurial energies. When party politics mixed with economics, the brew became potent indeed. The panics of 1819 and 1837 made many states nervous about their investments in "mixed" (quasi-public) enterprises, and in a few states, such as Pennsylvania, brought an angry popular impetus to the insistence that the states retreat entirely from their partnerships with major business ventures.[42] "The whole objective of government is negative," said one Jacksonian reformer. "It is to remove, and keep out of his way all obstacles to . . . natural freedom, unshackled by arbitrary vexations, and galling restrictions, untrammeled by human legislation."[43]

By the middle of the century, government was responding with growing frequency to the building pressure by enacting "general" incorporation laws. For a fee, these laws extended corporate status to most comers, and the newcomers increasingly were manufacturing interests and the young railroads. Under general incorporation laws, the legislature left much of the internal management of the corporation to the officers themselves. The forms for general charters were standardized, varying mainly with the field of enterprise. The emergence of the private business corporation, moreover, reflected an understanding that the purpose of corporate enterprise was beginning to change. While the special charters had recognized some public purpose behind incorporation, the new corporations served the needs primarily of investors. The duties and restrictions formerly placed on corporations were progressively relaxed and finally eliminated. More and more, it was the courts who filled in the gaps in law. Commensurately, the loyalties of the corporation shifted from the

---

[41] "Corporations," in *American Jurist,* reprinted in Haar, *Golden Age of American Law,* p. 336.
[42] Hartz, *Economic Policy and Democratic Thought,* pp. 161–175; Carter Goodrich, *Government Promotion of American Canals and Railroads, 1800–1890* (1960).
[43] Luther Hamilton, *Memoirs of Robert Rantoul* (1854), p. 283.

community to the stockholder, as officers pursued policies aimed at generating the highest rates of return on investment dollars.[44]

The advent of the private business corporation must be judged as one of the greatest stimuli to midcentury economic expansion. The new manufacturing corporations located American industry and urban development in the Northeastern states. Canal and railroad companies, increasingly wholly private ventures, funneled people and manufactures to the Northwest and beyond in exchange for foodstuffs destined for Eastern cities. Steamboats made possible upriver navigation of the Mississippi, linking new cotton fields in the Southwest with Midwestern transit points, New England mills, and Atlantic coast reexport centers. Over all hovered private banks of all stripes, ready to finance expansion and improvements by extending long-term promissory notes against the hope of great profits tomorrow.

The Legacy of Antebellum Public Policy

State governments were deeply involved in almost every level of the economy. It is worth pondering the nature of that involvement in order to come to grips with the logic, and the long-run consequences, of antebellum public policy.

A first question is whether the rate of return on government investment in such areas as banking, manufacturing, and transportation was of a magnitude actually to accelerate economic growth. Economic historians have attempted to answer such questions by applying a cost-benefit analysis to individual government projects. After years of study, though, few hard answers can be given. The difficulty comes with assigning a quantitative value to such vague concepts as benefits. The Erie Canal and its tributaries, the subject of especially intensive study, extended and integrated spatially separated markets. The benefit was indirect because it

---

[44] At the time of the Revolution, only a small number of chartered corporations were in existence. By 1800, the number of chartered corporations had climbed to about 300 and included primarily banking, insurance, canal, bridge, and turnpike concerns. By 1830, 1,300 business corporations had come into existence in New England alone. By the eve of the Civil War, most new corporations were private business entities, organized under general incorporation laws. Dodd, *American Business Corporations Until 1860*, pp. 11, 417–419; Schwartz, *The Law in America*, pp. 62–63.

was diffused throughout the Northeastern and Midwestern economies, and for this reason it is not susceptible to precise measurement.[45]

A more concrete question is how state public policy created an environment conducive to growth.

Supplementing the constitutional system and the early promotional role of the national government, state governments widened the market and thus expanded opportunity by granting subsidies to the transport industry. Market transactions required capital; states eased the perennial pinch by generously chartering and in some instances subsidizing banking institutions. Public health laws and the encouragement given to formal education and professional organizations enriched human capital. In an era of simple machines and scarce labor, the capacity, adaptability, and ingenuity of the work force counted for a great deal. Educational institutions also expanded and diffused the fund of technical knowledge, which worked its way back into the economy and rekindled growth. The modernization of the credit system and the corporate charter made possible the easy acquisition and disposition of property. The limitations on liability commonly written into charters further subsidized high-risk, high-value ventures. State regulatory measures, though inadequate and only sporadically enforced, added to the merchantability of state commodities. Finally, occupational licensing and the criminal system policed the outer limits of business activity.

The acts of governments constitute only one-half of the equation. Government was of the people, and it was the people who willed expansion. There existed in America a core structure of values that thrust society forward, impelling people on to self-enrichment. Commercial expansion, the market economy, and political ideology eventually became linked, and in a pronounced way after 1830. Americans viewed development and expansion as a phase in the unfolding glory of the republic. And many—although more as a matter of belief than of fact—expected a share of the benefits. Social and political changes as well seemed to confirm popular aspirations. Egalitarian reforms brushed aside many of the impediments to equality, while the early stages of industrialization rendered the social structure extraordinarily fluid. In this kind of atmosphere, where restrictions on individuals receded and opportunity burgeoned, the work ethic and the motivation to achieve flourished. Self-improvement became a veritable cult in nineteenth-century America, and government became one means to that end.

---

[45] Bruchey, *Roots of American Economic Growth*, pp. 210–212. Albert Fishlow, *Railroads and the Transformation of the Antebellum Economy* (1965), is perhaps the best study attempting to quantify results.

The popular foundations of political power gave to antebellum public policy its special élan and, ultimately, its peculiar history. State governments did not dictate policies from on high. Rather, they channeled the energies of the people. They remained, throughout the era, extremely responsive to local political forces. The official policies of government reflected this political fact of life: they favored those persons, groups, or interests who were best able to mobilize support for the laws they favored. In every political clash there are losers. The way in which the antebellum economy grew by no means benefited everyone. When government rejected universal taxation in favor of delegating quasi-governmental powers to private corporations, it decided that the costs of development would not be democratically assessed. Subsidization of growth, that is, fell predominantly on the injured private parties whose rights, if enforced, would limit the active use of contiguous property. Likewise, private corporations, because they possessed privileges that individuals lacked, were able to accumulate vast financial empires at the expense of lesser organized interests in the economy, and even at the expense of the state. Corporations were "*the* striking feature of American business life" in the nineteenth century, according to Charles and Mary Beard, "comparable in wealth and power and the number of its servants with kingdoms and states of old."[46]

Because official policies were the result of so many intersecting political forces, lawmakers were rarely mindful of the long-range implications of their actions. The emergence of the private business corporation out of the old charter form, staged by state legislators, had an enormous impact on postbellum society. General incorporation laws divested corporations of their old communal moorings, as Oscar and Mary Handlin have argued, gave them privilege but held them to few principles, gave them power but divorced them of responsibility.[47] By the eve of the Civil War, state governments had begun a slow process of withdrawal from the economy. The free-market idea, always potent, now triumphed. The new role of government was becoming that of removing barriers standing in the way of business enterprise, of ensuring the free play of the market.

The enormous financial constraints under which state governments operated, finally, must be added to politics and the shifting economic ideologies to explain the rise and fall of quasi-mercantilist policies. Regulations, public health laws, and criminal sanctions had the large in-

---

[46] Charles and Mary Beard, *History of the United States* (1923), p. 409. Emphasis added.
[47] Handlin and Handlin, *Commonwealth,* pp. 180–181, 187–189.

tention of protecting the public good. In practice, these laws often languished on the books. No state government was prepared to tax the people to support a bureaucracy or a class of civil servants whose full-time job was enforcement. Thus regulatory laws tended to be local, self-sustaining, political, and subject to all the hazards of personal arbitrariness. Under the circumstances, little else could be done. Capital scarcity vexed antebellum America. To divert the flow of capital into government would have been politically inadvisable, if not impossible. The America of 1800 had called on government to structure business; the America of 1830 had expected government to aid people in acquiring wealth; the America of the 1850s called on government to remove all restraints on competition. There was little room in antebellum social thought for government rule. Not until about 1900 did a new consensus on the role of government evolve, one emphasizing administrative oversight through bureaucratic structures run by civil servants. And by then, the urge for growth had been replaced by the problem of managing powerful, wealthy, large-scale industrial businesses.

FOUR

The Courts and the Common Law

The Transformation of Courts and Decision Making

The previous chapter examined the efforts of state legislatures to construct a legal environment within which economic growth, territorial expansion, and technological innovation could occur. The subject of this chapter is the distribution of rights within society. The focus is on the courts and the laws they made. The ends of antebellum common law were not unlike those of antebellum legislation. Judges created new rules of law that enlarged the sphere of private action and gave effect to the maximum assertion of individual will. Courts, however, differed from legislatures in that judges were not the elected representatives of the people. In theory, courts of law simply adjudicated disputes between private parties, relying on legal precedent (prior cases of the same nature) and the justice of each case. In reality, the same ideological and legal imperatives that transformed the legislature into an active law- and policymaking institution also influenced the judiciary. Vast areas of the common law inherited from England and carried over from the colonies were modified by judges during the first half of the century, and their decisions bore the imprint of the political, social, and economic forces that swept through the society. Yet legal change was not total. As Oliver Wendell Holmes stated in his classic work, *The Common Law*, the law is "forever adapting new principles from life at one end, and it always retains old ones from history at the other."[1]

Prior to the nineteenth century, English and American judges subscribed to a theory of decision making that cast the judge in the role of a "law finder." The common law was thought to comprise an elegant and complete system of rules and first principles reflective of natural law and the "wisdom of the ages." The first judicial precedent of a legal rule was thus explained as a declaration of some known preexisting standard, or, in the words of an early-nineteenth-century American judge, an emanation of "immutable truth and justice which arises from the eternal fitness of things . . . ."[2] The end of common law, under this theory, "is the dispensation of *justice*, the elucidation and enforcement of the idea of right."[3]

In a penetrating study of early-nineteenth-century legal thought, Morton Horwitz has described how a new "instrumentalist" conception of common law came into existence in the new republic. According to Horwitz,

> In eighteenth century America, common law rules were not regarded as instruments of social change; whatever legal change took place generally was brought about through legislation. During this period, the common law was conceived of as a body of essentially fixed doctrine to be applied in order to achieve a fair result. . . . Consequently, American judges before the nineteenth century rarely analyzed common law rules functionally or purposively, and they almost never self-consciously employed the common law as a creative instrument for directing men's energies toward social change. . . . What dramatically distinguished nineteenth century law from its eighteenth century counterpart was the extent to which common law judges came to play a central role in directing the course of social change.[4]

The force behind this change was republican political theory, and it began with the consideration by the judiciary of what parts of English common law should apply in the new American states.

The central problem confronted by state judges was how to obtain popular consent to a common-law rule. In the aftermath of the American Revolution, Americans believed that English common law,

---

[1] Oliver Wendell Holmes, Jr., *The Common Law* (1881), p. 36.
[2] Jesse Root, "The Origins of Government and Law in Connecticut," preface to Root's *Reports*, vol. 1 (Conn., 1798), p. iv; quoted in Horwitz, *Transformation of American Law*, p. 20.
[3] "The Independence of the Judiciary," *North American Review* (1843), p. 411.
[4] Horwitz, *Transformation of American Law*, p. 1.

and especially the common law of crimes, originated less in the divine order of things, as originally believed, than in the will of the judge. And judge-made law, it was reasoned, took as its meter the political thought, morals, and religion of the age. This was an insight of stunning intellectual significance. It was also a troubling one. If law was the product of social values and judicial will, what legitimacy did common law (with its feudal English origins and judge-made rules) have in a republican society that made popular consent the foundation of law?

One solution, as Jeremy Bentham put it in a series of letters to President James Madison offering his services to codify American law, was to "shut our ports against the Common Law, as we would against the plague," and enact a new code of legislation.[5] The virtue of codification was that lawmaking powers would be placed in the hands of the people's elected representatives. Uniformity and equality under law would be enhanced by the rational and comprehensive nature of a code. The arbitrariness of courts would be checked. The call for codification came first from the radical wing of the Jeffersonian Republican party and later from the supporters of the Jacksonian Democratic party.[6]

The critics of codification, most often judges and lawyers, countered that it would be practically impossible for legislators to enact codes that could meet every conceivable need and demand of a growing society. They were simply not up to the task. "The multitude of legislators," went one charge, included men of "learning, prudence, and experience, mixed up with a great deal of ignorance, vanity, and pretension." They were inclined to embark on projects "founded upon crude and visionary notions, superficial views of the delicate and various relations which each particular provision bears to the whole system."[7] Arguments for an expanded lawmaking power of courts clearly conflicted with republican and democratic theory; but the conflict was minimized when theorists and commentators took the next step and suggested that American common law, having broken the bonds of English precedent in the early decades of the century, had actually come to be the embodiment of the popular will. The advantage of common law, it was contended, was that it furnished "remedies according to growing wants, and varying circumstances of

---

[5] *The Works of Jeremy Bentham* (1962), p. 478; quoted in Schwartz, *The Law in America*, p. 72.
[6] See Robert Rantoul, "Oration at Scituate," and Timothy Walker, "Codification," Documents, pp. 84–96. See also Aumann, *Changing American Legal System,* pp. 120–137.
[7] Lemuel Shaw, "Profession of Law in the United States," Documents, p. 100.

man . . . without waiting for the slow progress of legislative interference."[8] Moreover, it was believed that the common law was "peculiarly well fitted to the rapidly advancing state of our country," since it

> possesses in an eminent degree the capacity of adapting itself to the gradual progress of improvement among us; and that this accommodating principle which pervades it, will adjust itself to every degree and species of improvement that may be suggested by practice, commerce, observation, study, or refinement.[9]

No court could for long ignore "reason" and "principle," the foundations of the common-law system of adjudication; nor could it run against the spirit of popular legislation. But it was possible, under the newly arising theory of law as an instrument of the people's will, for the judiciary to build an American common law that fulfilled popular needs and demands. The implications behind this dramatic rethinking of law were enormous. For one, it meant that precedent need not exert a restraining influence on American judges. "Bad" cases could be discarded as unsuited to American conditions. For another, it meant that American courts could legitimately shape legal rules into dynamic instruments for change.

Contract

The history of contract law in the first half-century is illustrative of the ways in which American common law changed.[10] A contract between two parties that ended up before a court in the eighteenth century was validated after meeting three tests. The court first determined whether a "meeting of the minds" existed between the parties. A second element of a valid contract was "consideration," the heart of the transaction,

[8] Zephaniah Swift, *A Digest of the Law of Evidence* (1810), p. v; quoted in Horwitz, *Transformation of American Law,* p. 23.
[9] Joseph Story, *Report of the Commission on Codification of the Law to the Governor of Massachusetts* (1837); reprinted in Presser and Zainaldin, *Law and American History,* pp. 398–405.
[10] See generally, Lawrence M. Friedman, *Contract Law in America, A Social and Economic Case Study* (1965); Horwitz, *Transformation of American Law,* pp. 160–210, on the conceptual development of American contract law; and Nelson, *Americanization of the Common Law,* pp. 136–144.

whereby one thing of value is given in exchange for another. Both these tests were essentially objective in nature and were made by reference to the terms of the, ordinarily written, agreement. The third test introduced an element of subjectivity: a valid contract must also be a fair one. The examination of fairness often turned on questions of fraud, false pretense, and undue advantage. The court, and in some cases the jury, scrutinized the agreement to determine that the things exchanged were of roughly equivalent value. Under this doctrine, known as "sound price," a thing of little or no value given in exchange for a thing of great value might result in the court's refusal to enforce the contract, or the refusal of the jury to award damages for nonperformance of the agreement. Discretion was key to the decision, for "sound price" resided solely in the minds of the judge and jury.

One of the clearest illustrations of the sound price doctrine appears in the 1822–1824 case of *Seymour v. Delancey.* A landowner had entered into a contract of sale in which two country farms were traded for a two-thirds interest in two town lots. The farm owner later attempted to back out of the contract, on the grounds that the agreement violated the sound price doctrine. The owners of the city lots sued for the enforcement of the contract. Chancellor Kent of New York, hearing the case, believed that a court "must be satisfied that the claim for a deed is fair and just, and reasonable." In his estimation the "village lots were not worth half the value of the country farms," and when the "consideration is so inadequate as to render it a hard bargain, the argument is strong against it."[11] He then declined to enforce the contract.

Several assumptions lie behind the ruling in *Seymour*—and behind the conception of contract on which that case rested. Most obvious is that law should not lend its support to agreements that violate the community's moral or ethical sense of fairness. In this view, law exists to maintain powers of control over the assertion of individual will. From an economic standpoint, there is a confidence in Kent's ruling that judges or juries can accurately ascertain the value of things traded, here farm and town land. Implicit in this confidence is a static vision of the economy, where the value of a thing yesterday is a good guide to the value of a thing tomorrow. Finally, the reluctance to enforce "hard bargains" reveals a preference in law for maintaining things as they are. The function of the court, then, is to monitor agreements and enforce only those that do not upset the order of things—whether of wealth, status, or morality.

[11] 6. Johns. Ch. 222 (1822); quoted in Presser and Zainaldin, *Law and American History*, pp. 291–293.

Kent's conception of contract in 1822 is a striking instance of a common-law rule caught between old and new ways of thinking. While his ruling was faithful to the precedent, it clashed with the spirit of development and individualism gaining ascendancy in the states. A law that preserved the status quo was hardly sufficient for a people engaged in ambitious enterprises. Resources were abundant but untapped, and the desire to exploit them was growing. Capital was scarce and in high demand. The new manufacturing and transportation projects held out the prospects of grand profits for investors, but the uncertain nature of new undertakings dictated caution. In much the same way that legislatures acted to harness national energies to the exploitation of resources by structuring the market, courts produced rules that governed the market's operation. But changes in common law were necessary. In the area of contract, individuals would have to be free to bargain and barter in their own self-interest. It was vitally important to the market-oriented model of contract, then, that courts enforce agreements without much inquiry into their speculative nature.

A second look at *Seymour v. Delancey* is revealing*, for in its eventual outcome we can see the emergence of a new doctrine of law in synchrony with social change. Senator Sudam reviewed Kent's decision and overruled each of his conclusions of law. Sudam believed that Kent's valuation of the town lots was based only on a finding of "mere inequality" of value. The town lots were situated near a proposed site for the construction of a navy yard, he noted. The lots would instantly increase in value if the yard were built. The transaction therefore was speculative in nature, he concluded, and as such was not susceptible to any objective evaluation. For this reason, it could not be predicted against whom the "hard bargain" would work. And since all parties seemed to have been aware of the risks, he asked, "what right have we to sport with" the agreement "fairly and deliberately entered into." He ended by restating the law: unfair contracts unworthy of court enforcement should include only those whose terms were "so flagrant and palpable as to convince a man at first blush that one of the contracting parties had been imposed upon by some false pretense."[12]

Sudam's language and reasoning followed the general outlines of a newly emerging contract law resting on the doctrine of *caveat emptor*

---

* The case arose in the New York Court for the Trial of Impeachment and Correction of Error. The entire senate, the state's chief justice, and the equity chancellor sat on the court.

[12] Seymour v. Delancey, 3 Cow. (1824), quoted in Presser and Zainaldin, *Law and American History*, p. 293.

(buyer beware). Under *caveat emptor*, which by 1840 had replaced the sound price doctrine in most courts, several of the earlier tests remained intact. There must still exist a meeting of the minds, and a consideration must be evident in the written agreement; but discretion to examine the fairness of the agreement was being withdrawn from the court.

There is a discrete link between developments in contract during the period and the economic and political changes sweeping society. "Americans . . . were a people going places in a hurry," Bernard Schwartz has written, and contract "was the legal instrument that helped them get there."[13]

The appearance of *caveat emptor* reflected the rising prominence of free-market forces in midcentury society. The value of property was becoming too inconstant to sustain objective evaluation, the interdependence of market transactions in a national economy too vital to permit community intervention. Behind this new law lay a sublime confidence that freedom to pursue self-interest would generate a multitude of day-to-day transactions, fueling commerce and bringing an ever larger portion of the population into the web of the market. The new law also accorded with social and political values in the Age of Jackson. It enthroned free will; it gave the individual the fullest opportunity for exercising his faculties in the employment of his property; and it maximized the sphere of private discretion in the utilization of resources. (See *White v. Flora and Cherry*, Documents, pp. 154–158.)

Property and Tort

Closely allied with developments in contract law were developments in the law of property and tort. Portions of the English common law of property held great sway over early-nineteenth-century American judges. Blackstone had summarized the essence of that law in two pithy maxims: "Use your own property in such a manner as not to injure that of another," and "the owner of the soil owns to the sky."[14] Although the two principles would seem contradictory, the one limiting and the other expanding rights in land, taken together they can be seen to express a high regard for the ideal of quiet, undisturbed possession. It would be a violation of the

---

[13] Schwartz, *The Law in America*, p. 59.
[14] William Blackstone, *Commentaries on the Laws of England* (1768), vol. 3, p. 218; quoted in Presser and Zainaldin, *Law and American History*, p. 297.

first rule, for example, "if a person keeps his hogs, or other noisome animals, so near the house of another, that the stench of them incommodes him and makes the air unwholesome."[15] For this was an injurious "nuisance," and enforceable by action of trespass on the case for nuisance, "as it tends to deprive" the neighbor "of the use and benefit of his house."[16] Blackstone did not mean to suggest that landowners were incapable of putting their property to use, only that they must be mindful of the rights of others, for "the law of England enforce[s] that excellent rule of gospel–morality, of 'doing for others, as we would they should do unto ourselves.'" In the case of hogs, one "must find some other place to do that act, where it will be less offensive."[17]

Early-nineteenth-century American property law recognized other kinds of rights. In some instances, the law awarded special privileges to those who improved their land. Thus, to take one example, a person who improved his property by building a dwelling house on it automatically obtained after twenty years a right to the sunlight washing over the premises. The right of "ancient light," as it was called, precluded neighbors from obstructing the flow of sunlight by building, say, tall or contiguous structures. Or a person who had erected a mill on a stream running over his property could obtain after twenty years' usage a right to have the same quantum of water always flowing through his mill. This prohibited upstream landowners from interfering with the flow of water, perhaps by building mills of their own. In both examples, the law protected an initial investment in property, and the effect was to favor first users or developers by granting them a monopoly over scarce resources.[18]

A final category of property rights in common law incorporated elements of competition and public benefit. In some cases, American and English common law sanctioned competitive uses of property that inflicted incidental damage on others, provided that some benefit accrued to the public. For example—and again English common law furnished the model—in some situations it was not considered a "nuisance" for one to erect a mill so close to another that it drew away the customary quantity of water that flowed downstream. Nor was it a nuisance "to set up any trade, or school, in neighborhood or rivalship with another."[19] For in both in-

---

[15] Ibid., p. 299.
[16] Ibid.
[17] Ibid.
[18] Ibid.
[19] Ibid.

stances the law recognized that by "such emulation the public are like to be gainers, and if the mill or school occasion a damage to the old one, it is damage without injury."[20]

Though most state courts recognized some or all features of this hierarchy of rights in property, changes in legal emphasis soon appeared, changes that favored certain types of property owners and businessmen—those whom judges identified with the "onward spirit of the age." These changes borrowed heavily from another area of law, the law of torts.

A "tort," simply defined, is a "wrong" committed against an individual's property, right, or person. The most important innovation in the nineteenth-century idea of tort was the development of the modern doctrine of "negligence." In common law, before the advent of modern negligence, a person causing damage to another was held absolutely liable for costs, and further bore the burden of proving his innocence, regardless of the damager's intent or the reason for the injury. "Under common law a man *acts* at his peril."[21] Known as strict or "absolute liability," few defenses could be made in a law suit in justification for damage (acts of God being the strongest).

The modern negligence doctrine, on the other hand, looked to the *cause* of the damage and held damagers liable only for injuries that flowed directly from some *fault*. In a classic statement of the new negligence doctrine, Chief Justice Lemuel Shaw of Massachusetts, in *Brown v. Kendall* (1850), declared that "the plaintiff must come prepared with evidence to show either that the *intention* was unlawful, or that the defendant was *in fault*; for if the injury was unavoidable, and the conduct of the defendant was free from blame, he will not be liable."[22] Thus pure accident, or the inability to foresee the consequences of a course of action—neither of which imply fault or culpability—under negligence doctrine became a good defense in a law suit. "No liability without culpability" was becoming a maxim of tort law. Conversely, damages that resulted from carelessness came within the category of fault and should result in compensation for the injured party. The law governing damages, which turned on causation, changed in like fashion. The traditional English rule that "Everyone who does an unlawful act is considered as the doer of all that follows" had given way by 1846 to a new rule that damages "must be the natural and proximate consequences of the wrongful act."[23] Liability for

---

[20] Ibid.
[21] Holmes, *The Common Law*, p. 82.
[22] Documents, pp. 174–179.
[23] *Scott v. Shepherd*, 2 W. Bl. 892, 899 (1773), for the English rule; Simon Greenleaf, *Treatise on the Law of Evidence*, vol. 2 (1846), sec. 265, for the American rule; see also Schwartz, *The Law in America*, pp. 56–57.

damages was therefore restricted by the requirement that a plaintiff must prove that a defendant's act was the "efficient producing cause." [24]

The conceptual innovations in the negligence and damage aspects of tort law profoundly affected property rights in the first half of the century. As as it did, the old hierarchy of property law collapsed, to be replaced by a unitary theory of rights founded on such codes of conduct as "reasonable use" and "reasonable care." Persons who used their property in a reasonable way or conducted their activities with prudence and care were exempted from the injuries they caused others. Liability was becoming founded on an "objective" measure based on how the "average man, the man of ordinary intelligence and prudence" could be expected to act. [25]

The new doctrines of reasonable use and care can be seen to have encouraged a spirit of competition among property owners, for it eroded priority of rights among property users by making liability contingent on the prudence and usefulness of action. As in the law of contract, the effect of the new tort rules was to expand the possibilities of action by limiting the damage liabilities of actors. This meant, for example, that technologically innovative enterprises, which in their nature inflicted some damage on neighbors, might be immunized from liability if they were reasonable in purpose and operation. And when judges defined reasonableness, they relied on objective standards (is the emission of noxious smoke and cinders incidental to the operation of a steam locomotive?) as well as considerations of public policy (should railroads be encouraged?) (See *Hentz v. The Long Island Railroad Company*, pp. 158–165.)

A good illustration of how changes in tort law might affect property use appears in the 1832 case of *Lexington & Ohio Railroad v. Applegate*. The decision of the Kentucky court is illustrative of how antebellum judges attempted to balance competing claims among developers and landowners, and it underscores the importance of public issues in private dispute resolutions.

The case was brought by a group of property owners in Louisville whose houses and store lots were situated along either side of a main street. The plaintiffs asked the court to issue an injunction against the operators of the railroad, the tracks of which ran down the middle of the street. The property owners argued that the railroad constituted a nuisance and, further, invaded their property rights (each lot extended to the middle

---

[24] *Marble v. Worcester*, 70 Mass. (4 Gray) 395, 406 (1855), quoted in Schwartz, *The Law in America*, p. 57.

[25] Holmes, *The Common Law*, p. 108.

of the street). The noise and smoke from the train made their homes less habitable, posed dangers to pedestrians, startled horses, and frightened away shoppers. The court, though, declined to issue an injunction that would have stopped the running of the train, since in its estimation the operation of the railroad constituted a "reasonable use" of the street "consistent with the purposes for which the street was established." They additionally determined that the operators were shown to have exercised "diligence" and "care" in running the train. But just as important as reasonableness in the court's decision was the explicit policy of protecting the young railroad:

> The onward spirit of the age must, to a reasonable extent, have its way. The law is made for the times, and will be made or modified by them. The expanded and still expanding genius of the common law should adopt it here, as elsewhere, to the improved and improving conditions of our country and countrymen. And, therefore, railroads and locomotive steam cars—the offspring, as they will also be the parents, of progressive improvement—should not, in themselves be considered as nuisances, although, in ages that are gone, they might have been held so.[26]

Land

If the uses to which land could be put changed, so too did the ways in which land could be owned and transferred. In a society that prized freedom of action, and made the free market a central institution in the economy, the legislative removal of restraints on the free acquisition and disposition of land became essential.

One of the early reforms in land law concerned tenure. Tenure is the "mode by which one holds an estate in land . . . importing any kind of holding, from mere possession to the owning of an estate of inheritance."[27] During the colonial period, the "ancient, complicated and barbarous" machinery of "monarchial . . . land tenure" was slowly reformed.[28] The movement was toward universal freehold tenure. The states completed this reform in the early decades of the nineteenth century by making all land tenure alloidial, whereby dominion is absolute and direct. The beauty of alloidial or "fee simple" tenure is its conceptual simplicity. The

---

[26] 38 Ky. (8 Dana) 289 (1839).
[27] Ballantine's *Law Dictionary,* s. v. "tenure."
[28] *Coster v. Lorillard* (1835) 12 New York Common Law Reports [14 Wend. 265].

freeholder is unburdened of any restrictions or conditions that attach to the more traditional tenures. Hand in hand with changes in tenure came changes in inheritance law. Soon after the Revolution, state legislatures abolished the old succession laws of primogeniture (inheritance of the land by the eldest son), widespread in the Southern and Middle states, and partible inheritance (the practice of giving sons of the deceased a double share in land), common in New England. New succession laws were instituted that distributed the property of the deceased equally to all the children. Also restricted was the practice of entailing land. An entail permitted a landowner, usually by means of a last will and testament, to lock his land in a family across several generations of heirs. One who possessed an entailed estate was, technically, barred from selling or otherwise alienating it outside the family.[29]

The developments in the law of tenure, succession, and entail dovetailed with developments in the law of property conveyance. The traditional methods of transferring title to land, with their archaic "deeds of enfeoffment" and "livery of seisin," made the sale of land costly if not risky. For any technical defect in the papers of conveyance, or failure to comply with certain customary procedures, might result in a transfer of clouded title. The traditional act of conveying a piece of land, therefore, required careful, knowledgeable, and usually expensive legal advice. At a time when land was becoming one of the principal articles of commerce, impatience with traditional procedures led to simpler, more streamlined practices of conveyance. By 1850, legislators and judges in most states, "eager to unclog the land market," had replaced older conveyancing practices with more rational and uniform procedures, and initiated the use of standardized, printed forms that could be mass produced and cheaply used.[30]

As burdensome as traditional conveyancing procedures was the traditional mode of trial in cases where title to land was disputed. The old common-law actions that initiated trial were stupendously complex and incurred enormous expenditures of time and money, and they therefore made the outcomes of trials unpredictable. The "action of ejectment" was adopted as a reform by most states by the middle of the century. Like freehold tenure, ejectment was the essence of simplicity and directness. It

[29] Stanley N. Katz, "Republicanism and the Law of Inheritance in the American Revolutionary Era," *University of Michigan Law Review*, 76 (1977), 1. A discussion of the legal changes appears in James Kent, *Commentaries on American Law*, 2nd ed. (1832), vol. IV, pp. 12–20.
[30] Friedman, *A History of American Law*, pp. 205–209.

dispensed with highly abstract technical pleadings, made possible the introduction of all sorts of evidence, expedited the trial, simplified the questions put to the jury, and rendered outcomes more certain.

The alterations in land law, conveyancing, and trial worked toward mutually inclusive ends. They made the ideal of property ownership paramount in law by removing restraints on its acquisition, and they favored movement over static possession by easing the restrictions on land's free alienation.

Family Relations

Like the law of contract, property, and tort, the law of the family underwent fundamental changes in the direction of privatization. In early America the law of the family took its shape from English legal practices, religious norms, and social customs peculiar to the conditions of New World settlement. And the image of the family projected by that law was both patriarchal and authoritarian. The legal relationship of the husband and wife is illustrative. In both English and early American law, the unmarried woman possessed the same legal rights as a man. But after marriage, her distinct and equal legal identity became submerged in the person of her husband (see Elizabeth Cady Stanton, p. 210). In the language of law, she ceased to be "femes sole" and became "femes covert." Through the quasi-religious fiction of marital unity, the husband and wife became a mystical "one" at the time of matrimony, but the "one" was in reality the husband. The symbolism of marital union was described in a highly descriptive passage from a seventeenth-century law tract:

> In this consolidation which we call wedlock is a locking together. It is true, that man and wife are one person; but understand in what manner. When a small brooke or little river incorporateth with Rhodanus, Humber, or the Thames, the poor rivulet looseth her name; it is carried and recarried with the new associate; it beareth no sway; it possesseth nothing during coverture. . . . I may more truly, farre way, say to a married woman, Her new self is her superior; her companion [is] her master.[31]

At marriage, then, the woman became, in effect, a legal nullity. Any land brought into the marriage by the wife passed under the control of

[31] *The Lawes Resolution of Womens Rights; or, The Lawes Provision for Women* (1632); quoted in Julia Cherry Spruill, *Women's Life and Work in the Southern Colonies* (1972 ed.), p. 340.

the husband; she could own no personal property outright, not even the clothing she wore; she could petition the legislature for divorce but only under the most extraordinary of circumstances; and she lost any privilege of custody over her children when she removed herself "from the protection" of her husband, whether legally through divorce or for any other reason.

The law did impose a moral obligation on husbands to cherish and support their wives, but it was merely a duty and as such could not be enforced in the courts. If the wife was "unruly," according to Sir William Blackstone, she could be chastised by her husband with a "rod no thicker than the thumb."[32] The American colonies did modify some of the harsher elements of English common law, and in practice, exceptions to the rule were tolerated. In some cases, for example, women could enter prenuptial agreements and thus own property, and as Richard B. Morris has found, postnuptial agreements providing for separate support and maintenance were recognized.[33] Nancy Cott, in a study of colonial Massachusetts divorce, discovered that on occasion the General Court would grant a divorce against an errant or absent husband.[34] But these are exceptions. For most of the population, the legal dominion of the husband was assumed, and jealously guarded in law.

Children had no greater share of legal rights. It is revealing that the law used the words "master" and "servant" interchangeably with the words "parent" and "child," borrowing from the language of apprenticeship. But children lacked the rights of the indentured servant. Conceptually, they were more like articles of property in which the father "possesses title," and over which the state could have little intervening power. In recognition of this parental autonomy, the law placed few restraints on parental treatment of children. If "correction" bordered on physical abuse, or if treatment approached neglect, children enjoyed few legal recourses. Full obedience to parental will was the rule, and some colonies even made youthful insubordination punishable by death. The law did recognize a community interest in the duty of parents to support and educate their children, but the duty gave birth to no enforceable right in

[32] Cited in Maxwell Bloomfield, *American Lawyers in a Changing Society, 1776–1876* (1976), p. 95.

[33] Richard B. Morris, *Studies in the History of American Law, with Special Reference to the Seventeenth and Eighteenth Centuries* (1930), p. 143.

[34] Nancy F. Cott, "Divorce and the Changing Status of Women in Eighteenth-Century Massachusetts," in *The American Family in Social-Historical Perspective,* ed. Michael Gordon, (1978), pp. 115–131; and Nancy F. Cott, "Eighteenth-Century Family and Social Life Revealed in Massachusetts Divorce Records," *Journal of Social History,* 10 (1976).

the child. God, according to Blackstone, protected children "more effectually than any laws, by implanting in the breast of every parent that . . . insuperable degree of affection which not even the deformity of person or mind, not even the wickedness, ingratitude, and rebellion of children, can totally suppress or extinguish."[35]

As in the case of married women, law and practice not infrequently diverged. Only a few instances exist of capital punishment for insubordinate children; extreme physical abuse of children now and then led to criminal prosecution; and some colonies, particularly in the seventeenth century, did make parental duties enforceable. It was also possible, of course, for the community to intervene in the family for the protection of children in ways that the law never could. But as in the legal fiction of marital unity, the relation of parent and child harbored no conception of familial rights divisible equally among the members. Authority and legal power gathered around the person of the household head.

The organization of the law of family relations (there was as yet no distinct branch of "family law") on patriarchal tenets made good sense in a society that valued authority over liberty, stability over change, and community values over individual self-interest. Relations in the family duplicated lines of authority in the society. The family thus functioned as a little community, an agent that brought prevailing social values to bear in the most personal of ways.[36]

The logic of patriarchy gradually became strained, and eventually collapsed, in the newer society of the nineteenth century. New forms of law appeared, with a new logic. They were slow in emerging, and reforms were piecemeal at best. But legal changes were emphatic and irreversible, as Maxwell Bloomfield has argued, and they moved in the direction of expanding rights for women and children and an enlarged power of the courts to intervene in family affairs.[37]

Developments in divorce, child custody, and property rights implicitly recognized a degree of autonomy in married women. The judicial divorce spread rapidly through the Northern states in the first half-century and made divorce more accessible and less expensive. Grounds for divorce were also expanded. Added to the traditional ground of adultery were the grounds of physical cruelty, desertion, and nonsupport. Some states made

---

[35] William Blackstone, *Commentaries on the Laws of England* (1889 ed.), vol. 1, p. 447; quoted in Bloomfield, *American Lawyers in a Changing Society*, p. 98.
[36] See, e.g., John Demos, *A Little Commonwealth: Family Life in Plymouth Colony* (1970).
[37] Bloomfield, *American Lawyers in a Changing Society*, pp. 91–135.

the grounds purposefully vague to encompass a wider gambit of marital behavior. Indiana was in the forefront of liberalized divorce law. Retaining
the traditional grounds of adultery, bigamy, and desertion, Indiana statutes
added the new grounds of cruelty, habitual drunkenness, conviction of a
felony, and "any other cause for which the Court shall deem it proper that
the divorce shall be granted."[38] A development common to most states was
the elimination of legislative divorce, which was expensive, and the im-
plementation of divorce by court decree, which was cheap and for the first
time brought legal divorce "within the reach of every taxpayer."[39]

Though divorce in the nineteenth century remained rare—and even as
a judicial procedure it remained beyond the financial reach of the poor—
the reformed divorce law did permit some women to escape unduly harsh
and unhappy alliances. It was also possible for women to retain custody of
children. New legislation directed judges to award custody with a view to
the child's needs and wishes, "on the principle that the rights of the
parents to their children, in the absence of misconduct, are equal, and the
happiness and welfare of the children are to determine the care and
custody."[40] And in states without custody legislation, there was nevertheless a marked tendency among the courts to refrain from enforcing the
husband's superior right of guardianship if the wife could prove a superior
ability to rear the children.

Perhaps the most significant gains for married women occurred in the
area of property rights. Here, more than anywhere else, the principle of
independence was recognized. Several states by the middle of the century
had enacted married women's property legislation.[41] The statutes departed from the common law and from equity by permitting wives to hold
property and enter into contracts for its sale and purchase independently
of their husbands. Some states steadfastly refused to enact such laws, confusing the economic issues with the more controversial questions of
morality, religion, and politics. As the attorney for one disgruntled
husband protested:

> The right sought . . . goes far beyond anything that has yet been conceded to
> the cause of woman's rights. To enable the wife to leave her husband at
> pleasure, and to take with her, in the retreat, all her property, of every kind
> and description, to be enjoyed by her, and managed and disposed of as her

---

[38] Quoted in ibid., p. 121.
[39] Ibid.
[40] "Married Women," *Monthly Law Reporter*, 23 (1860), 362, 370.
[41] Joel Bishop, *Commentaries on the Law of Married Women* (1875), vol. 2, p. 342 et seq.

own, apart from and to the entire exclusion of the husband, and in total disregard of the marital rights, is a monstrous proposition, that, among all the wild theories of improvements, has never yet been advocated in a civilized, Christian community, until the bringing of this suit, except by a few erratic and fanatical women, composing what is known as the "Woman's Rights Society."[42]

States that refused to enact liberalizing legislation did not shut their doors to courts of equity, which freely enforced nuptial property settlements and thereby arrived, though circuitously and with great expense, at a similar result.

Yet it must be observed that married women's property laws often served the interests of husbands by permitting them to shield family property from creditors, and courts often construed the legislation so narrowly as to defeat its intent. But the existence of the legislation, like developments in divorce and custody, contributed to the erosion of the fictional unity of marriage and buttressed a new conception of marriage as a partnership of equals.

Changes in the child's legal standing were less dramatic. The assumption of parental authority seems never to have been directly challenged. But in a marginal sense, the child's position did improve. For example, the evolving doctrines of child custody under the common law favored wives over husbands, but they also benefited children, since they were premised on a conception of the child's needs (see *Mercein v. The People,* Documents, pp. 224–229). Courts also demonstrated a reluctance to enforce parental guardianship rights against third-party custodians, if any alteration in custody would cause major harm to the child (see *Gilkeson v. Gilkeson,* Documents, pp. 229–233).[43]

More significant, perhaps, was the expansion of judicial power to entertain questions of the child's "rights." In English courts, and at least since the sixteenth century, the doctrine of *parens patriae* empowered judges to intervene in the family to protect the child's property from "waste" by parents or guardians. In America, courts redefined *parens patriae* to permit judicial intervention for the protection of the child's person or morals. A remarkable passage in the opinion written by Senator Paige in the case of *Mercein v. The People* (1840) attributed an explicitly republican foundation to the new power:

---

[42] *Schindel v. Schindel,* 12 Md. 294, 307–308 (1858); quoted in Bloomfield, *American Lawyers in a Changing Society,* p. 116.
[43] Jamil S. Zainaldin, "The Emergence of a Modern American Family Law: Child Custody, Adoption, and the Courts, 1796–1851," *Northwestern University Law Review,* 73 (1979).

By the law of nature, the father has no paramount right to the custody of his child. By that law the wife and child are equal to the husband and father; but inferior and subject to their sovereign. The head of a family, in his character of husband and father, has no authority over his wife and children; but in his character of sovereign he has. On the establishment of civil societies, the power of the chief of a family as sovereign, passes to the chief or government of the nation. And the chief or magistrate of the nation, not possessing the requisite knowledge necessary to a judicious discharge of the duties of guardianship and education of children, such portion of the sovereign power as relates to the discharge of these duties, is transferred to the parents, subject to such restrictions and limitations as the sovereign power of the nation think proper to prescribe. There is no parental authority independent of the supreme power of the state. . . . The moment a child is born, it owes allegiance to the government of the country of its birth, and is entitled to the protection of that government. And such government is obligated by its duty of protection, to consult the welfare, comfort and interests of such child in regulating its custody during the period of its minority.[44]

This expanded power under *parens patriae,* coupled with the state's police power, later was used to sustain compulsory education and child labor laws against the claims of parental sovereignty. These changes were more symbolic than real in the first half of the century, however. Not until 1900 was there a distinct conception of "children's rights"—the right not to be abused, mistreated, neglected or exploited, or denied support and education. But developments in custody law and *parens patriae* mark the beginning of a major reconception of parental rights in the courts as a power "held in trust" from political society, and thus within the scope of judicial regulation.[45]

In the areas of adoption and illegitimacy, judicial and legislative innovations were considerable. And again, the courts were the spearhead of reform.

Historically, members of communities, often neighbors and relatives, have taken in unattached children and treated them as family members. But under traditional common law these adopted sons and daughters possessed no clearly defined legal status. They could not inherit property from their de facto parents; nor could these parents claim any legal right of custody. Signs of change first appeared in the early decades of the nineteenth century, when American courts began recognizing limited rights in de facto adoptive parents and children. These rights were made more

---

[44] Documents, pp. 224–229.
[45] Zainaldin, "The Emergence of a Modern American Family Law," pp. 1084–1085.

secure, and the procedure for adoption formalized, by legislation—first in Massachusetts in 1851 and later in all states. These new laws gave adopted children rights of inheritance and imposed on parents the ordinary duties of providing protection, support, and education. Like adoptive children, children born outside marriage were considered nullities under law. *Filius nullius* was the legal description that Blackstone had affixed to these offspring; they were the children of nobody. First by judicial decision, and later by legislation, antebellum law softened the stigma of illegitimacy by recognizing reciprocal rights of custody and inheritance in children and unwed mothers.

The movement of law toward equality between husbands and wives, and the new concern for the needs and welfare of children, were pushed forward by values that originated outside law. Certainly early-nineteenth-century republicanism, with its heavy emphasis on rights of citizenship and liberty, and midcentury democratization, with its stress on equality, challenged the legitimacy of patriarchalism that had infused traditional common law. But developments in family law, which only at this period in history was becoming a distinct branch of law, may have owed just as much to the changing conception of childhood and family. Philippe Ariès has contended that in premodern society children were rarely differentiated from adults; they were seen simply as smaller versions with like attributes. By the nineteenth century a new view of children prevailed in Western culture. Now they were seen as distinct from adults in almost every imaginable way. In particular, children were thought to be innocent, delicate, and infinitely malleable; they possessed a psychology all their own.[46]

A similar change occurred in the conception of the family. In premodern society, according to John Demos and Peter Laslett, the family was an amorphous and changeable institution.[47] The family included not only parents and children, but kinsmen, those who boarded in the household, and indentured servants. In nineteenth-century America, the family gradually became a circle that encompassed only parents and children. And relationships in the family increasingly turned away from ascribed status to bonds of sentiment, feeling, and affection. To arbitrarily enforce superior rights through law, whether of the husband or the parents, may have been seen as opposed to the purpose of the family in nineteenth-century America.[48]

[46] Philippe Ariès, *Centuries of Childhood: A Social History of Family Life* (1962).
[47] Demos, *A Little Commonwealth;* Peter Laslett, *The World We Have Lost* (1965).
[48] Zainaldin, "The Emergence of a Modern American Family Law," p. 1084.

The growing attention paid to childhood and maternal power traces the outlines of a new image of sexual role. The new manufacturing economy of nineteenth-century America created barriers between work and home; labor became separated from household and family. Among the American middle class in this period, the father-husband increasingly was the one who worked outside the home, while the management of the family's internal affairs and child-rearing responsibilities gradually devolved upon the mother. Adding legitimacy to this social fact was a new intellectual stereotype of women. Supposedly, the woman had been endowed with endemic purity and innocence that suited her for the special tasks of child rearing and home management.[49] Within the circle of the family, the wife was becoming an equal of the husband; her "natural" empathy with children inevitably shattered the legal dominion of the father.

The Legacy of Legal Change: A Question of Neutrality

A major theme of antebellum common law is the redistribution of rights. And the nature of this redistribution was uniquely American: rights that in an earlier time had been considered essentially public in nature were now becoming private. Privatization of rights was accomplished through the creation by courts of relatively autonomous zones that held intrusive public power at bay. This was as true for contracting parties, property owners, and developers as it was for children and wives in families. The effect of changes in common law, then, was to erode the authority that communities had customarily enjoyed in overseeing daily life. "Man," to use the language of Walt Whitman, was becoming "a law, and series of laws, unto himself, surrounding and providing for, not only his own personal control, but all his relations to other individuals, and to the State."[50]

The privatization of rights, or making "man . . . [a] series of laws, unto himself," accorded well with the economic climate and the new democratic culture of antebellum America. Social changes in the second half of the century, however, wrenched it out of context and gave it new meaning. Late-Victorian America was a society at war with itself, propelled toward some unknown destination by forces that few could understand. Large-scale industrial capitalism was destroying free-market com-

[49] Nancy F. Cott, *The Bonds of Womanhood: "Women's Sphere" in New England, 1780–1835* (1977).
[50] *Democratic Vistas* (1871), p. 17.

petition; labor and management clashed in bloody confrontations; a squalid factory system was extending its reach over growing numbers of men, women, and children, many of whom were poor and powerless. The federal government and state legislatures attempted to resolve some of these problems by carving out a larger role for state planning and for monitoring, regulation, and control over the economy. Yet as legislatures did so they ran squarely up against now-hostile state and national courts that incorporated antebellum common law into their constructions of state and national constitutions. The doctrines of contractual freedom, the right to property, individual liberty—all were inflated beyond their original antebellum meaning and raised to a new constitutional plane; they became the shoal upon which much modern social legislation would founder.[51]

A second theme behind antebellum legal change relates to the shifting relationship between judge and jury and its implications for democratic theory. The jury in America traditionally possessed law-finding as well as fact-finding authority. The typical eighteenth-century judge, according to William E. Nelson and Morton J. Horwitz, instructed the jury on the law of the case at the conclusion of arguments in the trial and left the jury to decide the outcome through its verdict.[52] The jury was free to accept the judge's instructions uncritically, modify them, or even reject them. While in theory the jury was to accept the law as it was given, in reality it could do almost as it pleased, for the jury's deliberation was secret and beyond the court's immediate oversight. The jury's application of the law to the facts of a case resulted in what was called a "general verdict." The verdict took in the whole or "general" case, reflecting the jury's view on the validity of facts as well as law.

In the nineteenth century, a variety of procedural devices were introduced into American trial courts that tended to limit the jury to reviewing principally the factual evidence offered in support of plaintiff or defendant. Their verdict was a "special verdict," for it looked specifically to a part of the trial, the facts. The findings of law were left to the judge. And judges brought to this task a new professional competence and imagination, for now, unlike in the colonial era, they tended to come from the ranks of professional lawyers.

This new division of labor between judge and jury was part of the

[51] See, for example, Arnold Paul, *Conservative Crisis and the Rule of Law, Attitudes of Bench and Bar, 1887–1895* (1960); Morton Keller, *Affairs of State* (1978); Horwitz, *The Transformation of American Law*, pp. 253–266.
[52] Nelson, *Americanization of the Common Law*, pp. 69–88; Horwitz, *Transformation of American Law*, pp. 28–29, 141–143.

nineteenth century's rationalization of the trial process. Law-finding passed into the hands of professionals, the legal experts. When the new system of state law reports—the publication and circulation of the legal opinions of appellate judges—is added to the rationalization of the trial process, the end result was a more uniform system of law that contained, as well, an immense potential for the development of new legal rules. The emergence of a uniquely American law oblivious to state boundaries may also have acted as a force for unity and stability, laying the basis for a national legal culture at a time when social, political, and economic forces were atomizing the society.

The legal rationalization of the trial court and appellate decision-making process invested courts with a discretionary power that was essential to nineteenth-century common-law innovation, a third theme. Some, like the reformer Robert Rantoul, an ardent and radical Jacksonian Democrat, pictured the common law as "reason double distilled." He described "judge-made law" as "special legislation. The judge is human, and feels the bias which the coloring of the particular case gives. If he wishes to decide the next case differently, he has only to *distinguish*, and thereby make a new law."[53] The formality and complexity of legal proceedings, he believed, concealed from the public the capacity for judicial arbitrariness. Such defenders as Joseph Story believed that the common law was the "gathered wisdom of a thousand years," but even more, it was a "system having its foundations in natural reason; . . . built up and perfected by artificial doctrines, adapted and moulded to the artificial structure of society."[54] Under the shaping hand of the judiciary, he believed, the common law could be molded to American needs.

Critics and defenders of discretionary power in the common-law process were both right. The transformation of common law by the judiciary had its most salutary effect when a broad social consensus existed on the direction society should take. While the law was not "neutral," it did base its decisions on shared perceptions of the good of society and majority will. But within society there was not always consensus. Deep social divisions occasionally forced their way into courts, bringing out into the open some of the political premises behind decision-making.

The history of the law of conspiracy in America is revealing. The law

[53] Robert Rantoul, "Oration at Scituate," Documents, p. 84.
[54] Joseph Story, "Inaugural Address at the Harvard Law School," 1829; reprinted in Haar, *Golden Age of American Law*, p. 532. On the tendency of defenders of common law to equate antebellum law with science, see Perry Miller, *The Life of the Mind of America: From the Revolution to the Civil War* (1965), pp. 156-164.

of conspiracy is of English derivation and dates back in common law to at least the seventeenth century. The purpose of conspiracy law was to punish combinations of persons who perverted the legal process for purposes of extortion or for personal gain. It also punished coercive "confederacies"—those that by sheer numbers could impose their will. Obviously not all combinations or confederacies were illegal. When a combination crossed the line to become a conspiracy was a highly subjective determination for the court to make.

In the early nineteenth century, English conspiracy doctrine was imported and used by some American courts to stem the growth of the fledgling labor movement. Various arguments were advanced in support of such prosecutions, but the most frequent was that unions tended to hike wages "artificially," beyond what they would bring in the open market, and thus unions worked an "unlawful oppression" on employers and consumers. What a true wage should be is relative, and certainly not amenable to practical measurement. (There is no evidence of successful prosecution of businesses that combined to set ceilings on workers' wages.) At a time when there was general agreement that an unmodified English common law was inappropriate for a republican society, it is indeed striking that some courts resorted to a conspiracy law so hostile to the American principle of free association in cases brought against unionized workers (see the Cordwainers' case and *Commonwealth v. Carlisle*, Documents, pp. 125–138). The use of conspiracy prosecutions against unions eased after 1841, when Chief Justice Lemuel Shaw of Massachusetts, in a powerful opinion (*Commonwealth v. Hunt*) established stricter standards for conspiracy indictments (Documents, pp. 139–154).

Like conspiracy law, the law of "wrongful death" was an English import of uncertain origin. Traditional English law prohibited relatives of persons who had been killed negligently or unintentionally from suing the wrongdoer for damages. Courts believed that no monetary value should be placed on a human life, and that one person should not profit from the misfortune of another. The option seems to have been left open for the government to proceed by indictment against wrongdoers, and relatives might share in any punitive damages. Parliament overturned the rule of wrongful death in 1855, but in America it lived on. Wrongful death rules prevented next-of-kin of industrial accident victims from suing employers. In those cases where the deceased left a family with little or no means of support, the law surely stung. Common law eventually was altered by statutes to exempt classes of victims from the rule (notably passengers on trains).[55]

Judges can be seen to have favored some groups over others in yet other kinds of cases. The "fellow-servant" rule, stated most forcefully in the 1842 case of *Farwell v. The Boston and Worcester Railroad Corporation,* exempted employers from any liability to pay damages to workers injured on the job. (See Documents, pp. 166–174.) Prior to this time the rule that seems to have governed was *respondeat superior* ("let him above answer"), which held employers liable under the theory that employers were in the best position to maintain safety in the workplace. With the alarming increase in industrial accidents throughout the nineteenth century, the fellow-servant rule left large numbers of injured employees without meaningful remedy.[56]

Given the existence of judicial bias in the development of portions of American common law, it is perhaps surprising that radical reformers such as Rantoul had so little influence. It may be that those who cared about these issues were inclined to believe Story more than Rantoul. While biases affected parts of law, in other areas law served interests deemed vital to the society as a whole: it facilitated growth, valued personal liberty, enthroned democratic individualism, and served as a stabilizing and unifying force. If American justice fell short of its own highest ideals, it was because, in the end, American law was no more and no less fallible than the society of which it was a part.

---

[55] See, for example, *Carey v. Berkshire Railroad Co.,* 55 Mass. (1 Cush.) 475 (1848); Wex Malone, "The Genesis of Wrongful Death," *Stanford University Law Review,* 17 (1965), 1043.

[56] Lawrence M. Friedman and Jack Ladinsky, "Social Change and the Law of Industrial Accidents," *Columbia University Law Review,* 67 (1967), 50.

Documents

Introduction

The documents section uses a series of case studies to explore some of the broader themes and issues discussed in the essay.

Section 1, "The Nature and Purpose of Law," presents several nineteenth-century viewpoints on the American legal system. The first selection is an attack on common law by a sitting judge in his charge to the jury; it illustrates the political views of radical Republicans. The second and third selections, discussions by two prominent lawyers of the advantages and disadvantages of basing law exclusively on legislation, are also frank attacks on the common-law system. Robert Rantoul is writing from the perspective of an astute politician thoroughly familiar with the common-law process; Timothy Walker is interested primarily in republican theory. Walker's article is also useful as a concise introduction to the distinctions between written (legislative) and unwritten (decisional) law. Walker and Rantoul view the common law, and the method of decision-making by judges, as arbitrary, uncertain, and inconsistent with republican and democratic sentiments.

The fourth selection is a rebuttal to Walker by Washington Van Hamm. It displays one lawyer's deep distrust of the nonprofessional lawmaker. "Man is imperfect," writes Van Hamm. "He was imperfect in the middle and dark ages of the world. He is imperfect in the nineteenth century." It was a view distinctly out of step with the time, but a view that prevailed in the nineteenth-century legal world whenever questions about the feasibility of codifying the law were raised. It may have prevailed for other reasons, however, as the next selection by the eminent jurist Lemuel

77

Shaw suggests. Shaw believes that the common law is a "science" based on justice and principle, and that the process of judging (selecting from among conflicting and competing legal precedents to fit the facts of a case and the policy priorities of the time) is an inherently reasoned one. In Sections 2 and 3, there is an opportunity to compare Shaw's off-the-bench analysis of judging with his own performance as Chief Justice of the Massachusetts Supreme Court.

Section 1 closes with Alexis de Tocqueville's brilliant insights into the nature and function of law in America. Tocqueville is less concerned about the political implications of common-law decision making than about the ideology of law. He views law as the "conservative" balance wheel of democracy. In Tocqueville's view, law has supplanted the traditional institutions that customarily help maintain stability and order in any society, but which are missing in America. However, it is the American ideology of law that fascinates him most:

> As most public men are or have been legal practitioners, they introduce the customs and technicalities of their profession into the management of public affairs. . . . The language of the law thus becomes, in some measure, a vulgar tongue; the spirit of the law, which is produced in the schools and courts of justice, gradually penetrates beyond their walls into the bosom of society, where it descends to the lowest classes, so that at last the whole people contract the habits and the tastes of the judicial magistrate.

If Tocqueville is right, then the critics and defenders of common law are like the blind men who tried to describe the elephant: the parts bear pitifully little resemblance to the whole. Whether or not the law functioned as Tocqueville says it did, and whether the critics or defenders of common law were right, is left to the student.

The "reception" of English common law in America was a pervasive concern of early nineteenth-century intellectual and legal discourse. The question, most simply put, was to what extent Americans should base their still largely unformed common law on English legal precedents. To simply ask the question, as so many legislators and judges did, was to recognize that rules of law are derived from social and political considerations. This was an admission of striking significance. For if law were rooted in shifting social values, then what was the meaning of "principle," "justice," and "reason"? The *process* of lawmaking was unmasked. Naturally, in a society that viewed popular sovereignty and the will of the people as the foundation of governmental authority, the place of the judiciary in the political system became tenuous indeed. Yet, as the essay shows, the authority and power of the courts never really seemed threatened.

The three documents in Section 2, "Freedom, Economy, and Criminal Law," offer insight into these issues. All three are decisions in criminal cases that addressed the question of whether labor unions were "criminal conspiracies" under common law. Under traditional English common law, "combinations" or "confederacies" were illegal, even though the purpose of the combination may have been lawful. The law relating to combinations was a tortuous doctrine based on a strained logic, for certainly not *all* combinations could have been illegal. A business corporation was a combination, as were churches, local fire departments, social clubs, and such professional organizations as county bar associations—indeed practically any voluntary association fit the description of a combination as defined under English law. Nevertheless, technically—under English law—they were considered illegal, which actually meant that prosecutors and judges enjoyed a great deal of discretion in enforcing the law. No American court prior to the 1806 Philadelphia *Cordwainers'* case had used common law conspiracy doctrine to prosecute confederacies. The questions before the court in the *Cordwainers'* case, and in the *Carlisle* and *Hunt* cases that follow, were whether the English law of conspiracy applied in the states—when there had been no state legislation on combinations—and if so, whether labor unions were unlawful combinations.

Clearly, political questions could never be far from the surface of a case when a labor union became entangled in a conspiracy prosecution. Were unions free, voluntary associations, like churches and fire departments? Were they harmful, or beneficial, to the public good? Did union strikes against business establishments constitute an unlawful compulsion, an extralegal coercion of employers and nonunion employees? Were unions a "government within a government"? Of interest is not only how the courts answered these questions but also the reasoning process each court used to arrive at its answers. As such, the cases serve as evidence for assessing the various arguments raised by contemporary defenders and critics of common law. These cases further offer an opportunity for asking why, as Tocqueville observed, political questions in America "sooner or later" become resolved into judicial questions.

Individualism, as an ethic, was one of the highest expressions of nineteenth-century democratic culture. It was a source of the vast and enduring admiration Americans held for "Andy" Jackson. Walt Whitman enthroned the free and footloose man in his poetry, and market capitalism depended on the freedom of individuals to pursue their own economic self-interests. Section 3, "American Individualism," examines the idea of individualism as it influenced and appeared in the law of contract and tort.

By the end of the first half of the nineteenth century, contract law had become virtually synonymous with individualism. "Buyer beware" was the message telegraphed to the public, casting most of the risks of bargaining upon individual contractors. The values of the community and the community's interest in private contracts were pushed to the periphery as courts increasingly declined to examine the "fairness" and "equity" of contested contracts. Courts concentrated instead on the original understanding, the nature of the "bargain," that the parties had entered into. Freedom to compete in the marketplace meant freedom to act, to take large risks; and the contract, in the business world, was the lubricant of action. The first case in this section, *White v. Flora and Cherry,* highlights the new importance of the "risking bargain."

Preferences for action and the active use of property, even if such use caused damage to the rights or person of others, appeared in the law of tort during the same period. Two tort cases with vast implications for economic development are offered in this section. Both involve railroads. In the *Hentz* case, involving a statute as well as common law, the court forthrightly discusses the implications of its ruling for social policy. This case provides further evidence for assessing Rantoul's and Walker's charges that common-law decision making (and the construction of legislation) was arbitrary and uncertain, and Shaw's defense of the process as essentially reasoned and just.

The second case, *Farwell,* rules on the liability of the railroad corporation for an injury caused to one employee due to the negligence of another employee. The judge was Lemuel Shaw himself. Aside from the question of whether or not Shaw's ruling was "fair" to the plaintiff, *Farwell* shows how indefinite the boundaries between contract and tort could be. The case, on its face, is about a personal injury resulting from a negligent act, apparently a case "sounding in tort," yet Shaw chooses to analyze the case as one involving an "implied contract." That the law of tort involved much more than questions of economic policy, that it may also have required a revolutionary rethinking of the nature of human responsibility in an age when action and independent will were so highly valued, is suggested by the last case in this section, concerning a man who accidentally wounded another while trying to break up a fight between two dogs.

Some of the questions examined in Section 3 are raised again in Section 4, "Privilege or Competition?" Here the focus is the Supreme Court and the "contract clause" of the U.S. Constitution. Section 4 begins with Chief Justice Marshall's decision in the *Dartmouth College* case. This case can be examined from several vantages: Marshall's reasoning, the meaning of the contract clause, the nature of a corporation's property right, and the capacity of state legislatures to "take" property for some larger public purpose. While it is difficult to view Dartmouth College as a "privileged corporation," to the Jacksonians the case symbolized the evils of an arbitrary national judiciary and privileged economic interests. The case suggested that certain kinds of corporations, by virtue of legislative grants of "liberty and power" (the act of incorporation), occupied a vaulted and protected status in society. In other words, their "rights" (as interpreted by courts) acted as a bar on legislatures from later enacting other laws that might benefit the "common good" but which would be unconstitutional if they could be shown to diminish the value of the corporation's property. If in fact this was true, then corporations, as the next selection from John Vethake argues, enjoyed a practically autonomous status, removed from the superintending power of the people acting through their elected lawmakers. When the corporation's autonomy clearly ran against a strongly felt community need—when it hamstrung legislatures from enacting laws, such as chartering competing corporate ventures deemed in the best interest of commerce and community—then political and legal conflict quickly ascended to an ideological plane. What was the ultimate purpose of the government? Who ruled in society? It is, perhaps, these issues that Chief Justice Taney addresses in the closing case in this section, *Charles River Bridge.* Story's dissenting opinion (he concurred with Marshall in the *Dartmouth College* case) is offered here as a measure of how law had changed in the intervening eighteen years.

"Personal Autonomy," a subtheme running throughout the documentary materials, is the subject of Section 5, this time in the context of family law. It is customary to view developments in family law during this period as distinct from developments in other private-law areas, such as contract and tort. The one, it is believed, concerns social and cultural values, the other, economic values. While this is true in part, the essay attempts to show that the underlying and unifying theme in the transformation of common law was the expansion of private rights and powers. Individual autonomy was as much a concern to contractors and developers as to husbands, wives, and children. The trend in the economic sphere was to empower individuals; the trend in family law was to break up the "special privileges" of the husband and father and to redistribute rights more equitably among all family members. And in both spheres, inside and outside the home, the courts played leading roles.

The section begins with Elizabeth Cady Stanton's assault on the archaic law of divorce. Borrowing from the economic sphere, she suggests that the "matrimonial contract" be like all other contracts. This presupposes that the wife must have a "bargaining" power equal to the husband's. The *Nickerson, Mercein,* and *Gilkeson* cases apply the contract analogy to disputes over child custody. The application of principles of contract law to family law has far-reaching philosophical implications for the family. First, it means that the family is a copartnership. Second, the rights of family members become conditional. Third, the members of the family may "contract out" of obligations, either by seeking a divorce, relinquishing custody of a child, or releasing a child for adoption. And fourth, in a world where rights within the family are approaching (and *only* approaching) equality, the ultimate responsibility for the allocation and enforcement of rights must, of necessity, reside with the state. The section concludes with the Massachusetts adoption statute of 1851.

The organization of law into topical categories perhaps proves a point. Issues and questions surfacing in one documentary section, involving both doctrine and styles of reasoning, can be applied with equal validity to materials contained in other sections. The most startling fact about antebellum law is that the dimensions of change were nothing less than spectacular. Whether or not they were the "correct," or "just," or "fair" changes, as courts and legislators often claimed, is another question entirely. These materials are intended to prompt students to make their own judgments. A second fact, no less startling, is that the core values and interests in society that affected legal change in a sense mocked the intellectually immaculate legal categories and compartments that the trained legal minds of the era worked so hard to impose on law. In truth, the "order" in law is largely a mythical construct. The expansion and economic growth of nineteenth-century America was tumultuous, unbounded, and, as often as not, random and unplanned. The same can be said for much of its law.

1.

The Nature and Purpose of Law

"Justice" v. "Law": Judge John Dudley's Charge to the Jury [ca. 1805]

Judge Dudley, a trial court jurist whose views closely match those of the Jeffersonian radicals discussed in Chapter 1, was a farmer, later appointed to the New Hampshire Supreme Court. In the following excerpt, Dudley is "charging" the jury, that is, instructing them in the law that is to be applied to the facts the jury has heard in the course of the trial. What most interests us in this excerpt is his understanding of what "good law" is and his attitude toward the legal profession. In Dudley's opinion, what is law? What meaning do you give to his reference to Coke and Blackstone? Coke and Blackstone were English authors of legal treatises that purported to summarize the law of Parliament and of the English courts. How is the Bible relevant to law? What is the function of law, as Dudley sees it? The function of the jury? Why does Dudley distinguish between "law" and "justice"? Are they not the same thing?

• • •

"You've heered what has been said by the lawyers, the rascals! but no, I won't abuse 'em. 'Tis their business to make out a good case—they're paid for it, and they've done well enough in this case. But you and I, gentlemen, have sumthin else to think of. They talk about law—why, gentlemen, it's not law we want, but justice. They want to govern us by the common law of England; trust me for it, common sense is a much safer guide for us—the common sense of Raymond, Exeter, Ipin (Epping) and the other towns that sent us here to try this case between two of our neighbors. A clear head and an honest heart are wuth more than all the law of the lawyers. There was one good thing said by 'em though; 't was from one Shakspeare, an English stage-player, I believe. No matter for that; 't was e'enamost good enough to be in the Bible—"Be just and fear not." That's the law in this case, gentlemen, and law enough in any case in this court. It's our business to do justice between the parties; not by any quirks o' the law out of Coke or Blackstone—books that I never read and never will—but by common sense and common honesty between man and man. That's our business; and the curse of God is upon us if we neglect or turn aside from that. And now, Mr. Sheriff, take out the jury; and you,

* Reprinted from *American Law Review*, 40 (1906), 437.

Mr. Foreman, don't keep us waiting with idle talk—too much o' that
a'ready! about matters that have nothin' to do with the merits of this 'ere
case. Give us an honest verdict that common sense men needn't be
ashamed on.''

*All Law Must Be Legislation: Robert Rantoul, "Oration at Scituate"**

*Robert Rantoul (1805–1852) was a leading member of the Jacksonian Democratic
party in Massachusetts who practiced law first in Salem, Massachusetts, and later
in Boston. In an age when few lawyers had much formal education, Rantoul was a
graduate of Harvard (1826). He was a staunch and vocal opponent of slavery,
fought for a free public education system in his state, and vigorously attacked all
forms of corporate privilege. What do Rantoul's Jacksonian politics have to do with
the following passage on the common law? Why, exactly, does he describe the common law as an evil "sprung from the dark ages"? He is frightened by the power he
believes judges possess. What power do they possess? Why is this cause for alarm?
How is Rantoul like the radical Republicans discussed in Chapter 1? How is he different, say, from Judge Dudley? What kind of law and legal system does Rantoul
prefer? We ordinarily think of legislation and common law as two different entities.
Yet Rantoul speaks of common law as simply another manner of legislation. What
point is he making? And why was this an important issue in Rantoul's day? Why is it
an important issue in our own day? Compare Rantoul's attitude toward the common
law with Walker's, which follows. On the basis of what you have read, do you think
Rantoul was right?*

● ● ●

True independence requires us to forbear from longer aping foreign manners, when inconsistent with republican simplicity. It requires the corrupt
portion of the population of our great cities, to be kept in check by our
sound, substantial yeomanry, our intelligent mechanics, and our hardy
tars. These, we may safely trust, are uncontaminated.

Our legislation, also, should be of indigenous growth. The laws should
be intelligible to all, equal in their operation; and should provide prompt
and cheap remedies for their violation. The revision of the Statutes of this
Commonwealth, just completed, has done something towards this great
end,—how much, the public are hardly yet aware. It would have been

---

* Delivered July 4, 1836. Reprinted from Robert Rantoul, Jr., *Memoirs, Speeches and
Writings*, ed. Luther Hamilton (Boston: John P. Jewitt, 1854), pp. 277–282.

worth all the time, expense, and labor spent upon it, even though they had been ten times greater than they were. It is the most important act of our legislation since the revolution. Not only is the whole mass systematized, condensed, simplified, modernized, and made consistent with itself; but improvements, almost innumerable, have been introduced into every part, more in number and greater in value, than our general court [the state legislature] would have elaborated, in their ordinary mode of legislation, for many years.

But the Revised Statutes, excellent as they are, contrasted with the chaos for which they are substituted, still cover but a small part of the ground. We are governed principally, by the common law ; and this ought to be reduced, forthwith, to a uniform written code.

It is said by writers on the subject, that there are numerous principles of the common law, which are definitely settled and well known, and that the questionable utility of putting these into the form of a positive and unbending text, is not sufficient to outweigh the advantages of leaving them to be applied by the courts, as principles of common law, whenever the occurrence of cases should require it.

How can that which is definitely settled and well known, be applied otherwise than as a positive and unbending text? It is because judge-made law is indefinitely and vaguely settled, and its exact limits unknown, that it possesses the capacity of adapting itself to new cases, or, in other words, admits of *judicial legislation.*

Imperfect statutes are, therefore, commended because they leave the law, in the omitted cases, to be enacted by the judges. Why not carry the argument a little further, and repeal the existing statutes, so that the judges may make all the laws? Is it because the Constitution forbids judges to legislate? Why, then, commend the legislation of judges?

The law *should be* a positive and unbending text, otherwise the judge has an arbitrary power, or *discretion;* and the discretion of a good man is often nothing better than caprice, as Lord Camden has very justly remarked, while the discretion of a bad man is an odious and irresponsible tyranny.

Why is an *ex post facto* law, passed by the legislature, unjust, unconstitutional, and void, while judge-made law, which, from its nature, must always be *ex post facto*, is not only to be obeyed, but applauded? Is it because judge-made law is essentially aristocratical? It is said, the judge only applies to the case the principles of common law which exist already; but the legislature applies to a whole class of cases the principles of common sense and justice, which exist already, and which have existed from a much more remote antiquity.

The common law sprung from the dark ages; the fountain of justice is the throne of the Deity. The common law is but the glimmering taper by which men groped their way through the palpable midnight in which learning, wit, and reason were almost extinguished; justice shines with the splendor of that fulness of light which beams from the Ineffable Presence. The common law had its beginning in time, and in the time of ignorance; justice is eternal, even with the eternity of the allwise and just Lawgiver and Judge. The common law had its origin in folly, barbarism, and feudality; justice is the irradiance of divine wisdom, divine truth, and the government of infinite benevolence. While the common law sheds no light, but rather darkness visible, that serves but to discover sights of woe,—justice rises, like the Sun of Righteousness, with healing on his wings, scatters the doubts that torture without end, dispels the mists of scholastic subtilty, and illuminates with the light that lighteth every man that cometh into the world. Older, nobler, clearer, and more glorious, then, is everlasting justice, than ambiguous, base-born, purblind, perishable common law. That which is older than the creation may indeed be extolled for its venerable age; but among created things, the argument from antiquity is a false criterion of worth. Sin and death are older than the common law; are they, therefore, to be preferred to it? The mortal transgression of Cain was anterior to the common law: does it therefore furnish a better precedent?

Judge-made law is *ex post facto* law, and therefore unjust. An act is not forbidden by the statute law, but it becomes by judicial decision a crime. A contract is intended and supposed to be valid, but it becomes void by judicial construction. The legislature could not effect this, for the Constitution forbids it. The judiciary shall not usurp legislative power, says the Bill of Rights: yet it not only usurps, but runs riot beyond the confines of legislative power.

Judge-made law is special legislation. The judge is human, and feels the bias which the coloring of the particular case gives. If he wishes to decide the next case differently, he has only to *distinguish*, and thereby make a new law. The legislature must act on general views, and prescribe at once for a whole class of cases.

No man can tell what the common law is; therefore it is not law: for a law is a rule of action; but a rule which is unknown can govern no man's conduct. Notwithstanding this, it has been called the perfection of human reason.

The common law is the perfection of human reason,—just as alcohol is the perfection of sugar. The subtle spirit of the common law is reason double distilled, till what was wholesome and nutritive becomes rank poison. Reason is sweet and pleasant to the unsophisticated intellect; but this sublimated perversion of reason bewilders, and perplexes, and plunges its victims into mazes of error.

The judge makes law, by extorting from precedents something which they do not contain. He extends his precedents, which were themselves the extension of others, till, by this accommodating principle, a whole system of law is built up without the authority or interference of the legislator.

The judge labors to reconcile conflicting analogies, and to derive from them a rule to decide future cases. No one knows what the law is, *before* he lays it down; for it does not exist even in the breast of the judge. All the cases carried up to the tribunal of the last resort, are capable of being argued, or they would not be carried there. Those which are not carried up are not law, for the Supreme Court might decide them differently. Those which are carried up, argued, and decided, might have been decided differently, as will appear from the arguments. It is, therefore, often optional with the judge to incline the balance as he pleases. In forty per cent of the cases carried up to a higher court, for a considerable term of years, terminating not long ago, the judgment was reversed. Almost any case, where there is any difference of opinion, may be decided either way, and plausible analogies found in the great storehouse of precedent to justify the decision. The law, then, is the final will or whim of the judge, after counsel for both parties have done their utmost to sway it to the one side or the other.

No man knows what the law is *after* the judge has decided it. Because, as the judge is careful not to decide any point which is not brought before him, he restricts his decision within the narrowest possible limits; and though the very next case that may arise may seem, to a superficial observer, and even upon a close inspection by an ordinary mind, to be precisely similar to the last, yet the ingenuity of a thorough-bred lawyer may detect some unsuspected shade of difference, upon which an opposite decision may be founded. Great part of the skill of a judge consists in avoiding the direct consequences of a rule, by ingenious expedients and distinctions, whenever the rule would operate absurdly: and as an ancient maxim may be evaded, but must not be annulled, the whole system has been gradually rendered a labyrinth of apparent contradictions, reconciled by legal adroitness.

Statutes, enacted by the legislature, speak the public voice. Legislators, with us, are not only chosen because they possess the public confidence, but after their election, they are strongly influenced by public feeling. They must sympathize with the public, and express its will: should they fail to do so, the next year witnesses their removal from office, and others are selected to be the organs of the popular sentiment. The older portions of the common law are the work of judges, who held their places during the good pleasure of the king, and of course decided the law so as to suit the pleasure of the king. In feudal times, it was made up of feudal principles, warped, to be sure, according to the king's necessities. Judges now are appointed by the executive, and hold their offices during good behavior,—that is, for life, and are consequently out of the reach of popular influence. They are sworn to administer common law as it came down from the dark ages, excepting what has been repealed by the Constitution and the statutes, which exception they are always careful to reduce to the narrowest possible limits. With them, wrong is right, if wrong has existed from time immemorial: precedents are every thing: the spirit of the age is nothing. And suppose the judge prefers the common law to the Constitutions of the State and of the Union; or decides in defiance of a statute; what is the remedy? An astute argument is always at hand to reconcile the open violation of that instrument with the express letter of the Constitution, as in the case of the United States Bank,—or to prove an obnoxious statute unconstitutional, as would have happened in the case of the Warren Bridge, but for the firmness of Judge Morton. Impeachment is a bugbear, which has lost its terrors. We must have democratic governors, who will appoint democratic judges, and the whole body of the law must be codified.

It is said, that where a chain of precedents is found running back to a remote antiquity, it may be presumed that they originated in a statute which, through lapse of time, has perished. Unparalleled presumption this! To suppose the legislation of a barbarous age richer and more comprehensive than our own. It was without doubt a thousand times more barren. But what if there were such statutes? The specimens which have survived do not impress us with a favorable opinion of those that may have been lost. Crudely conceived, savage in their spirit, vague, indeterminate, and unlimited in their terms, and incoherent when regarded as parts of a system, the remains of ancient legislation are of little use at present, and what is lost was probably still more worthless. If such laws were now to be found in our statute book, they would be repealed at once; the innumerable judicial constructions which they might have received would not save them. Why then should supposed statutes, which probably never had any but an imaginary existence, which if they ever existed were the rude work of barbarians, which cannot now be ascertained, and if they could be, would be despised and rejected as bad in themselves, and worse for our situation and circumstances,—why should such supposed statutes govern, in the nineteenth century, the civilized and intelligent freemen of Massachusetts?

These objections to the common law have a peculiar force in America, because the rapidly advancing state of our country is continually presenting new cases for the decision of the judges; and by determining these as they arise, the bench takes for its share more than half of our legislation, notwithstanding the express provisions of the Constitution that the judiciary shall not usurp the functions of the legislature. If a common law system could be tolerable anywhere, it is only where every thing is stationary. With us, it is subversive of the fundamental principles of a free government, because it deposits in the same hands the power of first making the general laws, and then applying them to individual cases; powers distinct in their nature, and which ought to be jealously separated.

But even in England, common law is only a part of a system, which, as a whole, would be incomplete without *equity*. We strive to make the part supply the place of the whole. Equity is the correction of that wherein the law by reason of its generality is deficient; yet we have taken the law, deficient as it confessedly is, without the correction, except in certain cases, where by degrees, and almost without the knowledge of the people, equity powers have been given to the courts. A court of chancery would not be tolerated here, for reasons which I have not time to enter upon; and without that adjunct, the common law system would not be tolerated in England. The remedy is to fuse both into one mass, adopting such principles of equity as are really necessary, simplifying the whole, enacting the result in the form of statutes, and, from time to time, supplying defects and omissions, as they are discovered. It is hardly necessary to observe, that in doing this, opportunity should be taken to reform and remodel the great body of the law, which stands in need of such a revision more than any other science. Some immense advances, it is true, have been made within the last two years, of which the total abolition of special pleading is not the least remarkable. But instead of being satisfied with what has been gained, it should only encourage us to step forward more boldly in what remains to do. All American law must be statute law.

● ● ●

Timothy Walker, Codification*   ════════════════

Timothy Walker was one of the leading and most respected spokesmen for codification. If Rantoul was a fighter and a radical, Walker was an impeccable member of the legal establishment. He was editor of the influential Western Law Journal *and a professor of law in Cincinnati, Ohio. Rantoul's attack, delivered as a July Fourth oration, was a calculatedly popular one; Walker's was aimed at a very different audience—lawyers. Walker deftly takes the reader by the hand and unravels the intricacies of the issues surrounding codification. He thus provides an excellent perspective on Rantoul's arguments and on the defenders of the common-law system and tradition.*

Walker is concerned with the practicalities of codification. In this respect he differs from Rantoul. But how is he like Rantoul? Walker seems to view judicial discretion as a necessary feature of common-law decision making. Why? And why does he find it objectionable? (Review the discussion at the end of Chapter 4.) Is Walker's article "political"? Can Walker be compared to other antebellum reformers? Is Walker concerned with social justice in the way that Rantoul is? How would businessmen react, do you suppose, to Walker's arguments? Walker attempts to place his opposition to common law within the framework of republican political theory. What is the connection? What does Walker mean when he says that the common law originated in an age of barbarism?

Perhaps the most arresting part of Walker's blast at the process of common-law decision making is his discussion of certainty in law. After describing how he believes judges "make law," he attempts to turn the argument against codification on its head. Codes, it was often contended, were the work of despots and absolutist governments. They gave the "Prince's pleasure. . . the force of law." But, continues Walker, "under the wide latitude assumed in Ohio, as to the common law, you have but to substitute judge *in the place of* prince, *to make the proposition a maxim here." Walker, in other words, views the common law as a cancer of arbitrary power buried deep in the vitals of republican government. He concludes his article by writing that making law certain is a positive duty of the state, for only certain laws "have a just claim upon our obedience." Several questions can be posed. First, based upon what you have read in the essay, do you believe that the American common law was ruled by the "hoary antiquity" of past centuries? Second, was the process of judging as arbitrary as Walker claims? And third, was judicial discretion necessarily arbitrary? Was there too much discretion left to judges under the common-law method of deciding cases? How much is too much?*

A rebuttal to Walker, contained in a later issue of the Western Law Journal, *appears below.*

• • •

---

* "Codification—Its Practicability and Expediency—Being a Report made to the Cincinnati Legislative Club, in 1835," *Western Law Journal*, 1 (July 1844).

We are not lovers of innovation for its own sake. We know that the mere fact of being *untried* is no recommendation to any scheme. Great respect is always due to the experience of past ages. We freely admit, that in the unparalleled mental activity of the present time, the tendency is to think *too little*, rather than too much, of present institutions. When about to propose any radical reform, this fact should be borne in mind. Otherwise, we may unintentionally give the wheel such an impetus, that it will revolve too far. But, on the other hand, there may be such a thing as too much contentment with things as they are. That sluggish disposition of mind, which desires no change, is as much to be deprecated, as its opposite. Let it be universal, and the progress of human improvement would cease; the world would come to a final pause; and a deep and hopeless lethargy would settle down upon the race of men. There is, however, a golden medium between these two extremes. It is that disposition of mind which neither reveres what is old, nor admires what is new, merely on account of its being old or new; but submits every question to the test of strict examination, upon its intrinsic merits. With such a disposition we desire to approach the subject referred to us.

The proposition is to supersede the common, or unwritten law, by enlarging the boundaries of written law. Now, the common law comes down to us with letters of commendation from remote antiquity. Sage after sage, through a long lapse of time, has paid it the tribute of lofty panegyric. It has not only been said to embody "the hoarded wisdom of a thousand years," but also to be in reality, "the perfection of reason." Americans are called upon especially to revere it, as the parent of modern liberty. Because it withstood, with genuine Saxon obstinacy, the early encroachments of Norman power, we are required to believe that it breathes throughout the very soul of indomitable freedom; and that, for this reason, our ancestors brought it over to this country, and cherished it as their most precious birthright. But to all such suggestions, it is sufficient here to reply, that if hoary antiquity and unbounded encomium had been permitted to preclude scrutiny, the philosophy of Aristotle would still enslave the human mind.

• • •

What then is meant by *written law?* By written law we understand the formal and solemn enactments of Legislation. It comprehends both *constitutions, treaties,* and *statutes*; but is chiefly made up of the last. Now as we elect and compensate a body of men, for the exclusive purpose of providing us with laws, it would seem, at first glance, as if we need have no other laws than those which some time or other had passed through the regular forms of enactment by the Legislature. But the truth is, that not one fiftieth part of the laws by which our rights are regulated, have ever been promulgated from a legislative hall, so as to come within the definition of written law.

What then is meant by *unwritten law*, and whence does it derive its authority? The common law is called unwritten, because there is no record of its formal enactment by any legislative body. The theory sometimes maintained, is, that its principles must once have been enacted in due form, but that the record of such enactment has been lost. This, however, is mere theory. The fact is that the whole body of common law is the vast work of *Judicial Legislation.* In other words, it has been made from first to last by *Judges;* and the only record of it is to be found in the *Reports* of their decisions. The system has grown up to its present enormous bulk, by gradual accretions, from the earliest periods of English history down to the present moment. The *Reports* of decisions in England and America, together with *Indexes, Digests,* and *Abridgments,* all of which go to make up the records of the common law, already amount to a *thousand volumes*; and the number is increasing every year more rapidly than before. To illustrate the formation of the system, let us suppose that a question arose in times far back, concerning which the written laws contained no provision. In such a case, if the judge could find a reported decision in point, he was governed by it. If not, he sought for cases analogous, and moulded his decision according to their principles. If neither of these, then, rather than let a wrong go unredressed, he threw himself upon his best discretion, and made a law to suit the case. In this way every principle of the common law has been adjudicated, and each adjudication forms a *precedent* for subsequent cases. Accordingly it may happen that the rights of an American citizen, in the nineteenth century, will depend upon the opinion of a British judge, pronounced in the tenth century. For if a question now arises, concerning which our written law is silent, we go to the *Reports*. If those of our state contain nothing in point, we ransack the other American reports. If none of these settle the question, we consult the English reports, searching back to the earliest times.

• • •

It will be seen from this description, that in the theory of the common law, precedents when once established, are *absolutely binding,* and that consequently *judicial discretion* is limited to new cases. But this is far from being practically true. Judges feel at liberty, on what appears to them good reason, not only to *overrule* the decisions of other courts, but even their own prior decisions.

• • •

And this wide liberty is taken for the purpose of avoiding an evil inherent in the system. It results from the very nature of things, that many of the doctrines established centuries ago, in states of society altogether different from the present, must be totally unsuitable to our condition.

• • •

Now in such cases, where a rigid adherance to precedents would induce a decision at war with present fitness and propriety, the judge assumes the province of a legislator, and overrules the ancient authority. In fact, the Supreme Court of this state has laid down, upon this subject, the broad position, that it will be governed by what we call the common law, only so far as it is adapted to our circumstances. So that the question, what is the law of Ohio, can only be answered by saying, that it is what our judges please to determine.

Having thus ascertained the difference between the two kinds of law, we are prepared to answer the first question propounded by the resolution; namely, is it practicable to make such a code as is contemplated?

On this point we do not entertain a doubt. The whole body of law, in whatever form it exists, must be composed of a series of principles, and surely it cannot be impossible to collect these principles together, arrange them into a system, and give them a legislative sanction. This is all the resolution contemplates.

• • •

We turn, then, to the question of *expedience*—and here we are met at once by the chilling assertion, that it would be impossible to render a code *complete*, and therefore we had better retain the common law. Let us examine this position. Is the common law complete? Does it contain well settled principles enough to meet every future case? If so, the objection vanishes at once; for we have shown that all these principles might be incorporated into the code. But the truth is, that in the nature of things no system, whether of written or unwritten law, can be, in this sense, complete. Take away from the common law the *judicial discretion*, which makes the law for new cases, as fast as they arise, and its manifold deficiencies would soon be felt. Now what is there to hinder this same judicial discretion from supplying, in the same way, the deficiencies of a code?

That the most elaborate code would be deficient, we may safely admit; since no human sagacity could anticipate all future cases. In the ever multiplying relations of human affairs, the imagination cannot run forward to the time when new cases will not present themselves. But are these now provided for by the common law? Certainly not. So far, then, as respects *new cases,* the imperfection of our nature creates the same necessity for judicial discretion, whether we have a code or not. But the advantage of a code would be, that judicial discretion would then be confined to new cases only, which is not the case now. We have seen that judicial precedents have not the binding authority of legislative acts. Now, although it may be generally true, that when a precedent has been overruled, the principle substituted is abstractly better than that which is abrogated, yet every such instance must be attended with the evil of a *retroactive law.* It takes the world by suprize. What men have considered settled, they suddenly find unsettled; and they begin to lose confidence in the stability of their rights.

• • •

Let us now glance at some of the positive advantages. And first, instead of searching, as we now must, through a thousand volumes, to ascertain what our rights are, we should find them perhaps in eight or ten volumes.

• • •

A second advantage would be, increased *certainty* as to what the law is. Now, as we have seen, all is doubtful. Two thousand cases may arise, in which authorities can be found on both sides. In fact, the common law may be truly said to lie hidden in the breast of the judge. It is usual to rail at that fundamental proposition of the Justinian code, which declares, that the Prince's pleasure has the force of law. But under the wide latitude assumed in Ohio, as to the common law, you have but to substitute *judge* in the place of *prince*, to make the proposition a maxim here. Now, the code proposed, would do away with this uncertainty—and instead of wasting a long life in unavailing efforts to be able to declare with certainty what the law is, we might turn at once to the very page and section.

The third advantage would be, that, by leaving out of the code, all that portion of the common law, which, because it was well adapted to the age of barbarism in which it originated, is, for that very reason, totally unfit for us, we should have a system of laws in harmony with each other, and with the general spirit of our institutions. Now, the Common and Statute law, taken together, form but an ill assorted and chaotic mass of incongruities and technicalities. We dislike to deal in such broad assertions; but time will not permit us to enumerate particulars. A well reasoned code would call forth order from this confusion, and entitle the law to be called a science. Now it enjoys that name only by courtesy. Could we but hold up in their true colors, all the *fictions* which are made necessary, in order to attain any thing like justice under the common law—all those arbitrary and yet wonderfully subtle distinctions in the forms of action and the doctrines of pleading, which occasion almost as many cases to be decided upon mere points of form, as upon their real merits—and all those abuses which have been tolerated from age to age, by reason of the unconscionable length and redundancy given to all legal instruments and forms of proceeding—had we time to exhibit these rank deformities of the common law, now understood only by the initiated, to the unhackneyed common sense of the public at large, it would be in vain to tell them that the common law is "the perfection of reason." They would feel the contrary. They would at once perceive, that it was framed more for the benefit of lawyers than litigants. They would realize, what is the unquestionable truth, that in all those qualities which should characterize a science, the common law is immeasurably behind every other art and science.

• • •

We would not, however, be understood as saying that the common law has no good features. We speak of it as a system considered with reference to this age and country. We are not surprised that the first emigrants prized it so highly. It was not only the rule under which they had been reared, but it was infinitely better than no rule at all. They were not prepared at once to frame a code for themselves; and did well to take that which was ready furnished to their hands. But we are surprised that two centuries have been suffered to elapse, with so little effort to improve our legal condition. We can only account for the fact, by reflecting that the mass of the community wait for lawyers to take the lead in legal reform, and that lawyers have reason to be well contented with the system as it is. A clear, concise, and well arranged code, to which all who can read might have access would not, to say the least, tend to increase their business.

• • •

We shall advert to but one further argument. The prevalence of laws never enacted by legislators, is inconsistent with the theory of our social compact. The people, in their primary, free, and sovereign capacity, have organized themselves into a body politic, upon certain fundamental principles, declared in their constitution. One of these principles is, that a body of men, representing the people, and speaking in their name, shall, in the mode pointed out, frame laws for their government. The constitution recognizes no other legislative power, and no other mode of making laws. It supposes that laws derive their authority from the fact of being enacted in due form by the body constituted for that purpose. Now all we ask is to have this principle carried out universally into practice. Let us have a code of laws emanating from this authority, so comprehensive that we shall have no occasion to resort to the feudal ages for rules of conduct. Let us have the means of knowing with certainty what laws have a just claim upon our obedience, by reference to the rolls of state. Let no citizen be able to say, even with the appearance of plausibility, that he is not bound to submit to a given law, because it has never been enacted by the legislative power, and therefore he has no evidence that it is a law.

• • •

*Washington Van Hamm, In Answer to Judge Walker's Report**

• • •

It is very difficult, in an old, settled community, like our own, to undo all the customs and habits of the people, and introduce among them an entirely new order of things. For such would be the case if a regular code of law were adopted. Old laws, and old decisions of our Courts, would be cast aside for new enactments and new rules; for it the code consisted simply of a collection of our present laws, and an adoption of the present decisions of our Courts, I would ask, of what benefit could it be? It would be merely a republication of what we already have in a sufficiently convenient form. I take it, that by *codification* is meant, not merely a collection of all our present laws into one or more volumes, but an enlargement of our present laws, whether legislative or judicial, so as to include within the system a remedy for every injury, whether public or private. A scheme like this, if it were practicable to bring it about, would be of

---

* "In Answer to Judge Walker's Report," *Western Law Journal*, 1 (September 1844), 529–537.

inestimable importance to our people. But how can it be done? Man is imperfect. He was imperfect in the middle and dark ages of the world. He is imperfect in the nineteenth century. And he will continue to be imperfect so long as he continues to be an inhabitant of this globe. And although from time immemorial, legislative bodies, both in monarchical and free governments, have been constantly engaged in enacting laws, still, with every succeeding year, the necessities and circumstances of man have deemed new and very different laws absolutely essential to the preservation of life, liberty, and property.

Such having been the case in all previous time, it is not to be expected, that any number of men, however learned they may be in philosophy and law, should be able to establish a system of law more perfect than the one under which we at present live. It is true, our present statute laws are defective; our judicial decisions are full of imperfections; and our judges are but men, and as liable to err as any other individuals in the community. To prove this, it is only necessary to refer for a moment to the amendatory laws and new enactments of our Legislature, and to the overruled decisions of our Courts. But a new code would be made by the same men, or by those living in the same age, and in the same condition, and surrounded by the same imperfections.

Now let us suppose that the Legislature, in their wisdom, should select three or five of the most learned members of the bar, for the purpose of "so enlarging and systematizing the written law, as to reduce it to a regular code." And let us suppose further, that these learned gentlemen should so well succeed in the accomplishment of the object proposed, as to send forth to the good people of Ohio, under legislative sanction, eight or ten volumes, containing the whole civil and criminal law of the State, and receive therefor the plaudits of the whole population, learned and unlearned. And suppose, further, that this object was so admirably effected as to induce every lawyer in the State to throw aside or destroy every book of Reports (including the Ohio Reports), in his library, and rely solely on the *Code*, what would be the condition of our people? Why, says Judge Walker, in substance at least, not only the lawyer, but the plain unlettered man would know the law of the State with very little trouble; all would be certain and fixed, and "the glorious uncertainty of the law" would no longer exist.

Now let us look calmly at this state of things, and see whether this would be the result. I am willing to admit, that such might be the result if all men could think alike, and construe codes and statutes alike; and if the condition of our people should remain precisely as at the time of the taking effect of the supposed code; but, fortunately or unfortunately, for us, we are prone to differ in our views of the plainest things; we are not disposed to think alike, talk alike, or to construe codes and statutes alike; nor is it possible for the people of Ohio, with all their energy, enthusiasm of character, and industry, to remain even for a single year in the same condition. We are moving forward with telegraphic speed to greatness and glory. Nothing, save war, pestilence, or famine, can stay the march of this wonderful people.

To show in the clearest light, that no additional certainty would arise from the establishment of a code, I will take the liberty of offering the following illustration. Upon the very day of the publication and taking effect of this supposed code, Mr. John Doe, a plain, unlettered man, reads in plain letters from a plain paragraph, a single section of this new and untried code, and puts, as he supposes, a plain, common sense construction upon it, and thereupon concludes, that he has a remedy for an injury sustained. He directs his steps towards the office of a learned counsellor, who puts precisely the same interpretation upon this same section that his client has done before him. Suit is accordingly commenced, and every thing goes on swimmingly until the attorney of the defendant, Mr. Richard Roe, files his demurrer or plea*, and argues before the Court, on the trial of the case, that the construction put upon the code is entirely erroneous. The Court, upon mature deliberation, taking into consideration the circumstances under which the code was enacted, and the probable intention of the Legislature, are of opinion, that the law is with the defendant, and adjudge costs against the plaintiff. This decision of this honorable Court is reported to the people of the State, in another volume, as explanatory of a single section of the new code. Henceforward, not only plain, unlettered men, but learned counsellors and jurists, are compelled to look up a volume of reports, containing judicial constructions put on this new code. Thus it will be with almost every section of the new code. Judicial constructions of the new code must be hunted up to know exactly the meaning of the Legislature. I put this case to the judgment of any man, whether learned or unlearned. As a fair instance of the condition of the law, immediately after the taking effect of this new code. And if such be the case immediately afterwards, how many volumes of reports, construing this new code, would we have in Ohio, in the course of ten years? Again: in the course of a year, owing to the change of the circumstances and condition of our people, an injury arises for which no remedy is to be

---

* His answer, disagreeing either with the plaintiff's interpretation of law or recitation of facts.

found in the code. What is to be done? Either the judge is to go beyond the pale of written law and make a remedy for the particular case, or the injured party must go unredressed. And who, I would respectfully ask, can foresee the many hundreds and thousands of cases which may arise, and which are not provided for in the code?

• • •

Indeed, in my apprehension, there is no mode so well calculated to produce litigation, as the placing of law books in the hands of those who have never made the science of law their particular study. It is like placing a medical work in the hands of one who knows nothing of the science of medicine. The patient reads and prescribes for himself, and in ninety-nine cases out of a hundred, he is compelled to employ a physician to undo the mischief done by his own rash prescriptions. As an apt illustration of the injury done by placing law books in the hands of those who are unacquainted with the science, I would respectfully refer the reader to Swan's Treatise—and I do so without disrespect to the learned author, for whom as a man and as a judge I have the highest regard—but it does seem to me, that this book, gotten up for the very purpose of enabling every man to be his own lawyer, has been productive of more trouble and litigation and costs to the people, than all the hidden mysteries of the law prior to its publication. Individuals who were previously in the habit of applying to lawyers for advice, after the publication of Swan's Treatise, immediately flew to its pages as a sovereign remedy for all their troubles; and being unable to put a proper construction upon the law, as laid down in that excellent work, they get into the very midst of litigation, and then are compelled to apply to a lawyer for his assistance in getting them out. Just so it is with professional men, when they attempt to take upon themselves mechanical and agricultural employments. Knowing but little, practically at least, without the sphere of their own professions, they make poor farmers, and poor mechanics. A *jack-at-all-trades* is generally esteemed a good-for-nothing-sort of man. Let each individual in society attend strictly to his own profession or trade, without attempting to take upon himself the duties of all professions and trades, and men will be more prosperous and happy. It is said, and wisely said, that a man can be great in only one thing. If he attempt to be great in every thing, he is very apt to fail in all things.

• • •

This thing of certainty is the great argument in favor of codification. If it can be established, that there is no more certainty in our statute or written law, than in our unwritten or common law, the main argument falls to the ground. So long as *judicial discretion* remains, there can be no absolute certainty in the law. And *judicial discretion* must remain, so long as legislators and judges are imperfect human beings. An honest judge can only be governed by precedent, whether that precedent arise under a written or unwritten law, so long as it is consistent with reason and justice, and applicable to our condition. I am, therefore, clearly of opinion, that the Supreme Court of this State are right in saying, that they "will be governed by the common law only so far as it is adapted to our circumstances." I cannot conceive that greater danger can arise from *judicial discretion*, in the administration of justice under a statute law, than under the common law, as it at present exists. If the common law were now, in fact, an unwritten law, and not contained in the hundreds and thousands of volumes of reports, danger might be apprehended from *judicial discretion*. But as the common law does in fact exist, *judicial discretion* is as much limited by common as by statute law.

• • •

"The Science of Law": Lemuel Shaw, Profession of the Law in the United States*

Lemuel Shaw was Chief Justice of the Massachusetts Supreme Court, and two of his most significant opinions are reprinted in Sections 2 and 3. "The Science of Law," delivered as an address before the members of the Suffolk County bar in 1827 and considered one of Shaw's finest off-the-bench statements on the nature of law and decision making, offers a strong defense of the system of common law in America. It should be read along with the selections from Rantoul, Walker, and Van Hamm. In your opinion who was right?

Shaw begins, like Walker, by expressing the belief that the greatest threat to "liberty" and republican government is arbitrary laws. "A stern, inexorable, or capricious will, stands in the place of reason, of justice, and principle," he says. Walker and Shaw are also in implicit agreement on the value of change in society. Neither, to use Shaw's words, are "fond of ease and quiet." Similarly, both agree on the value of known and certain laws. Walker, like Shaw, refers to the necessity of constructing a "scientific" law.

It is on the specifics of common law that the three men differ. To Shaw, the common law is the essence of "reason and natural justice." To Rantoul, it is a reason "double distilled." To Walker, it is a "perfection of reason" filled with "rank

* *American Jurist and Law Magazine* (Boston), 7 (January 1832), 56–70. Punctuation modified.

deformities. " *Shaw does not respect tradition for tradition's sake. As a judge, he is best known for fashioning new or modified rules of law to fit American circumstances. But to Shaw this is not arbitrary lawmaking. To Walker, each new decision is a promulgation of some new law. By its very nature, judicial decision making is "legislation." Can you reconcile these two points of view? What is the primary function of a judge, according to Shaw? What is Shaw's attitude toward legislatures? Why, in the opinion of Shaw, must there be a judiciary, and a common law, in the kinds of state republics that existed at the time? Walker and Rantoul are avowedly democratic in their sentiments: they favor the radical democratization of lawmaking by placing all power in the hands of the legislature. Does this mean that Shaw is antidemocratic? Perhaps most intriguing is Shaw's understanding of the common law as a "science." What did Shaw mean by science?*

• • •

There are two very different modes of governing mankind; the one by the will of a superior, either absolute, as in the case of a naked despotism, or more or less modified and restrained, as in the case of a limited monarchy; the other, by laws fixed and certain, binding upon the whole people, being the will of the whole people, deliberately expressed in the mode established by fundamental laws, and openly promulgated, by which . . . every citizen is entitled to seek his rights, and bound to regulate his conduct. And this description applies not only to his civil rights, but emphatically to those which in a much higher degree awaken the interest and engage the affections of freemen, because they are the only safe pledge and guaranty of all the rest; I mean his political rights.

In a mere naked, absolute despotism, whatever appearance it may exhibit of splendor or of greatness, it is manifest that law and its professors would be entirely out of place. A stern, inexorable, or capricious will, stands in the place of reason, of justice, and principle. Both legislation and jurisprudence are lamentably concise. . . .

Reason would in vain waste her profoundest researches into the moral nature and social condition of man in seeking for the deduction of rights, which are never recognised; justice would as vainly urge the existence and obligation of duties where the forms of justice are not seldom perverted to the purposes of confiscation and judicial robbery; and eloquence would raise her persuasive voice in vain where her tones are unfelt, and her language is unintelligible.

• • •

[Having argued that] the absolute and entire supremacy of law [is] the distinguishing characteristic of free government, it may be interesting and

important to trace somewhat more particularly, the true distinction between the two systems [of arbitrary and free government]. In practical
operation the difference, perhaps, may not be so striking as in the theory
and principle. An arbitrary government, whether it claims to derive its
prerogatives from divine right, or from paternal authority, or from a right
of conquest, transmitted by hereditary descent, or whether it rest solely
upon actual possession and enjoyment, is assumed to depend upon
powers, extrinsic, and superior to the authority and will of the people
governed. The power of governing necessarily implies and presupposes
an entire independence and supremacy on the one side, and subjection and
obedience on the other. Hence the maxim, so apparently absurd to us, that
the king can do no wrong. A sovereign amenable to his subjects, is a
solecism in the theory of arbitrary government. Where a monarch, either
actuated by a naturally kind disposition, or yielding a reluctant assent to a
force which he is unable or unwilling to resist, consents to the adoption of
a constitution, so far from its being considered as a fundamental law
founded upon the will and assent of the whole people, equally binding on
the whole, and the source from which all other authority is derived, is on
the contrary considered solely as an expression of the will of the
sovereign, as the annunciation of his gracious determination to regulate
his own unlimited powers, and to direct his own supreme authority in the
manner prescribed by such constitution. The rights and privileges of the
subject are regarded as concessions emanating from the grace and bounty
of the sovereign. . . .

In the theory of free government, all this is exactly reversed. It regards
men as by nature social and endowed with powers adequate to enable
them, by the establishment of government, to provide for defining and
securing their social rights, and under a natural obligation to respect those
of others, and it presupposes that all power resides originally in the whole
people as a social community, that all political power is derived from
them, is designed to be exercised solely for the general good, and limited
to the accomplishment of that object; that no powers are, or ought to be,
vested in the government, beyond those which are necessary and useful to
promote the general security, happiness, and prosperity; and that all
powers not delegated remain with the people. The natural rights of persons being equal, no natural distinctions are acknowledged, except those
which flow from the disposition and ability to do good and to promote the
general welfare, that inherent distinction which belongs to the possession
and exercise of moral and intellectual powers. . . .

• • •

But the true point of view in which the obvious distinction in the principle and practice of the two systems, . . . is this. Under an arbitrary government, the corrupting influence of uncontrolled power on the hearts of those who exercise it, the discouragement of education and general intelligence among the great body of the people, the debasing effect produced by the employment of physical force and coercion as the means and instrument of governing, the discouragement of patriotism and public virtue by rendering them useless or contemptible, the repression of enterprise, industry, and intellectual exertion, by the establishment of artificial ranks; these circumstances produce a perpetual tendency on the part of the people to degradation, . . .

Whilst under a free government, every advance in general intelligence and improvement adds something to the strength, security, and perfection of its institutions; all the aspirings of the most gifted minds are awakened and encouraged, all the efforts of enterprise are sustained by the assurance that its rewards are near and certain, that all the honors and privileges which society can confer, are open to those who, by their virtues, talents, and public services, shall best deserve them. These circumstances have a constant tendency to advance society to the highest state of moral and intellectual improvement, of which it is capable, and to ensure the greatest happiness of the greatest numbers.

Perhaps, gentlemen, in thus enlarging upon the nature and principles of government, it may appear that I am departing too widely from that range of topics which properly belong to the place and to the occasion. But, if I am not entirely mistaken, the practical consequences to be drawn from this view of the supremacy of law in a free government, and the immediate and direct influence which this consideration must necessarily exert upon the character, condition, and duties of those who are professionally engaged in its actual administration, this must be a subject of deep and peculiar interest to the American lawyer. Our government, throughout its entire fabric, professes to be a free, representative government. It is peculiarly, exclusively, and emphatically a government of laws. The constitutions of the United States and of the several states. . . are regarded . . . as a part of the laws. Indeed they possess this character in a peculiar and eminent degree, because they are of general obligation, of a fixed and determinate character, controlling and modifying all the ordinary acts of legislation, binding and imperative upon all courts and tribunals of justice, and subject to be repealed or changed only by a peculiar and complicated mode, in which the deliberate will of the whole people is cautiously expressed. To these fundamental laws, every individual citizen has a right to appeal, and does constantly appeal, in the discussion and establishment of his rights, civil as well as political. In an equal degree, they regulate and control the highest functions of government, determine the just sources and limits, and regulate the distribution of all powers, executive, legislative, and judicial. These principles may, at any time, be drawn in question before the tribunals of justice, and are subject to the same rules of judicial interpretation, with all other legal provisions. It is difficult to conceive of the vast extent to which this consideration enlarges the field of American jurisprudence, and increases the functions, and elevates the duties and character of the American lawyer.

'If,' says Sir William Jones, 'Law be a science, and really deserve so sublime a name, it must be founded on principle, and claim an exalted rank in the empire of reason.' If such be the just character of law, . . . how much more eminently does it maintain that character when, in addition to those subjects, it embraces within its range the whole science of political philosophy. Hence we daily witness, under the head of '*constitutional law,*' a title hardly known in any other system of jurisprudence, the profoundest discussions at the bar and the ablest decisions from the bench, almost without the aid of precedent, because they involve questions which have never before been raised, in which the principles of social duty, of natural and conventional obligation are considered, distinguished, and applied, with that sagacity, reach of thought, and scientific skill, which can be derived only from a thorough and intimate acquaintance with the philosophy of the mind.

It is impossible, in this brief address, to do more than slightly glance at some of the various modes in which this view of the law, connected with the actual state of society in the United States, must affect the character and condition of the American lawyer. I know it is much the fashion to extol our own country and our own times, to display our rapid increase in wealth and population, our national greatness, and the purity and excellence of our laws, in a tone of exultation somewhat bold and extravagant. It is not my province either to censure or commend this disposition, . . . In various states of society there are, no doubt, respective advantages and disadvantages, and many just compensations. There are, no doubt, many persons, fond of ease and quiet, who would desire to pursue the tranquil tenor of their lives, in the same steps with their fathers, because their fathers walked in them, and yield a ready submission to any laws, which were the laws of their fathers. Of this class there are no doubt lawyers educated in a profound reverence for things established, who could never think of questioning the authority of a black-letter maxim, and who would regard a rule of law found in a dictum of Coke or Lord Hobart, as much sounder and wiser than any new rule, though drawn by the most exact deduction from a series of well established principles of natural justice. But were we to sympathize ever so deeply in the tastes and feelings of those with whom a love of repose, and an abhorrence of all change are predominant sentiments, still it would be useless to regret the existence of changes which are now irrevocable, . . . which we can neither alter nor control. We can no more bring back past institutions, with the maxims and habits which belong to them, than we can restore past time. Without therefore stopping to consider whether the present state of things in the United States is better or worse than any other, . . . it belongs to the American lawyer to form a just estimate of the appropriate duties of his profession, and to cherish an ardent desire to perform them in the manner most honorable to himself and useful to his age and country.

One of the most remarkable characteristics of the age, and which cannot be overlooked in this estimate, is a prodigious activity and energy in every department of life, especially in every thing that appertains to the faculties of the mind. Every body is taught to read, and every body does read, upon every sj bject. Seminaries are every where established, of every grade, from the university to the primary school, for teaching every branch of knowledge, and other seminaries are founded for the purpose of instructing instructors in the art of conducting seminaries. Nor is the appropriate food wanting, of every variety, both in quantity and quality, to satisfy the cravings of the mental appetite thus created. Every body writes, discusses, and prints. Patent presses, themselves the product of extraordinary ingenuity, driven with astonishing rapidity by mechanical power, groan under the weight of every species of publication, from the Cyclopedia in thirty quartos, to the penny pamphlet. Periodical publications in every variety of form, upon every subject, adapted as well to the taste as to the pecuniary ability of every reader, are diffused through the community to an extent hitherto entirely unexampled. The fruit of all this extraordinary activity of mind, combined with the utmost latitude and freedom of discussion, is an eager, perserving and insatiable spirit of inquiry, upon every subject which can deeply affect the interests and passions of men. . . . This earnest spirit of inquiry applies, perhaps, with still greater force to the laws, than to any other subject. The principles of every legislative enactment, and the reason of every judicial decision, are made the subject of discussion, and brought to the test of the severest scrutiny.

The popular and representative character of our legislative bodies render it of the utmost importance that this restless spirit of inquiry should be duly estimated, and properly guarded and directed, in order to prevent its pernicious effects upon the character and stability of the laws. Twenty-five busy and active legislatures are at work a great portion of every year in making, altering, and amending the laws. These are composed of men of every diversity of character, talent, learning, and experience, many of whom are desirous of distinguishing themselves by proposing changes in the laws, more or less radical. It surely cannot be a matter of surprise that the eager and inquisitive spirit, so busy in every other department, should be in full activity here. Those who value the character of the laws cannot evade or disregard it. It is not enough to say, that the law is so established, that so it was enacted by the statute of Edward I. or so it was ruled in a case in the Year Books. The rule may be a good rule, because it is an essential and component part of a complicated and well devised system, and completes the symmetry of a noble body of laws. But some better reason must be given for it, than that so it was enacted, or so it was decided. The question will still be put, 'upon what principle is it founded?' This question must be fairly met and answered. Nothing short of this will preserve that character of purity, stability, and firmness, without which laws would be worse than useless.

I have already remarked that in a free representative government, our profession, as a body, if true to themselves, if they are characterized by learning, industry, moderation, disinterestedness, and genuine love of country, must always possess in a great degree the confidence and attachment of the people, and enjoy a proportionate influence in their representative bodies. To the extent of this influence, they are unquestionably responsible for the character of the laws, particularly of all those which affect private rights, and relate to the administration of justice.

In the multitude of legislators, among whom there is much learning, prudence, and experience, mixed up with a great deal of ignorance, vanity, and pretension, it is not always easy to distinguish between a restless impatience of things as they are, a wanton love of innovation, and a sincere and ardent zeal for improvement. It is manifest, therefore, that with many propositions which would be really useful and beneficial . . . there will also be multitudes of projects, founded upon crude and visionary notions, superficial views of the delicate and various relations which each particular provision bears to the whole system.

Under these circumstances, it obviously requires great experience, sagacity and sound judgment, to distinguish what is really useful and beneficial from what is useless or pernicious, . . . and great firmness and decision in resisting the encroachments of innovation. It is due to the spirit of the age, that whilst a rapid progress is making in every other department of knowledge, as much should be done for the science of law, as the subject will admit. So far as this demands greater industry and perseverance, more thorough and exact knowledge, more enlarged, comprehensive and liberal views of the law, and the various and incidental branches of knowledge with which it is connected, the duty of the American lawyer cannot be mistaken, and, unless I have entirely mistaken the spirit and character of our profession, will not be disregarded.

Gentlemen, it was my intention in this connexion to have made some observations upon those characteristics of law which should be kept steadily in view, both in legislation and jurisprudence; to have considered how far a gradual and judicious amelioration of the law may be consistent with that stability which is so essential to the security of property and other rights,—to have inquired how far the law may be probably improved by the construction of codes, with some collateral topics; but I have already trespassed too far upon your patience, and must forbear.

There is, however, one topic, intimately connected with this part of the subject, too important to be overlooked, to a few observations upon which, I must still further ask your indulgence.

In assigning to the law the character of a science, founded upon the principles of reason and natural justice, it would be a false and unreasonable conclusion to infer that natural reason is sufficient to furnish a rule in every particular case. I am aware that there are some persons who maintain that the law is a system of artificial and technical rules, having very little regard to principle, . . . Others again maintain that natural justice is sufficient to settle all controverted questions, and that every case may be well settled upon its own particular equities. Both of these views are unquestionably partial and erroneous. Whilst the law is a science founded upon reason and principle, and no law can stand the test of strict inquiry which palpably violates the dictates of natural justice, yet it is also a system of precise and practical rules, adapted to regulate the rights and duties of persons in an infinite variety of cases, in which natural law is silent or indifferent, and yet where it is of the utmost importance that there should be a fixed rule. An instance or two will sufficiently illustrate this position. It is an obvious dictate of natural justice, that an infant of tender years cannot be bound by a contract, and that a man of mature age shall be. But such is the gradual progress from infancy to manhood, that natural law furnishes no rule for determining when the one terminates and the other begins. Still less can it determine that a young man on the last day of his twenty-first year is incapable of contracting, but acquires such capacity on the next day. The same remark applies to the statute of limitations. Such is the loss of life, and memory, and other sources of evidence, that it is obviously quite fit, that simple contracts, if enforced at all, should be enforced within some limited time. But whether within five, six, or seven years, this consideration of fitness affords no means of determining. The same observation applies to the vast variety of rules founded on judicial precedent. There are multitudes of cases where, when the question is first drawn into judicial discussion, it is nearly indifferent, whether the law be decided one way or the other, and yet when the rule is once fixed, it is of the greatest importance that it be steadily adhered to. . . .[T]he rule being once settled by a judicial decision, how important it is to the mercantile world that it should be strictly and steadily enforced. In all these cases, and multitudes will readily present themselves to the mind of every experienced lawyer, natural justice furnishes the general principle, and positive enactment, or judicial precedent, the precise rule. The great object of this precision and exactness, in the rule itself, and steadiness in applying it, is to afford security and prevent litigation. . . . But if each case were to be decided upon considerations of equity and natural justice, every transaction might lead to a judicial controversy, because each party would have ground to hope that the judge or jury would be in his own favor, where there was no rule to guide him.

The positive and practical rules of jurisprudence bear the same relation to the principles of natural law, that a well contrived constitution of government bears to the natural principles of society. It is a plain and manifest dictate of the social nature of man, that there should be an established government. But no natural principle requires that there should be a President, a Senate, or House of Representatives, or Supreme Court. In both cases, natural justice furnishes the general principle, positive or conventional law the exact rule. But in both cases, when established, and because established, it is of the greatest importance that the exact rule be adhered to and enforced, because the general principle is consistent with reason and natural justice, and the precise practical rule is essential to the stability of the government, and the utility of the laws. This character of the law, therefore, as a science founded on principle, has no tendency to disparage the importance of positive enactment, nor to weaken the authority of judicial precedent.

Permit me, in conclusion, to express a hope that these views, hasty and superficial as they are, will not be without their practical utility. If the law be justly regarded as a liberal science, intimately connected with the existence, and essential to the maintenance of free government, embracing an enlarged and profound study of the principles of moral and political philosophy, if its utility and importance be justly regarded by a free and enlightened community, these considerations cannot fail to excite the interest and industry of the student, to encourage the honorable exertions of the practitioner, and to awaken and cherish those feelings of sympathy and mutual respect, which should ever characterize the associates and members of an honorable and liberal profession.

The Americans and Their Law: Alexis de Tocqueville, Democracy in America*

Alexis de Tocqueville, a French aristocrat, lawyer, and legislator, was sent to America to study penal reform. His travels furnished the material for a penetrating analysis of American society. He was a member of European nobility fascinated with the democratic experiment in America, but at the same time troubled by what he saw as strong and ambivalent tendencies in democracy toward anarchy and majoritarian tyranny. It was the derivative nature of American society that held a special appeal for Tocqueville, the fact that it was new, experimental, boundless in energy and resourcefulness, and possibly a portent of the future.

The excerpt below contains his discussions of law, courts, and the legal profession. For the most part, Tocqueville admired what he saw. Law was the balance wheel of democracy, he believed, embodying elements of liberation and restraint; the judiciary was seen as protecting fundamental rights, and the legal profession was described as a salutary and mediating force between classes with inherently antagonistic interests.

Can you reconcile Tocqueville's description of judicial power with the outcome of state judicial reform analyzed in Chapter 1? He believes that the judiciary in America is more powerful than judiciaries in other nations. Why? Does he see any conflict between judicial power and majority rule? American courts, he believes, are "at once favorable to liberty and to public order." How can this be so? Is it not a contradiction? In what ways do courts protect the people from tyranny?

Tocqueville contrasts class interests in aristocracies and democracies. In all societies, classes form "distinct communities." Yet legal institutions in America, he

---

* Alexis de Tocqueville, *Democracy in America*, ed. Phillips Bradley (1945), vol. 1, pp. 103–107, 246–250, 256–259, 283–290.

believes, have managed to avoid giving "a dangerous or exclusive tendency to the government." The "constant influence of the government is beneficial." How so? On the basis of what you have read in the essay, do you agree?

According to Tocqueville, what is the role of the legal profession in America? Why does he attribute such immense power to the profession? He describes lawyers as a natural force of conservatism—in the defense of propertied interests, in the defense of the state, and in the defense of the public order. Why should they be naturally *so? Does Tocqueville see a potential for danger in the profession's power and influence?*

Two points in this passage should prompt special thought. First, Tocqueville notes that virtually every major political question in the United States is eventually resolved into a legal question for determination by a court. Second, he believes that the "legal spirit" extends far beyond courts of justice. It permeates government and administration, schools and communities, "so that the language of the law thus becomes, in some measure, a vulgar tongue." The chapters of the essay indirectly make a similar point: that much of the social and economic change occurring in antebellum America proceeded within and through law. How can one explain what perhaps can be described as a uniquely American infatuation with law, legal processes, and legal forms?

JUDICIAL POWER IN THE UNITED STATES, AND ITS INFLUENCE ON POLITICAL SOCIETY

• • •

I have thought it right to devote a separate chapter to the judicial authorities of the United States, lest their great political importance should be lessened in the reader's eyes by merely incidental mention of them. Confederations have existed in other countries besides America; I have seen republics elsewhere than upon the shores of the New World alone: the representative system of government has been adopted in several states of Europe; but I am not aware that any nation of the globe has hitherto organized a judicial power in the same manner as the Americans. The judicial organization of the United States is the institution which a stranger has the greatest difficulty in understanding. He hears the authority of a judge invoked in the political occurrences of every day, and he naturally concludes that in the United States the judges are important political functionaries; nevertheless, when he examines the nature of the tribunals, they offer at the first glance nothing that is contrary to the usual habits and privileges of those bodies; and the magistrates seem to him to interfere in public affairs only by chance, but by a chance that recurs every day.

• • •

The Americans have retained these three distinguishing characteristics of the judicial power: an American judge can pronounce a decision only when litigation has arisen, he is conversant only with special cases, and he cannot act until the cause has been duly brought before the court. His position is therefore exactly the same as that of the magistrates of other nations; and yet he is invested with immense political power. How does this come about? If the sphere of his authority and his means of action are the same as those of other judges, whence does he derive a power which they do not possess? The cause of this difference lies in the simple fact that the Americans have acknowledged the right of judges to found their decisions on the *Constitution* rather than on the *laws*. In other words, they have permitted them not to apply such laws as may appear to them to be unconstitutional.

I am aware that a similar right has been sometimes claimed, but claimed in vain, by courts of justice in other countries; but in America it is recognized by all the authorities; and not a party, not so much as an individual, is found to contest it. This fact can be explained only by the principles of the American constitutions. In France the constitution is, or at least is supposed to be, immutable; and the received theory is that no power has the right of changing any part of it. In England the constitution may change continually, or rather it does not in reality exist; the Parliament is at once a legislative and a constituent assembly. The political theories of America are more simple and more rational. An American constitution is not supposed to be immutable, as in France; nor is it susceptible of modification by the ordinary powers of society, as in England. It constitutes a detached whole, which, as it represents the will of the whole people, is no less binding on the legislator than on the private citizen, but which may be altered by the will of the people in predetermined cases, according to established rules. In America the Constitution may therefore vary; but as long as it exists, it is the origin of all authority, and the sole vehicle of the predominating force.

It is easy to perceive how these differences must act upon the position and the rights of the judicial bodies in the three countries I have cited. If in France the tribunals were authorized to disobey the laws on the ground of their being opposed to the constitution, the constituent power would in fact be placed in their hands, since they alone would have the right of interpreting a constitution of which no authority could change the terms. They would therefore take the place of the nation and exercise as absolute a sway over society as the inherent weakness of judicial power would allow them to do. Undoubtedly, as the French judges are incompetent to declare a law to be unconstitutional, the power of changing the constitution is indirectly given to the legislative body, since no legal barrier would oppose the alterations that it might prescribe. But it is still better to grant the power of changing the constitution of the people to men who represent (however imperfectly) the will of the people than to men who represent no one but themselves.

It would be still more unreasonable to invest the English judges with the right of resisting the decisions of the legislative body, since the Parliament which makes the laws also makes the constitution; and consequently a law emanating from the three estates of the realm can in no case be unconstitutional. But neither of these remarks is applicable to America.

In the United States the Constitution governs the legislator as much as the private citizen: as it is the first of laws, it cannot be modified by a law; and it is therefore just that the tribunals should obey the Constitution in preference to any law. This condition belongs to the very essence of the judicature; for to select that legal obligation by which he is most strictly bound is in some sort the natural right of every magistrate.

In France the constitution is also the first of laws, and the judges have the same right to take it as the ground of their decisions; but were they to exercise this right, they must perforce encroach on rights more sacred than their own: namely, on those of society, in whose name they are acting. In this case reasons of state clearly prevail over ordinary motives. In America, where the nation can always reduce its magistrates to obedience by changing its Constitution, no danger of this kind is to be feared. Upon this point, therefore, the political and the logical reason agree, and the people as well as the judges preserve their privileges.

Whenever a law that the judge holds to be unconstitutional is invoked in a tribunal of the United States, he may refuse to admit it as a rule; this power is the only one peculiar to the American magistrate, but it gives rise to immense political influence. In truth, few laws can escape the searching analysis of the judicial power for any length of time, for there are few that are not prejudicial to some private interest or other, and none that may not be brought before a court of justice by the choice of parties or by the necessity of the case. But as soon as a judge has refused to apply any given law in a case, that law immediately loses a portion of its moral force. Those to whom it is prejudicial learn that means exist of overcoming its authority, and similar suits are multiplied until it becomes powerless. The alternative, then, is, that the people must alter the Constitution or the legislature must repeal the law. The political power which the Americans have entrusted to their courts of justice is therefore immense, but the evils of this power are considerably diminished by the impossibility of attacking the laws except through the courts of justice. If the judge had been empowered to contest the law on the ground of theoretical generalities, if he were able to take the initiative and to censure the legislator, he would play a prominent political part; and as the champion or the antagonist of a party, he would have brought the hostile passions of the nation into the conflict. But when a judge contests a law in an obscure debate on some particular case, the importance of his attack is concealed from public notice; his decision bears upon the interest of an individual, and the law is slighted only incidentally. Moreover, although it is censured, it is not abolished; its moral force may be diminished, but its authority is not taken away; and its final destruction can be accomplished only by the reiterated attacks of judicial functionaries. It will be seen, also, that by leaving it to private interest to censure the law, and by intimately uniting the trial of the law with the trial of an individual, legislation is protected from wanton assaults and from the daily aggressions of party spirit. The errors of the legislator are exposed only to meet a real want; and it is always a positive and appreciable fact that must serve as the basis of a prosecution.

I am inclined to believe this practice of the American courts to be at once most favorable to liberty and to public order. If the judge could attack the legislator only openly and directly, he would sometimes be afraid to oppose him; and at other times party spirit might encourage him to brave it at every turn. The laws would consequently be attacked when the power from which they emanated was weak, and obeyed when it was strong; that is to say, when it would be useful to respect them, they would often be contested; and when it would be easy to convert them into an instrument of oppression, they would be respected. But the American judge is brought into the political arena independently of his own will. He judges the law only because he is obliged to judge a case. The political question that he is called upon to resolve is connected with the interests of the parties, and he cannot refuse to decide it without a denial of justice. He performs his functions as a citizen by fulfilling the precise duties which belong to his profession as a magistrate. It is true that, upon this system, the judicial censorship of the courts of justice over the legislature cannot extend to all laws indiscriminately, inasmuch as some of them can never give rise to that precise species of contest which is termed a lawsuit; and even when such a contest is possible, it may happen that no one cares to bring it before a court of justice. The Americans have often felt this inconvenience; but they have left the remedy incomplete, lest they should give it an efficacy that might in some cases prove dangerous. Within these limits the power vested in the American courts of justice of pronouncing a statute to be unconstitutional forms one of the most powerful barriers that have ever been devised against the tyranny of political assemblies.

• • •

WHAT ARE THE REAL ADVANTAGES WHICH AMERICAN SOCIETY DERIVES FROM A DEMOCRATIC GOVERNMENT

• • •

GENERAL TENDENCY OF THE LAWS UNDER AMERICAN DEMOCRACY, AND INSTINCTS OF THOSE WHO APPLY THEM.

The defects and weaknesses of a democratic government may readily be discovered; they can be proved by obvious facts, whereas their healthy influence becomes evident in ways which are not obvious and are, so to speak, hidden. A glance suffices to detect its faults, but its good qualities can be discerned only by long observation. The laws of the American democracy are frequently defective or incomplete; they sometimes attack vested rights, or sanction others which are dangerous to the community; and even if they were good, their frequency would still be a great evil. How comes it, then, that the American republics prosper and continue?

In the consideration of laws a distinction must be carefully observed between the end at which they aim and the means by which they pursue that end; between their absolute and their relative excellence. If it be the intention of the legislator to favor the interests of the minority at the expense of the majority, and if the measures he takes are so combined as to accomplish the object he has in view with the least possible expense of time and exertion, the law may be well drawn up although its purpose is bad; and the more efficacious it is, the more dangerous it will be.

Democratic laws generally tend to promote the welfare of the greatest possible number; for they emanate from the majority of the citizens, who are subject to error, but who cannot have an interest opposed to their own advantage. The laws of an aristocracy tend, on the contrary, to concentrate wealth and power in the hands of the minority; because an aristocracy, by its very nature, constitutes a minority. It may therefore be asserted, as a general proposition, that the purpose of a democracy in its legislation is more useful to humanity than that of an aristocracy. This, however, is the sum total of its advantages.

Aristocracies are infinitely more expert in the science of legislation than democracies ever can be. They are possessed of a self-control that protects them from the errors of temporary excitement; and they form far-reaching designs, which they know how to mature till a favorable opportunity arrives. Aristocratic government proceeds with the dexterity of art; it understands how to make the collective force of all its laws converge at the same time to a given point. Such is not the case with democracies, whose laws are almost always ineffective or inopportune. The means of democracy are therefore more imperfect than those of aristocracy, and the measures that it unwittingly adopts are frequently opposed to its own cause; but the object it has in view is more useful.

Let us now imagine a community so organized by nature or by its constitution that it can support the transitory action of bad laws, and that it can await, without destruction, the general tendency of its legislation: we shall then conceive how a democratic government, notwithstanding its faults may be best fitted to produce the prosperity of this community. This is precisely what has occurred in the United States; and I repeat, what I have before remarked, that the great advantage of the Americans consists in their being able to commit faults which they may afterwards repair.

• • •

No political form has hitherto been discovered that is equally favorable to the prosperity and the development of all the classes into which society is divided. These classes continue to form, as it were, so many distinct communities in the same nation; and experience has shown that it is no less dangerous to place the fate of these classes exclusively in the hands of any one of them than it is to make one people the arbiter of the destiny of another. When the rich alone govern, the interest of the poor is always endangered; and when the poor make the laws, that of the rich incurs very serious risks. The advantage of democracy does not consist, therefore, as has sometimes been asserted, in favoring the prosperity of all, but simply in contributing to the well-being of the greatest number.

The men who are entrusted with the direction of public affairs in the United States are frequently inferior, in both capacity and morality, to those whom an aristocracy would raise to power. But their interest is identified and mingled with that of the majority of their fellow citizens. They may frequently be faithless and frequently mistaken, but they will never systematically adopt a line of conduct hostile to the majority; and they cannot give a dangerous or exclusive tendency to the government.

The maladministration of a democratic magistrate, moreover, is an isolated fact, which has influence only during the short period for which he is elected. Corruption and incapacity do not act as common interests which may connect men permanently with one another. A corrupt or incapable magistrate will not combine his measures with another magistrate simply because the latter is as corrupt and incapable as himself; and these two men will never unite their endeavors to promote the corruption and inaptitude of their remote posterity. The ambition and the maneuvers of the one will serve, on the contrary, to unmask the other. The vices of a magistrate in democratic states are usually wholly personal.

But under aristocratic governments public men are swayed by the interest of their order, which, if it is sometimes confused with the interests of the majority, is very frequently distinct from them. This interest is the common and lasting bond that unites them; it induces them to coalesce and combine their efforts to attain an end which is not always the happiness of the greatest number; and it serves not only to connect the persons in authority with one another, but to unite them with a considerable portion of the community, since a numerous body of citizens belong to the aristocracy without being invested with official functions. The aristocratic magistrate is therefore constantly supported by a portion of the community as well as by the government of which he is a member.

The common purpose which in aristocracies connects the interest of the magistrates with that of a portion of their contemporaries identifies it also with that of future generations; they labor for the future as well as for the present. The aristocratic magistrate is urged at the same time towards the same point by the passions of the community, by his own, and, I may almost add, by those of his posterity. Is it, then, wonderful that he does not resist such repeated impulses? And, indeed, aristocracies are often carried away by their class spirit without being corrupted by it; and they unconsciously fashion society to their own ends and prepare it for their own descendants.

The English aristocracy is perhaps the most liberal that has ever existed, and no body of men has ever, uninterruptedly, furnished so many honorable and enlightened individuals to the government of a country. It cannot escape observation, however, that in the legislation of England the interests of the poor have often been sacrificed to the advantages of the rich, and the rights of the majority to the privileges of a few. The result is that England at the present day combines the extremes of good and evil fortune in the bosom of her society; and the miseries and privations of her poor almost equal her power and renown.

In the United States, where public officers have no class interests to promote, the general and constant influence of the government is beneficial, although the individuals who conduct it are frequently unskillful and sometimes contemptible. There is, indeed, a secret tendency in democratic institutions that makes the exertions of the citizens subservient to the prosperity of the community in spite of their vices and mistakes; while in aristocratic institutions there is a secret bias which, notwithstanding the talents and virtues of those who conduct the government, leads them to contribute to the evils that oppress their fellow creatures. In aristocratic governments public men may frequently do harm without intending it; and in democratic states they bring about good results of which they have never thought.

• • •

RESPECT FOR LAW IN THE UNITED STATES.

It is not always feasible to consult the whole people, either directly or indirectly, in the formation of law; but it cannot be denied that, when this is possible, the authority of law is much augmented. This popular origin, which impairs the excellence and the wisdom of legislation, contributes much to increase its power. There is an amazing strength in the expression of the will of a whole people; and when it declares itself, even the imagination of those who would wish to contest it is overawed. The truth of this fact is well known by parties, and they consequently strive to make out a majority whenever they can.

• • •

In the United States, except slaves, servants, and paupers supported by the townships, there is no class of persons who do not exercise the elective franchise and who do not indirectly contribute to make the laws. Those who wish to attack the laws must consequently either change the opinion of the nation or trample upon its decision.

A second reason, which is still more direct and weighty, may be adduced: in the United States everyone is personally interested in enforcing the obedience of the whole community to the law; for as the minority may shortly rally the majority to its principles, it is interested in professing that respect for the decrees of the legislator which it may soon have occasion to claim for its own. However irksome an enactment may be, the citizen of the United States complies with it, not only because it is the work of the majority, but because it is his own, and he regards it as a contract to which he is himself a party.

In the United States, then, that numerous and turbulent multitude does not exist who, regarding the law as their natural enemy, look upon it with fear and distrust. It is impossible, on the contrary, not to perceive that all classes display the utmost reliance upon the legislation of their country and are attached to it by a kind of parental affection.

I am wrong, however, in saying all classes; for as in America the European scale of authority is inverted, there the wealthy are placed in a position analogous to that of the poor in the Old World, and it is the opulent classes who frequently look upon law with suspicion. I have already observed that the advantage of democracy is not, as has been sometimes asserted, that it protects the interests of all, but simply that it protects those of the majority. In the United States, where the poor rule, the rich have always something to fear from the abuse of their power. This natural anxiety of the rich may produce a secret dissatisfaction; but society is not disturbed by it, for the same reason that withholds the confidence of the rich from the legislative authority makes them obey its mandates: their wealth, which prevents them from making the law, prevents them from withstanding it. Among civilized nations, only those who have nothing to lose ever revolt; and if the laws of a democracy are not always worthy of respect, they are always respected; for those who usually infringe the laws cannot fail to obey those which they have themselves made and by which they are benefited; while the citizens who might be interested in their infraction are induced, by their character and station, to submit to the decisions of the legislature, whatever they may be. Besides, the people in America obey the law, not only because it is their own work, but because it may be changed if it is harmful; a law is observed because, first, it is a self-imposed evil, and, secondly, it is an evil of transient duration.

ACTIVITY THAT PERVADES ALL PARTS OF THE BODY POLITIC IN THE UNITED STATES; INFLUENCE THAT IT EXERCISES UPON SOCIETY.

On passing from a free country into one which is not free the traveler is struck by the change; in the former all is bustle and activity; in the latter everything seems calm and motionless. In the one, amelioration and progress are the topics of inquiry; in the other, it seems as if the community wished only to repose in the enjoyment of advantages already acquired. Nevertheless, the country which exerts itself so strenuously to become happy is generally more wealthy and prosperous than that which appears so contented with it lot; and when we compare them, we can scarely conceive how so many new wants are daily felt in the former, while so few seems to exist in the latter.

If this remark is applicable to those free countries which have preserved monarchical forms and aristocratic institutions, it is still more so to democratic republics. In these states it is not a portion only of the people who endeavor to improve the state of society, but the whole community is engaged in the task; and it is not the exigencies and convenience of a single class for which provision is to be made, but the exigencies and convenience of all classes at once.

It is not impossible to conceive the surprising liberty that the Americans enjoy; some idea may likewise be formed of their extreme equality; but the political activity that pervades the United States must be seen in order to be understood. No sooner do you set foot upon American ground than you are stunned by a kind of tumult; a confused clamor is heard on every side, and a thousand simultaneous voices demand the satisfaction of their social wants. Everything is in motion around you; here the people of one quarter of a town are met to decide upon the building of a church; there the election of a representative is going on; a little farther, the delegates of a district are hastening to the town in order to consult upon some local improvements; in another place, the laborers of a village quit their plows to deliberate upon the project of a road or a public school. Meetings are called for the sole purpose of declaring their disapprobation of the conduct of the government; while in other assemblies citizens salute the authorities of the day as the fathers of their country. Societies are formed which regard drunkenness as the principal cause of the evils of the state, and solemnly bind themselves to give an example of temperance.

The great political agitation of American legislative bodies, which is the only one that attracts the attention of foreigners, is a mere episode, or a sort of continuation, of that universal movement which originates in the lowest classes of the people and extends successively to all the ranks of society. It is impossible to spend more effort in the pursuit of happiness.

● ● ●

In visiting the Americans and studying their laws, we perceive that the authority they have entrusted to members of the legal profession, and the influence that these individuals exercise in the government, are the most powerful existing security against the excesses of democracy. This effect seems to me to result from a general cause, which it is useful to investigate, as it may be reproduced elsewhere.

The members of the legal profession have taken a part in all the movements of political society in Europe for the last five hundred years. At one time they have been the instruments of the political authorities, and at another they have succeeded in converting the political authorities into their instruments. In the Middle Ages they afforded a powerful support to the crown; and since that period they have exerted themselves effectively to limit the royal prerogative. In England they have contracted a close alliance with the aristocracy; in France they have shown themselves its most dangerous enemies. Under all these circumstances have the members of the legal profession been swayed by sudden and fleeting impulses, or have they been more or less impelled by instincts which are natural to them and which will always recur in history? I am incited to this investigation, for perhaps this particular class of men will play a prominent part in the political society that is soon to be created.

Men who have made a special study of the laws derive from [that] occupation certain habits of order, a taste for formalities, and a kind of instinctive regard for the regular connection of ideas, which naturally render them very hostile to the revolutionary spirit and the unreflecting passions of the multitude.

The special information that lawyers derive from their studies ensures them a separate rank in society, and they constitute a sort of privileged body in the scale of intellect. This notion of their superiority perpetually recurs to them in the practice of their profession: they are the masters of a science which is necessary, but which is not very generally known; they serve as arbiters between the citizens; and the habit of directing to their purpose the blind passions of parties in litigation inspires them with a certain contempt for the judgment of the multitude. Add to this that they naturally constitute *a body*; not by any previous understanding, or by an agreement that directs them to a common end; but the analogy of their studies and the uniformity of their methods connect their minds as a common interest might unite their endeavors.

Some of the tastes and the habits of the aristocracy may consequently be discovered in the characters of lawyers. They participate in the same instinctive love of order and formalities; and they entertain the same repugnance to the actions of the multitude, and the same secret contempt of the government of the people. I do not mean to say that the natural propensities of lawyers are sufficiently strong to sway them irresistibly; for they, like most other men, are governed by their private interests, and especially by the interests of the moment.

I do not . . . assert that *all* the members of the legal profession are at *all* times the friends of order and the opponents of innovation, but merely that most of them are usually so. In a community in which lawyers are allowed to occupy without opposition that high station which naturally belongs to them, their general spirit will be eminently conservative and anti-democratic. When an aristocracy excludes the leaders of that profession from its ranks, it excites enemies who are the more formidable as they are independent of the nobility by their labors and feel themselves to be their equals in intelligence though inferior in opulence and power. But whenever an aristocracy consents to impart some of its privileges to these same individuals, the two classes coalesce very readily and assume, as it were, family interests.

• • •

Lawyers are attached to public order beyond every other consideration, and the best security of public order is authority. It must not be forgotten, also, that if they prize freedom much, they generally value legality still more: they are less afraid of tyranny than of arbitrary power; and, provided the legislature undertakes of itself to deprive men of their independence, they are not dissatisfied.

I am therefore convinced that the prince who, in presence of an encroaching democracy, should endeavor to impair the judicial authority in his dominions, and to diminish the political influence of lawyers, would commit a great mistake: he would let slip the substance of authority to grasp the shadow. He would act more wisely in introducing lawyers into the government; and if he entrusted despotism to them under the form of violence, perhaps he would find it again in their hands under the external features of justice and law.

The government of democracy is favorable to the political power of lawyers; for when the wealthy, the noble, and the prince are excluded from the government, the lawyers take possession of it, in their own right, as it were, since they are the only men of information and sagacity, beyond the sphere of the people, who can be the object of the popular choice. If, then, they are led by their tastes towards the aristocracy and the prince, they are brought in contact with the people by their interests. They like the government of democracy without participating in its propensities and without imitating its weaknesses; whence they derive a two-fold authority from it and over it. The people in democratic states do not mistrust the members of the legal profession, because it is known that they are interested to serve the popular cause; and the people listen to them without irritation, because they do not attribute to them any sinister designs. The lawyers do not, indeed, wish to overthrow the institutions of democracy, but they constantly endeavor to turn it away from its real direction by means that are foreign to its nature. Lawyers belong to the people by birth and interest, and to the aristocracy by habit and taste; they may be looked upon as the connecting link between the two great classes of society.

The profession of the law is the only aristocratic element that can be amalgamated without violence with the natural elements of democracy and be advantageously and permanently combined with them. I am not ignorant of the defects inherent in the character of this body of men; but without this admixture of lawyer-like sobriety with the democratic principle, I question whether democratic institutions could long be maintained; and I cannot believe that a republic could hope to exist at the present time if the influence of lawyers in public business did not increase in proportion to the power of the people.

This aristocratic character, which I hold to be common to the legal profession, is much more distinctly marked in the United States and in England than in any other country. This proceeds not only from the legal studies of the English and American lawyers, but from the nature of the law and the position which these interpreters of it occupy in the two countries. The English and the Americans have retained the law of precedents; that is to say, they continue to found their legal opinions and the decisions of their courts upon the opinions and decisions of their predecessors. In the mind of an English or American lawyer a taste and a reverence for what is old is almost always united with a love of regular and lawful proceedings.

This predisposition has another effect upon the character of the legal profession and upon the general course of society. The English and American lawyers investigate what has been done; the French advocate inquires what should have been done; the former produce precedents, the latter reasons. A French observer is surprised to hear how often an English or an American lawyer quotes the opinions of others and how little he alludes to his own, while the reverse occurs in France. There the most trifling litigation is never conducted without the introduction of an entire system of ideas peculiar to the counsel employed; and the fundamental principles of law are discussed in order to obtain a rod of land by the decision of the court. This abnegation of his own opinion and this implicit deference to the opinion of his forefathers, which are common to the English and American lawyer, this servitude of thought which he is obliged to profess, necessarily gives him more timid habits and more conservative inclinations in England and America than in France.*

* Tocqueville is here comparing the civil law tradition of France, founded on codes, with England's and America's common law tradition.

The French codes are often difficult to comprehend, but they can be read by everyone; nothing, on the other hand, can be more obscure and strange to the uninitiated than a [law] founded upon precedents. The absolute need of legal aid that is felt in England and the United States, and the high opinion that is entertained of the ability of the legal profession, tend to separate it more and more from the people and to erect it into a distinct class. The French lawyer is simply a man extensively acquainted with statutes of his country; but the English or American lawyer resembles the hierophants of Egypt, for like them he is the sole interpreter of an occult science.

The position that lawyers occupy in England and America exercises no less influence upon their habits and opinions. The English aristocracy, which has taken care to attract to its sphere whatever is at all analogous to itself, has conferred a high degree of importance and authority upon the members of the legal profession. In English society, lawyers do not occupy the first rank, but they are contented with the station assigned to them: they constitute, as it were, the younger branch of the English aristocracy; and they are attached to their elder brothers, although they do not enjoy all their privileges. The English lawyers consequently mingle the aristocratic tastes and ideas of the circles in which they move with the aristocratic interests of their profession.

And, indeed, the lawyer-like character that I am endeavoring to depict is most distinctly to be met with in England: there laws are esteemed not so much because they are good as because they are old; and if it is necessary to modify them in any respect, to adapt them to the changes that time operates in society, recourse is had to the most inconceivable subtleties in order to uphold the traditionary fabric and to maintain that nothing has been done which does not square with the intentions and complete the labors of former generations. The very individuals who conduct these changes disclaim any desire for innovation and had rather resort to absurd expedients than plead guilty to so great a crime. This spirit appertains more especially to the English lawyers; they appear indifferent to the real meaning of what they treat, and they direct all their attention to the letter, seeming inclined to abandon reason and humanity rather than to swerve one tittle from the law. English legislation may be compared to the stock of an old tree upon which lawyers have engrafted the most dissimilar shoots in the hope that, although their fruits may differ, their foliage at least will be confused with the venerable trunk that supports them all.

In America there are no nobles or literary men, and the people are apt to mistrust the wealthy; lawyers consequently form the highest political class and the most cultivated portion of society. They have therefore nothing to gain by innovation, which adds a conservative interest to their natural taste for public order. If I were asked where I place the American aristocracy, I should reply without hesitation that it is not among the rich, who are united by no common tie, but that it occupies the judicial bench and the bar.

The more we reflect upon all that occurs in the United States, the more we shall be persuaded that the lawyers, as a body, form the most powerful, if not the only, counter-poise to the democratic element. In that country we easily perceive how the legal profession is qualified by its attributes, and even by its faults, to neutralize the vices inherent in popular government. When the American people are intoxicated by passion or carried away by the impetuosity of their ideas, they are checked and stopped by the almost invisible influence of their legal counselors. These secretly oppose their aristocratic propensities to the nation's democratic instincts, their superstitious attachment to what is old to its love of novelty, their narrow views to its immense designs, and their habitual procrastination to its ardent impatience.

The courts of justice are the visible organs by which the legal profession is enabled to control the democracy. The judge is a lawyer who, independently of the taste for regularity and order that he has contracted in the study of law, derives an additional love of stability from the inalienability of his own functions. His legal attainments have already raised him to a distinguished rank among his fellows; his political power completes the distinction of his station and gives him the instincts of the privileged classes.

Armed with the power of declaring the laws to be unconstitutional, the American magistrate perpetually interferes in political affairs. He cannot force the people to make laws, but at least he can oblige them not to disobey their own enactments and not to be inconsistent with themselves. I am aware that a secret tendency to diminish the judicial power exists in the United States; and by most of the constitutions of the several states the government can, upon the demand of the two houses of the legislature, remove judges from their station. Some other state constitutions make the members of the judiciary elective, and they are even subjected to frequent re-elections. I venture to predict that these innovations will sooner or later be attended with fatal consequences; and that it will be found out at some future period that by thus lessening the independence of the judiciary they have attacked not only the judicial power, but the democratic republic itself.

It must not be supposed, moreover, that the legal spirit is confined in the United States to the courts of justice; it extends far beyond them. As the lawyers form the only enlightened class whom the people do not mistrust, they are naturally called upon to occupy most of the public stations. They fill the legislative assemblies and are at the head of the administration; they consequently exercise a powerful influence upon the formation of the law and upon its execution. The lawyers are obliged, however, to yield to the current public opinion, which is too strong for them to resist; . . .

It is curious for a Frenchman to hear the complaints that are made in the United States against the stationary spirit of legal men and their prejudices in favor of existing institutions.

The influence of legal habits extends beyond the precise limits I have pointed out. Scarcely any political question arises in the United States that is not resolved, sooner or later, into a judicial question. Hence all parties are obliged to borrow, in their daily controversies, the ideas, and even the language, peculiar to judicial proceedings. As most public men are or have been legal practitioners, they introduce the customs and technicalities of their profession into the management of public affairs. The jury extends this habit to all classes. The language of the law thus becomes, in some measure, a vulgar tongue; the spirit of the law, which is produced in the schools and courts of justice, gradually penetrates beyond their walls into the bosom of society, where it descends to the lowest classes, so that at last the whole people contract the habits and the tastes of the judicial magistrate. The lawyers of the United States form a party which is but little feared and scarcely perceived, which has no badge peculiar to itself, which adapts itself with great flexibility to the exigencies of the time and accommodates itself without resistance to all the movements of the social body. But this party extends over the whole community and penetrates into all the classes which compose it; it acts upon the country imperceptibly, but finally fashions it to suit its own purposes.

• • •

2.
Freedom, Economy, and Criminal Law

*The Cordwainers' Case**   ===================

Commonwealth v. Pullis, *or the Cordwainers' Case (the name Cordwainer was taken from the Cordovan leather shoemakers worked), offers an excellent insight into Tocqueville's commentary about courts—illustrating how the important social,*

---

* Reprinted from John R. Commons, Editor, *A Documentary History of American Industrial Society,* Vol. 3. First published, 1910; reissued, with new prefaces, New York: Russell & Russell, 1958. Reprinted by permission.

political, and economic issues of the day became encapsulated in legal forms for resolution by courts. This case involved the potentially explosive question of whether or not labor unions were illegal under common law. It was explosive because the political feelings on both sides of the issue were so strong (with Federalists tending to oppose and Republicans tending to favor unions); because the social welfare of the working class and the economic future of Philadelphia were said to be at stake; because the issues touched on deep questions of liberty; and perhaps most important, because the common law, as often was the case, provided no clear precedent for deciding the legal issues.

In 1794 Philadelphia's shoemakers organized the Federal Society of Journeyman Cordwainers. The purpose of the organization was to prevent employers from "knocking down" wages and to close the gap in the pay scales between different classes of workers in the industry. Through a series of strikes in the 1790s, the union attempted to peg wages for all shoemakers to the highest prevailing wage for the most skilled of the artisans. The success of these early strikes was mixed. Several moderate wage increases were won, but not for all the city's shoemakers. In the spring of 1805 the society struck, demanding an across-the-board increase for the city's shoemakers. The strike failed. In the summer of 1805 the city's shoemakers agreed to accept a slight reduction in wages from their employers (the master journeymen) because of a slowdown in sales of shoes. In the fall they demanded a return to the former higher wages, but the merchants refused. Thus the society struck again in November 1805. This strike collapsed with the indictment and arrest of the leaders for "conspiracy." The passage below is the charge to the jury by Recorder (judge) Levy in the leaders' trial.

It is the political backdrop that makes this case so fascinating. The trial became a showcase of radical Republican grievances in Philadelphia and in the nation; it occurred in a period when Pennsylvania's constitution was under revision, and it highlighted, and foretold, the growing divisions between manufacturers and the nascent class of urban workers. The trial essentially concerned whether the English common law of conspiracy applied in Pennsylvania. The broader issue concerned the nature of liberty and compulsion, and the apparent threat that labor unions posed to social order. The prosecution objected to the union because its members were "a government unto themselves," imposing an arbitrary power on employers and prejudicing the interest of the community. Defense counsel responded that the employers' freedom to repress wages for the sake of profits was no less an exercise of arbitrary power that denied the common "rights of man"; that the union was one of the few means available to workers to protect the dignity and value of their labor.

What is Recorder Levy's attitude toward common law? Can you link Levy's attitudes with those discussed in Chapter 1? What is the function of the jury, according to Levy? What is his attitude toward the legal profession? Toward lawyers involved in the legal process? Levy's understanding of the way the free market operates seems to influence his conclusions of law. Does this seem fair to you in a criminal proceeding? Do you agree with his interpretation of the motives of the union? Is he fair in his definition of what constitutes a "free" market? Why is Levy so concerned with protecting the authority of courts and preserving respect for common law? Has Levy answered the question of why the English common law of conspiracy should be held applicable in Pennsylvania? Is Levy's charge about politics, law, or economics?

The report of Recorder Levy's charge to the jury, and the arguments of counsel on both sides of the case, were privately printed and distributed by a Philadelphia printer for Thomas Lloyd. Apparently, Lloyd had attended the trial and taken notes in shorthand. The subsequent printed account is the only full record we have of the proceedings. On the frontis-piece of the printed book, Lloyd had the printer append the following statement:

> To Thomas M'Kean, Governor, and
> The General Assembly of Pennsylvania,
> Is dedicated the report of the most interesting law case, which has occurred in this state since our revolution . . . with the hope of attracting their particular attention, at the next meeting of the Legislature.
> "It is better that the law be known and certain, than that it be right." With respect, I am, fellow citizens, your most obedient,   Thomas Lloyd.

● ● ●

[Recorder Levy's charge to the jury:] Very able research has been made in this enquiry, and every principle necessary for your information has been laid before you. As far as the arguments of counsel apply to your understanding and judgment, they should have weight: but, if the appeal has been made to your passions, it ought not to be indulged. You ought to consider such appeals as an attack upon your integrity, as an attempt to enlist your passions against your judgment, and, therefore, listen to them with great distrust and caution. . . . An attempt has been made to shew that the spirit of the revolution and the principle of the common law, are opposite in this case. That the common law, if applied in this case, would operate an attack upon the rights of man. The enquiry on that point, was unnecessary and improper. Nothing more was required than to ascertain what the law is. The law is the permanent rule, it is the will of the whole community. After that is discovered, whatever may be its spirit or tendancy, it must be executed, and the most imperious duty demands our submission to it.

It is of no importance whether the journeymen or the masters be the prosecutors. What would it be to you if the thing was turned round, and the masters were the defendants instead of the journeymen? It is immaterial to our consideration whether the defendants are employers or employed; poor or rich. . . .

There are only two objects for your consideration. First. What the rule of law is on this subject? Second. Whether the defendants acted in such a manner as to bring them within that rule?

• • •

No matter what their motives were, whether to resist the supposed oppression of their masters, or to insist upon extravagant compensation. No matter whether this prosecution originated from motives of public good or private interest, the question is, whether the defendants are guilty of the offences charged against them? . . . If the defendants are guilty of the crime, [it does not matter] whether the prosecutor brings his action from motives of public good, or private resentment. The prosecutors are not on their trial, if they have proved the offence, alleged in the indictment against the defendants; and if the defendants are guilty, will any man say, that they ought not to be convicted: because the prosecution was not founded in motives of patriotism? Certainly the only question is, whether they are guilty or innocent. . . .

• • •

It is proper to consider, is such a combination consistent with the principles of our law, and injurious to the public welfare? The usual means by which the prices of work are regulated, are the demand for the article and the excellence of its fabric. Where the work is well done, and the demand is considerable, the prices will necessarily be high. Where the work is ill done, and the demand is inconsiderable, they will unquestionably be low. If there are many to consume, and few to work, the price of the article will be high: but if there are few to consume, and many to work, the article must be low. Much will depend too, upon these circumstances, whether the materials are plenty or scarce; the price of the commodity, will in consequence be higher or lower. These are the means by which prices are regulated in the natural course of things. To make an artificial regulation, is not to regard the excellence of the work or quality of the material, but to fix a positive and arbitrary price, governed by no standard, controuled by no impartial person, but dependent on the will of few who are interested; this is the unnatural way of raising the price of goods or work. This is independent of the number of customers, or of the quality of the material, or of the number who are to do the work. It is an unnatural, artificial means of raising the price of work beyond its standard, and taking an undue advantage of the public. Is the rule of law bottomed upon such principles, as to permit or protect such conduct? Consider it on the footing of the general commerce of the city. Is there any man who can calculate (if this is tolerated) at what price he may safely contract to deliver articles, for which he may receive orders, if he is to be regulated by the journeymen in an arbitrary jump from one price to another? It renders it impossible for a man, making a contract for a large quantity of such goods, to know whether he shall lose or gain by it. If he makes a large contract for goods to-day, for delivery at three, six, or nine months hence, can he calculate what the prices will be then, if the journeymen in the intermediate time, are permitted to meet and raise their prices, according to their caprice or pleasure? Can he fix the price of his commodity for a future day? It is impossible that any man can carry on commerce in this way. There cannot be a large contract entered into, but what the contractor will make at his peril. He may be ruined by the difference of prices made by the journeymen in the intermediate time. What then is the operation of this kind of conduct upon the commerce of the city? It exposes it to inconveniences, if not to ruin; therefore, it is against the public welfare. How does it operate upon the defendants? We see that those who are in indigent circumstances, and who have families to maintain, and who get their bread by their daily labour, have declared here upon oath, that it was impossible for them to hold out; the masters might do it, but they could not: and it has been admitted by the witnesses for the defendants, that such persons, however sharp and pressing their necessities, were obliged to stand to the turn-out, or never afterwards to be employed. They were interdicted from all business in future, if they did not continue to persevere in the measures, taken by the journeymen shoemakers. Can such a regulation be just and proper? Does it not tend to involve necessitous men in the commission of crimes? If they are prevented from working for six weeks, it might induce those who are thus idle, and have not the means of maintenance, to take other courses for the support of their wives and children. It might lead them to procure it by crimes—by burglary, larceny, or highway robbery! A father cannot stand by and see, without agony, his children suffer; if he does, he is an inhuman monster; he will be driven to seek bread for them, either by crime, by beggary, or a removal from the city. Consider these circumstances as they affect trade generally. Does this measure tend to make good workmen? No: it puts the botch incapable of doing justice to his work, on a level with the best tradesman. The master must give the same wages to each. Such a practice would take away all the excitement to excel in workmanship or industry. Consider the effect it would have upon the whole community. If the masters say they will not sell under certain prices, as the journeymen declare they will not work at certain wages, they, if persisted in, would put the whole body of the people into their power. Shoes and boots are articles of the first necessity. If they could stand out three or four weeks in winter, they might raise the price of boots to thirty, forty, or fifty dollars a pair, at least for some time, and until a competent supply could be got from other places. In every point of view, this measure is pregnant with public mischief and private injury . . . tends to demoralize the workmen . . . destroy the trade of the city, and leaves the pockets of the whole community to the discretion of the [workers]. If these evils were unprovided for by the law now existing, it would be necessary that laws should be made to restrain them.

What has been the conduct of the defendants in this instance? They belong to an association, the object of which is, that every person who follows the trade of a journeyman shoemaker, must be a member of their body. The apprentice immediately upon becoming free, and the journeyman who comes here from distant places, are all considered members of this institution. If they do not join the body, a term of reproach is fixed upon them. The members of the body will not work with them, and they refuse to board or lodge with them. The consequence is, that every one is compelled to join the society. . . . If the purpose of the association is well understood, it will be found they leave no individual at liberty to join the society or reject it. They compel him to become a member. Is there any reason to suppose that the laws are not competent to redress an evil of this magnitude? The [by-]laws of this [organization] are grievous to those not inclined to become members . . . they are injurious to the community, but they are not the laws of Pennsylvania. We live in a community, where the people in their collective capacity give the first momentum, and their representatives pass laws on circumstances, and occasions, which require their interference, as they arise.

But the acts of the legislature form but small part of that code from which the citizen is to learn his duties, or the magistrate his power and rule of action. These temporary emanations of a body, the component members of which are subject to perpetual change, apply principally to the political exigencies of the day.

It is in the volumes of the common law we are to seek for information . . . as well as the most important causes that come before our tribunals. That invaluable [common law] has ascertained and defined, with a critical precision, and with a consistency that no fluctuating political body could or can attain, not only the civil rights of property, but the nature of all crimes from treason to trespass, has pointed out the rules of evidence and the mode of proof, and has introduced and perpetuated, for their investigation, that admirable institution, the freeman's-boast, the trial by jury. Its profound provisions grow up, not from the pressure of the only true foundations of all knowledge, long experience and practical observation at the moment, but from the common law matured into an elaborate connected system. Law is by the length of time, it has been in use and the able men who have administered it. Much abuse has of late [been] teemed upon its valuable institutions. Its enemies do not attack it as a system: but they single out some detached branch of it, declare it absurd or intelligible, without understanding it. To treat it justly they should be able to comprehend the whole. Those who understand it best entertain the highest opinion of its excellence. . . No other persons are competent judges of it. As well might a circle of a thousand miles diameter be described by the man, whose eye could only see a single inch, as the common law be characterized by those who have not devoted years to its study. Those who know it, know that it regulates with a sound discretion most of our concerns in civil and social life. Its rules are the result of the wisdom of ages. It says there may be cases in which what one man may do with offence, many combined may not do with impunity. It distinguishes between the object so aimed at in different transactions. If the purpose to be obtained, be an object of individual interest, it may be fairly attempted by an individual. . . Many are prohibited from combining for the attainment of it.

What is the case now before us? . . A combination of workmen to raise their wages may be considered in a two fold point of view: one is to benefit themselves . . . the other is to injure those who do not join their society. The rule of law condemns both. If the rule be clear, we are bound to conform to it even though we do not comprehend the principle upon which it is founded. We are not to reject it because we do not see the reason of it. It is enough, that it is the will of the majority. It is law because it is their will—if it is law, there may be good reasons for it though we cannot find them out. But the rule in this case is pregnant with sound sense and all the authorities are clear upon the subject. Hawkins, the greatest authority on the criminal law, has laid it down, that a combination to maintaining one another, carrying a particular object, whether true or false, is criminal . . . the authority cited from 8 *Mod. rep.* does not rest merely upon the reputation of that book. He gives you other authorities to which he refers. It is adopted by Blackstone, and laid down as the law by Lord Mansfield [in] 1793, that an act innocent in an individual, is rendered criminal by a confederacy to effect it.

In the profound system of law, (if we may compare small things with great) as in the profound systems of Providence . . . there is often great reason for an institution, though a superficial observer may not be able to discover it. Obedience alone is required in the present case, the reason may be this. One man determines not to work under a certain price and it may be individually the opinion of all: in such a case it would be lawful in each to refuse to do so, for if each stands, alone, either may extract from his determination when he pleases. In the turn-out of last fall, if each member of the body had stood alone, fettered by no promises to the rest, many of them might have changed their opinion as to the price of wages and gone to work; but it has been given to you in evidence, that they were bound down by their agreement, and pledged by mutual engagements, to persist in it, however contrary to their own judgment. The continuance in improper conduct may therefore well be attributed to the combination. The good sense of those individuals was prevented by this agreement, from having its free exercise. Considering it in this point of view, let us take a look at the cases which have been compared to this by the defendant's counsel. Is [the agreement to organize, and combine, to effect a particular purpose or goal] like the formation of a society for the promotion of the general welfare of the community, such as to advance the interests of religion,* or to accomplish acts of charity and benevolence? Is it like the society for extinguishing fires? or those for the promotion of literature and the fine arts, or the meeting of the city wards to nominate candidates for the legislature or the executive? These are for the benefit of third persons the society in question to promote the selfish purposes of the members. The mere mention of them is an answer to all, that has been said on that point. There is no comparison between the two; they are as distinct as light and darkness. How can these cases be considered on an equal footing? The journeymen shoemakers have not asked an encreased price of work for an individual of their body; but they say that no one shall work, unless he receives the wages they have fixed. They could not go farther than saying, no one should work unless they all got the wages demanded by the majority; is this freedom? Is it not restraining, instead of promoting, the spirit of '76 when men expected to have no law but the constitution, and laws adopted by it or enacted by the legislature in conformity to it? Was it the spirit of '79, that either masters or journeymen, in regulating the prices of their commodities should set up a rule contrary to the law of their country? General and individual liberty was the spirit of '76. It is our first blessing. It has been obtained and will be maintained . . . we will not leave it to follow an *ignus fatius,* calculated only to mislead our judgment. It is not a question, . . . whether we shall have, besides our state legislature a new legislature consisting of journeymen

* Refers to the bylaws of a local religious sect that prohibited its members from marrying outside the church (author's note).

shoemakers. It is of no consequence, whether the prosecutors are two or three, or whether the defendants are ten thousand, their numbers are not to prevent the execution of our laws . . . though we acknowledge it is the hard hand of labour that promise the wealth of a nation, though we acknowledge the usefulness of such a large body of tradesmen and agree they should have every thing to which they are legally entitled; yet we conceive they ought to ask nothing more. They should neither be the slaves nor the governors of the community.

The sentiments of the court, not an individual of which is connected either with the masters or journeymen; all stand independent of both parties . . . are unanimous. They have given you the rule as they have found it in the book, and it is now for you to say, whether the defendants are guilty or not. The rule they consider as fixed, they cannot change it. It is now, therefore, left to you upon the law, and the evidence, to find the verdict. If you can reconcile it to your consciences, to find the defendants not guilty, you will do so; if not, the alternative that remains, is a verdict of guilty.

The jury retired, about 9 o'clock, and were directed by the court to seal up their verdict. . . . the verdict was entered on the back of the bill of indictment—guilty. And the court fined the defendants eight dollars each, with costs of suit, and to stand committed till paid.

Can Employers "Combine"?*
Commonwealth vs. Carlisle
(1821)

One of the arguments of defense counsel in the Cordwainers' case was that the merchants had formed their own "combination" in 1789 (five years before the society) and that the Society of Cordwainers was actually intended to restore free dealings between workers and manufacturers. The defense counsel quoted from Adam Smith's Wealth of Nations *to show that the formation of combinations was a common business practice and one defended by a man who advocated removal of restraints on free trade. The court, though, believed the evidence insufficient to support such claims. Yet Recorder Levy was quite clear that the law, when conspiracy is involved, must be "blind," favoring neither merchant nor worker.*

Precisely these questions are raised in Carlisle, *which again involves Philadelphia shoe merchants and members of the shoemakers' union. One Peter Voorhees, a member of the shoemakers' union, under oath charged a group of "master ladies shoemakers" (merchant manufacturers) with combining and agreeing with one another not to employ any journeyman who refused to work "at reduced*

* Brightly's Nisi Prius Reports, 36

wages. " *But it also appeared that the object of the merchants' organization* "*went no further than to reestablish certain rates which had prevailed a few months before, from which, there was reason to believe, the employers had been compelled to depart, by a combination among the journeymen.* " *The merchants were taken under custody and placed in jail under a commitment from a city alderman. The question presented before the court in this case was of a technical nature: whether the judge was bound to bail or remand the merchants on habeas corpus. Our interest is in what Justice Gibson has to say about what constitutes a conspiracy under Pennsylvania common law, and in particular about the excusability of merchant confederacies.*

A most interesting feature of this case is that the merchant manufacturers sought a "*motion to discharge [the case against them] on the ground that a combination to regulate wages is no offense by the common law of Pennsylvania.* " *Had they not read Recorder Levy's instructions? Or did they mean that such a combination was no offense when formed by manufacturers, as opposed to journeymen?*

Justice Gibson was one of the most distinguished jurists to sit on the Pennsylvania Supreme Court in the nineteenth century. His review of the law of conspiracy in Carlisle *was the most rigorous yet, and he was the first American judge to attempt to peel away the layers of ambiguity within the law in search of a* "*general*" *principle. He begins by stating that English conspiracy law as it applied to journeymen* "*may be entirely unfitted to the condition and habits of the same class here.* " *What does he mean by this? He then describes how the extension of conspiracy in England to a greater variety of cases gave rise to an* "*unsettled state of the law of conspiracy.* " *What do you suppose Gibson means by* "*unsettled*"? *It does not seem to have appeared that way to English judges. Does this concern have anything to do with American republican values?*

The principle Gibson offers, to clarify the precedent, is motive, or intention. What do these concepts mean? What is "*bad*" *motive? In what way is the view that Gibson brings to conspiracy more congenial to the political and economic concerns in the United States than Recorder Levy's understanding of conspiracy?*

Like Recorder Levy, Gibson relies on a free-market model of the economy that incorporates the wage-fund theory of capital and labor—that there is a limited amount of money in the economy with which to pay workers' wages—in analyzing combinations. He clearly believes that under some circumstances a merchants' combination would be criminal. What are those circumstances? Consider, for the moment, that Gibson believed it impossible that merchants could permanently depress wages through a combination, since others in the business would find it in their interest to offer workers "*more liberal terms; and these, by just compensation for labour, would have a monopoly of all the journeyman—they would ultimately ruin those who should adhere to the system of depression.* " *In Gibson confining his speculation to merchants within a single town, a county, a state, the nation as a whole? Can you see why this might be important? Are you as confident as Gibson that a free market will always be self-correcting? Consider also the matter of competition. He tells us that the ferry boat operators who combine "to ruin or injure the owner of a neighboring ferry" are engaging in unlawful behavior, whereas "it is otherwise where capital is combined, not for the purposes of oppression, but fair competition with others of the same calling." Do you believe this distinction is really quite so clear? What if the intent of a combination was to accumulate wealth, but the result of that combination was the destruction of all competition? Would it be reasonable to suggest that Gibson is thinking of corporations when he describes "combinations" in this context? What language in the opinion can you point to as evidence for the point? "Intent," incidentally, is said to be a question purely of fact that the jury must decide. Would there be problems of evidence in proving such a fact? In whose interests would such problem cases most likely be resolved? If you consider that the interests of capital would prevail, do you think Gibson intended this?*

How is this case resolved? If one reads Carlisle *with Levy's instructions, the impression of course is that employers may almost always combine to further an end, whereas labor may never combine. Yet Gibson takes pains to harmonize Levy's stand with his own. Is he persuasive? Has Gibson, by concentrating on "intent" and then defining its good and bad elements, advanced the "just" operation of conspiracy law? In other words, is Gibson's "general" principle free of political or economic bias?*

[Justice Gibson] In no book of authority has the precise point before me been decided. . . . In the trial of the boot and shoemakers of Philadelphia, there was no general principle distinctly asserted, but the case was considered only in reference to its particular circumstances, and in these it materially differed from that now under consideration. . . . There are, indeed, a variety of British precedents of indictments against journeymen for combining to raise their wages; and precedents rank next to decisions as evidence of the law; but it has been thought sound policy in England to put this class of the community under restrictions so severe, by statutes that were never extended to this country, that we ought to pause before we adopt their law of conspiracy. . . . An investigation of the principles of the law which declares the offence, then, becomes absolutely necessary to a correct decision in this particular instance; and I at once proceed to it[.]

The unsettled state of the law of conspiracy has arisen, as was justly remarked in the argument, from a gradual extension of the limits of the offence; each case having been decided on its own peculiar circumstances, without reference to any pre-established principle. When a combination had for its direct object to do a criminal act; as to procure the conviction of an innocent man (the only case originally indictable, and which afterwards served as a nucleus for the formation of the entire law of the subject) the mind at once pronounced it criminal. So where the act was lawful, but the intention was to accomplish it by unlawful means; as where the conviction of a person known to the conspirators to be guilty, was to be procured by any abuse of his right to a fair trial in ordinary course. But when the crime became so far enlarged as to include cases where the act was not only lawful in the abstract, but also to be accomplished exclusively by the use of lawful means, it is obvious that distinctions as complicated and various as the relations and transactions of civil society, became instantly involved, and to determine on the guilt or innocence of each of this class of the cases, an examination of the nature and principles of the offence became necessary. This examination has not yet been very accurately made; for there is in the books an unusual want of precision in the terms used to describe the distinctive features of guilt or innocence. It is said the union of persons in one common design is the gist of the offence: but that holds only in regard to a supposed question of the necessity of actual consummation of the meditated act; for if combination were, in every view, the essence of the crime, it would necessarily impart criminality to the most laudable associations. It is said . . . that the conspiracy is the gist of the charge, and that to do a thing lawful in itself by conspiracy is unlawful; but that is begging the very question, whether a conspiracy exists, and leaves the inquiry of what shall be said to be doing a lawful act by conspiracy, as much in the dark as ever. [After reviewing what treatise writers have said about conspiracy, Gibson concludes that] it will therefore be perceived that the *motive* for combining, or, what is the same thing, the nature of the object to be attained as a consequence of the lawful act is, in this class of cases, the discriminative circumstance. Where the act is lawful for an individual, it can be the subject of a conspiracy, when done in concert, only where there is a [direct] *intention* that injury shall result from it, or where the object is to benefit the conspirators to the prejudice of the public or the oppression of individuals, and where such prejudice or oppression is the natural and necessary consequence. To give appropriate instances respectively referable to each branch of this classification of criminal intention:—if a number of persons should combine to establish a ferry, not from motives of public or private utility, but to ruin or injure the owner of a neighbouring ferry, the wickedness of the motive would render the association criminal, although it is otherwise where capital is combined, not for the purposvs of oppression, but fair competition with others of the same calling. So with respect to the other branch: if the bakers of a town were to combine to hold up the article of bread, and by means of a scarcity thus produced, extort an exorbitant price for it, although the injury to the public would be only collateral to the object of the association, it would be indictable; and to one or other of these, may the motive in every decided case be traced. . . . I take it, then, a combination is criminal wherever the act to be done has a necessary tendency to prejudice the public or to oppress individuals by unjustly subjecting them to the power of the confederates, and giving effect to the purposes of the latter, whether of extortion or mischief.

According to this view of the law, a combination of employers [moving now into a discussion of the facts before the court] to depress the wages of journeymen below what they would be, if there was no recurrence to artificial means by either side, is criminal. There is between the different parts of the body politic a reciprocity of action on each other, which, like the action of antagonizing muscles in the natural body, not only prescribes to each its appropriate state and condition, but regulates the motion of the whole. The effort of an individual to disturb this equilibrium can never be perceptible, nor carry the operation of his interest on that of any other individual, beyond the limits of fair competition; but the increase of power by combination of means, being in geometrical proportion to the number concerned, an association may be able to give an impulse, not only oppressive to individuals, but mischievous to the public at large; and it is the employment of an engine so powerful and dangerous, that gives criminality to an act that would be perfectly innocent, at least in a legal view, when done by an individual. The combination of capital for purposes of commerce, or to carry on any other branch of industry, although it may in its consequences indirectly operate on third persons, is unaffected by this consideration, because it is a common means in the ordinary course of human affairs, which stimulates to competition and enables men to engage in undertakings too weighty for an individual. It would, I grant, be impossible for the employers in any branch of manufactures to produce a permanent depression of wages, because others would find it their interest to embark in the business on more liberal terms; and these, by a just compensation for labour, would have a monopoly of all the journeymen—they would ultimately ruin those who should adhere to the system of depression. The competition of interest must eventually break up every combination of the kind.

But though every plan of coercion must recoil on those who put it in practice, it may occasion much temporary mischief to others. The journeymen are compelled to enter, with their employers, into the unprofitable contest of who can do the other most harm, or submit to work for such prices as the latter may choose to give. Hence, precisely the same oppressive consequences to this class, as would result to the community from a confederacy among the bakers to extort an exorbitant price for bread, which everyone will acknowledge to be indictable. . . . It must be evident therefore, that an association is criminal when its object is to depress the price of labour below what it would bring, if it were left without artificial excitement by either masters or journeymen, to take its chance in the market.

But the motive may also be as important to avoid, as to induce an inference of criminality. The mere act of combining to change the price of labour is, perhaps, evidence of impropriety of intention, but not conclusive; for if the accused can show that the object was not to give an undue value to labour, but to foil their antagonists in an attempt to assign to it, by surreptitious means, a value which it would not otherwise have, they will make out a good defence. In the [*Cordwainers'* case], the Recorder [Levy], a lawyer of undoubted talents, instructed the jury that it was "no matter what the defendants' motives were, whether to resist the supposed oppression of their masters, or to insist upon extravagant wages;" but this, although perfectly true as applicable to that case, where the combination was intended to coerce not only the employers but third persons, is not of universal application. A combination to resist oppression, not merely supposed but real, would be perfectly innocent; for where the act to be done and the means of accomplishing it are lawful, and the object to be attained is meritorious, combination is not conspiracy. . . . It must therefore be obvious that the point in this case is, whether the [merchants who have entered into a combination and have been arrested for conspiracy] have been actuated by an improper motive; and that, being a question purely of fact, I am bound to refer its decision to a jury. . . . but as I was necessarily led into an examination of principles that might have an unfavourable operation on the [combining merchants], I owed it to them, particularly as there was some evidence of combination on the part of the journeymen who prosecute, to state also those principles that may possibly operate in [the merchants'] favour. . . .

Unions as Free Associations: Commonwealth v. Hunt*

Like the Cordwainers' *case of 1806,* Hunt *straddled the major social, political, and economic issues of the day. The case arrayed the Jacksonian Democrats against the more "conservative" Whigs. The Democrats, taking their name from President Andrew Jackson, inherited the mantle of Jeffersonian Republicanism. As we observed in Chapters 1 and 4 of the essay, the early Republicans and later the Democrats both held strong convictions about the nature and purpose of law: as far as possible it should be codified, and above all it should serve the interests of the majority of citizens. The Whigs formed in opposition to Jackson's reelection as President. They favored a strong national government and vigorous economic expansion, but unlike the old Federalist party, they had made their peace with democracy.*

The Whig district attorney of Boston, Samuel D. Parker, procured an indictment charging conspiracy against the Boston Journeymen Bootmakers' Society, at the behest of Jeremiah Horne, a disgruntled worker who had been fined and expelled from the society for violating its bylaws. Parker was well known in Boston for his antipathy toward workers' organizations. Defending the bootmakers was Robert Rantoul (see pp. 84–89).

Judge Peter O. Thacher presided over the trial of the bootmakers in Boston's municipal court. Thacher's sympathies matched Parker's. Only eight years earlier he had instructed a jury that any combination among "laborers and mechanics," either to raise wages or alter hours of work, constituted a "conspiracy" and was indictable at common law. This meant that the state of Massachusetts could still move against workers' "confederacies," even though no Massachusetts statute had pronounced judgment on the matter. After Parker and Rantoul had presented their cases, Thacher turned to the jury and practically directed a verdict of guilty (although a judge in a criminal case may only direct an acquittal and should leave conviction to the jury), when he indicated that a verdict of innocence would have disastrous consequences for Massachusetts:

> all industry and enterprise would be suspended, and all property would become insecure. It would involve in one common, fatal ruin, both laborer and employer, and the rich as well as the poor. It would tend directly to array them against each other, and to convulse the social system to its centre. A frightful despotism would soon be erected on the ruins of this free and happy commonwealth.

The jury, faced with the specter of a commonwealth in ruins, perhaps not surprisingly rendered a verdict of guilty. Rantoul appealed the case to the Supreme

* 45 Mass. (4 Met.) 111 (1842).

Judicial Court, questioning Judge Thacher's instructions, which found the mere combination of workmen a crime at common law. (Rantoul's objections are part of the "bill of exceptions" discussed in the opinion below.) The question before the appeals court, then, is whether or not workers' combinations to regulate their wages are illegal conspiracies. Chief Justice Shaw, one of the great state judges of the day, delivered the opinion for the court. He "arrested" (in essence overruled) the trial court judgment.

As you read Shaw's opinion on the first and third counts of the indictment, see if you can figure out why he objects to the language in these counts. He notes that the indictment against the workers is a violation of the Massachusetts Declaration of Rights. Why is this so? What does this tell you about Shaw's regard for personal liberty and state power? Can you see now why a person such as Robert Rantoul would favor the codification of the criminal law—and why he lent his services as counsel to the workers?

In Shaw's view, what are the bootmakers "guilty" of? Is that a crime? What purposes does he attribute to the Bootmakers' Society? Can you detect in Shaw's analysis of the union any political or economic policy preferences? What does he think about the idea of competition in the marketplace? Recall the discussion, in Chapter 3, about the rise of the business corporation and, in Chapter 4, about the "instrumentalism" of antebellum judicial decision making. Can an argument be made that Shaw is simply treating the union like any other business venture? If Shaw, citing the state's Declaration of Rights, is concerned about liberty, what could Thacher possibly have meant when he said that labor unions would erect a "frightful despotism" on top of the "ruins of this free and happy commonwealth"? Does Shaw say anything about Thacher?

Let us look back now at what Recorder Levy and Judge Gibson had to say about combinations. Why should those two judges have reached such a radically different conclusion from Shaw concerning the legality of unions? You might think about the analogies that two of the judges use in showing why a "combination" is legal or illegal: Gibson's analogy to the damaged ferry boat operator and extortionist baker; and Shaw's analogy to the the damaged baker and extortionist farmhands. Are they not using the same analogies? Why then do we have different rulings?

Do you think Shaw's opinion is "prolabor"? If so, does this mean that his ruling is also "antibusiness"? Are skilled workmen not interested in the prosperity of business? What would Recorder Levy have said? Does this tell you now why Shaw and Levy differ? In assessing Levy, recall Chapter 1 and the radical Republicans' view of commerce and law.

Is this a case about criminal law? About politics? About economics? Have Levy and Gibson and Shaw reached their conclusions purely through the application of logic? If you were the judge in each of these cases, what "pressures" would have been brought to bear on your determination? Keep in mind the years in which you would have been living.

[Court Reporter's Statement on the indictment]

This was an indictment against the defendants, (seven in number,) for a conspiracy. The first count alleged that the defendants, together with divers other persons unknown to the grand jurors, "on the first Monday of September 1840, at Boston, being workmen and journeymen in the art and manual occupation of boot-makers, unlawfully, perniciously and deceitfully designing and intending to continue, keep up, form, and unite themselves into an unlawful club, society and combination, and make unlawful by-laws, rules and orders among themselves, and thereby govern themselves and other workmen in said art, and unlawfully and unjustly to extort great sums of money by means thereof, did unlawfully assemble and meet together, and, being so assembled, did then and there unjustly and corruptly combine, confederate and agree together, that none of them should thereafter, and that none of them would, work for any master or person whatsoever, in the said art, mystery or occupation, who should employ any workman or journeyman, or other person in the said art, who was not a member of said club, society or combination, after notice given him to discharge such workman from the employ of such master; to the great damage and oppression, not only of their said masters employing them in said art and occupation, but also of divers other workmen and journeymen in the said art, mystery and occupation; to the evil example of all others in like case offending, and against the peace and dignity of the Commonwealth."

The second count charged that the defendants, and others unknown, at the time and place mentioned in the first count, "did unlawfully assemble, meet, conspire, confederate and agree together, not to work for any master or person who should employ any workman not being a member of a club, society or combination, called the Boston Journeymen Bootmakers' Society in Boston, in Massachusetts, or who should break any of their by-laws, unless such workman should pay to said club and society such sum as should be agreed upon as a penalty for the breach of such unlawful rules, orders and by-laws; and by means of said conspiracy, they did compel one Isaac B. Wait, a master cordwainer in said Boston, to turn out of his employ one Jeremiah Horne, a journeyman boot-maker, because said Horne would not pay a sum of money to said society for an alleged penalty of some of said unjust rules, orders and by-laws."

The third count averred that the defendants and others unknown, "wickedly and unjustly intending unlawfully, and by indirect means, to impoverish one Jeremiah Horne, a journey-man boot-maker, and hinder him from following his trade, did'' (at the time and place mentioned in the former counts) ''unlawfully conspire, combine, confederate and agree together, by wrongful and indirect means to impoverish said Horne, and to deprive and hinder him from following his said art and trade of a journeyman boot-maker, and from getting his livelihood and support thereby; and in pursuance of said conspiracy, they did wrongfully, unlawfully and indirectly prevent him, the said Horne, from following his said art, occupation, trade and business, and did greatly impoverish him.''

In the fourth count it was alleged that the defendants, (at the time and place before mentioned) ''unjustly intending to injure and impoverish one Jeremiah Horne, and to deprive him of work and employment, and to prevent his earning a livelihood and support by following his trade of a journeyman boot-maker, did unlawfully conspire, combine, confederate and agree together, by indirect means wrongfully to prejudice the said Horne and prevent him from exercising his trade as a journeyman boot-maker, and impoverish him.''

The fifth count set forth, that the defendants, at Boston, on the first Monday of November 1839, ''unlawfully, designedly to prejudice and impoverish one Isaac B. Wait, one Elias P. Blanchard, one David Howard, and divers other persons, whose names to the jurors are not known, all being master cordwainers and boot-makers in said Boston, employing journeymen boot-makers, did unlawfully, wrongfully and corruptly conspire, combine, confederate and agree together, by indirect means unjustly to prejudice and impoverish said Wait, Blanchard, Howard, and said other master cordwainers, whose names are unknown as aforesaid, and to prevent and hinder them from employing any journeymen boot-makers, who would not, after being notified, become members of a certain club, society or combination, called the Boston Journeymen Bootmakers' Society in Boston, Massachusetts, or who should break or violate any of the rules, orders or by-laws of said society, or refuse or neglect to pay any sum of money demanded from them, by said society, as a penalty for such breach of said by-laws.''

The defendants were found guilty, at the October term, 1840, of the municipal court, . . .

A printed copy of the constitution of the Boston Journeymen Bootmakers' Society was given in evidence against the defendants, at the trial; and it was agreed that the same might be referred to by the counsel, in the argument, and by the court, . . .

This case was argued, at the last March term, on all the exceptions alleged at the trial; but the argument on those points only, which were decided by the court, is here inserted.

Rantoul, [attorney] for the defendants. As we have no statute concerning conspiracy, the facts alleged in the indictment constitute an offence, if any, at common law. But the English common law of conspiracy is not in force in this State. We have not adopted the whole mass of the common law of England, indiscriminately, nor of the English statute law which passed either before or after the settlement of our country. So much only of the common law has been adopted, as is applicable to our situation, excluding "the artificial refinements and distinctions incident to the property of a great commercial people; the laws of revenue and police; such especially as are enforced by penalties." 1 Bl. Com. 107, & *seq.* 1 Tucker's Black. Appx. 406. Statutes do not bind colonies, unless they are expressly named. The English law, as to acts in restraint of trade, is generally local in its nature, and not suited to our condition. It has never been adopted here, and the colonies are not named in the statutes on that subject which have been passed in England since they were settled. . . .

The original of the law of conspiracy is in *St.* Edw. I, (A. D. 1304) and includes in its definition only false and malicious indictments.*

The next stage of the law of conspiracy appears in the early editions of 1 Hawk. *c.* 72, § 2: "That all confederacies wrongfully to prejudice a third person are criminal at common law; as a confederacy by indirect means to impoverish a third person, or falsely and maliciously to charge a man with being the reputed father of a bastard child; or to maintain one another in any matter, whether it be true or false." By "indirect means," unlawful means are meant.

The case of *The King* v. *Journeymen Tailors,* 8 Mod. 10, was decided after Hawkins's work was published, and is not a part of the law laid down by him, in his first editions. In that case, it was held that a conspiracy among workmen, to refuse to work under certain wages, is an indictable offence. This case, if correctly reported, introduced new law, unless it was decided on the statutes of laborers. The doctrine of that case, therefore, is not a part of the law adopted in this State. It was not the doctrine of the common law, when our ancestors came hither, and is not suited to our condition.

But the report of the case in 8 Mod. 10, is not to be depended upon. The book is of not authority, and is entitled to no respect. The doctrine of

---

* A statute of Parliament (author's note).

the case is not supported by any previous decision. Yet this is the only authority for the repetition of the same doctrine in the numerous books in which it is now found.

Probably the indictment, in that case, was sustained on the statutes of laborers. . . .

The statutes of laborers were blind struggles of the feudal nobles to avert from themselves the effects of great national calamities. Every one of these statutes had a local and temporary cause. In the famine of 1315, and the plague of 1316, parliament vainly strove to alleviate the universal distress, by fixing a legal price for provisions. Yet the scarcity increased, so that the king, going to St. Albans, "had much ado to get victuals to sustain his family." 1 Parl. Hist. 152. And some months later, mothers ate their children. Monk of Malmsb. 166. Walsingham's Chronicles, 107, 108. From the same motives, and with no better success, the plague of 1349 was followed by that remarkable statute *de servientibus,* from which have been derived all subsequent statutes of laborers. *St.* 25 Edw. III. 1 Parl. Hist. 274. 2 Reeves Hist. (2d ed.) 388. This pestilence was as general and destructive as any recorded in history. The deaths in London were mostly of the laboring classes: *Maxime operariorum et servientum.* 5 Rymer's Fœd. 693. King Edward had just been debasing his coin. Daniel in 1 Kennet's Hist. 224. From these causes, the wages of labor rose rapidly, and the law undertook to fix them. But in spite of fines, imprisonment and the pillory, wages and prices continued to rise. Knyghton's Chronicles, 2600.*

• • •

All the counts in the present indictment are fatally defective; *first*, in not averring any unlawful acts or means; *secondly*, if any such acts or means are averred, in not setting them forth. The vagueness and generality

---

* Mr. Rantoul examined, in the same manner, the subsequent statutes of laborers—34 Edw. III. *c.* 10. 12 Rich. II. *c.* 4.   7 Hen. IV. *c.* 17.   4 Hen V. *c.* 4.   2 Hen. VI. *c.* 18.   3 Hen. VI. *c.* 1. 23 Hen. VI *c.* 12.—and especially 1 Edw. VI. *c.* 3. (A. D. 1547.) 2 & 3 Edw. VI. *c.* 15. 3 & 4 Edw. VI. *c.* 16; which statutes, continued or modified by 5 Eliz. *c.* 4, (A. D. 1562,) & 1 Jac. I. *c.* 6, (A. D. 1604) were the law of England at the time of the settlement of Massachusetts, and were afterwards continued by 3 Car. I. *c.* 5, & 16 Car. I. *c.* 4, and were unrepealed at the time of the American revolution.

By these statutes, (said Mr. R.) a mere refusal to work was criminal *in an individual*; and by 2 & 3 Edw. VI. *c.* 15, a *combination* to refuse to work became criminal, for the first time. Such combinations are now legalized by 4 & 5 Wm. IV. *c.* 40.

In 1355, the commons petitioned, "that the points of confederacy may be declared; considering how the judges judge rashly thereof." The king made answer: "None shall be punished for confederacy, but where the statute speaketh expressly upon the point contained in the same statute." 1 Parl. Hist. 289. This petition related to rash judgments on *St.* Edw. I. concerning confederacies.

of the charges are such, that *autrefois convict* could not be pleaded to a second indictment for the same acts. When the end is not unlawful, the means should be set forth. *Commonwealth* v. *Warren,* 6 Mass. 74. *Lambert* v. *The People,* 9 Cow. 578. Mere combination is nowhere said to be unlawful, expect in 8 Mod. 10.

Austin, (Attorney General,) [prosecuting the case] for the Commonwealth. The common law doctrine of conspiracy is part of the law of this Commonwealth. It has been recognized by the legislature, in Rev. Sts. *c.* 82, § 28, and *c.* 86, § 10; and was long since enforced by this court. *Commonwealth* v. *Boynton* and *Commonwealth* v. *Pierpont,* 3 Law Reporter, 295.

The charge against the defendants is, in effect, an attempt to monopolize by them certain labor, on their own terms, and to prevent others from obtaining or giving employment. This is an indictable offence.

The case in 8 Mod. 10, (whatever may be the authority of the book,) shows the *fact,* that defendants were convicted of an offence like that with which the present defendants are charged; and that decision is cited by text writers, and by judges, without any question as to its soundness, or as to the accuracy of the report.

The old statutes of laborers, which have been referred to, do not at all affect the common law doctrine. No reference is made to them in the English books of criminal law, or in the reports of the cases of conspiracy by workmen.

A conspiracy to raise wages is indictable in England, not because it is unlawful for an individual to attempt to raise his wages—as the defendants' counsel suggests—but because a combination for that purpose is criminal and punishable. 6. T. R. 636, per Grose, J. So there are many other cases, in which an act, done by a single person, would not be cognizable by law, but which becomes the subject of indictment, if effected by several with a joint design.

Where the means of carrying a conspiracy into effect are alleged, in the indictment, to be unlawful, it is not necessary to set forth those means. . . .

It is not necessary, in order to render a conspiracy indictable, that the means, devised to carry it into effect, should be acts that are indictable. It is sufficient if they are unlawful. In *Commonwealth* v. *Boynton,* already cited, the conspiracy was to cheat by false pretences. Yet false pretences were not then indictable in Massachusetts. 6 Mass. 73.

• • •

Shaw, [Chief Justice]. Considerable time has elapsed since the argument of this case. It has been retained long under advisement, partly because we were desirous of examining, with some attention, the great number of cases cited at the argument, and others which have presented themselves in course, and partly because we considered it a question of great importance to the Commonwealth, and one which had been much examined and considered by the learned judge of the municipal court.

We have no doubt, that by the operation of the constitution of this Commonwealth, the general rules of the common law, making conspiracy an indictable offence, are in force here, and that this is included in the description of law which had, before the adoption of the constitution, been used and approved in the Province, Colony, or State of Massachusetts Bay, and usually practised in the courts of law. Const. of Mass. *c.* VI. § 6. . . . Still, it is proper in this connexion to remark, that although the common law in regard to conspiracy in this Commonwealth is in force, yet it will not necessarily follow that every indictment at common law for this offence is a precedent for a similar indictment in this State. The general rule of the common law is, that it is a criminal and indictable offence, for two or more to confederate and combine together, by concerted means, to do that which is unlawful or criminal, to the injury of the public, or portions or classes of the community, or even to the rights of an individual. This rule of law may be equally in force as a rule of the common law, in England and in this Commonwealth; and yet it must depend upon the local laws of each country to determine, whether the purpose to be accomplished by the combination, or the concerted means of accomplishing it, be unlawful or criminal in the respective countries. All those laws of the parent country, whether rules of the common law, or early English statutes, which were made for the purpose of regulating the wages of laborers, the settlement of paupers, and making it penal for any one to use a trade or handicraft to which he had not served a full apprenticeship—not being adapted to the circumstances of our colonial condition—were not adopted, used or approved, and therefore do not come within the description of the laws adopted and confirmed by the provision of the constitution already cited. This consideration will do something towards reconciling the English and American cases, and may indicate how far the principles of the English cases will apply in this Commonwealth, and show why a conviction in England, in many cases, would not be a precedent for a like conviction here. *The King* v. *Journeymen Tailors of Cambridge,* 8 Mod. 10, for instance, is commonly cited as an authority for an indictment at common law, and a conviction of journeymen mechanics of a conspiracy to raise their wages. It was there held, that the indictment need not [be based on the statute] because the gist of the offence was the conspiracy, which was an offence at common law. At the same time it was conceded, that the unlawful object to be accomplished was the raising of wages above the rate fixed by a general act of parliament. It was therefore a conspiracy to violate a general statute law, made for the regulation of a large branch of trade, affecting the comfort and interest of the public; and thus the object to be accomplished by the conspiracy was unlawful, if not criminal.

But the rule of law, that an illegal conspiracy, whatever may be the facts which constitute it, is an offence punishable by the laws of this Commonwealth, is established as well by legislative as by judicial authority. Like many other cases, that of murder, for instance, it leaves the definition or description of the offence to the common law, and provides modes for its prosecution and punishment. The Revised Statutes, *c.* 82, § 28, and *c.* 86, § 10, allowed an appeal from the court of common pleas and the municipal court, respectively, in cases of a conviction for conspiracy, and thereby recognized it as one of the class of offences, so difficult of investigation, or so aggravated in their nature and punishment, as to render it fit that the party accused should have the benefit of a trial before the highest court of the Commonwealth. And though this right of appeal is since taken away, by *St. of* 1839, *c.* 161, this does not diminish the force of the evidence tending to show that the offence is known and recognized by the legislature as a high indictable offence.

But the great difficulty is, in framing any definition or description, to be drawn from the decided cases, which shall specifically identify this offence—a description broad enough to include all cases punishable under this description, without including acts which are not punishable. Without attempting to review and reconcile all the cases, we are of opinion, that as a general description, though perhaps not a precise and accurate definition, a conspiracy must be a combination of two or more persons, by some concerted action, to accomplish some criminal or unlawful purpose, or to accomplish some purpose, not in itself criminal or unlawful, by criminal or unlawful means. We use the terms criminal or unlawful, because it is manifest that many acts are unlawful, which are not punishable by indictment or other public prosecution; and yet there is no doubt, we think, that a combination by numbers to do them would be an unlawful conspiracy, and punishable by indictment. Of this character was a conspiracy to cheat by false pretences, without false tokens, when a cheat by false pretences only, by a single person, was not a punishable offence. *Commonwealth* v. *Boynton*, before referred to. So a combination to destroy the reputation of an individual, by verbal calumny which is not indictable. So a conspiracy to induce and persuade a young female, by false representations, to leave the protection of her parent's house, with a view to facilitate her prostitution. *Rex* v. *Lord Grey,* 3 Hargrave's State Trials, 519.

But yet it is clear, that it is not every combination to do unlawful acts, to the prejudice of another by concerted action, which is punishable as conspiracy. . . .

• • •

Let us, then, first consider how the subject of criminal conspiracy is treated by elementary writers. The position cited by Chitty from Hawkins, by way of summing up the result of the cases, is this: "In a word, all confederacies wrongfully to prejudice another are misdemeanors at common law, whether the intention is to injure his property, his person, or his character." And Chitty adds, that "the object of conspiracy is not confined to an immediate wrong to individuals; it may be to injure public trade, to affect public health, to violate public police, to insult public justice, or to do any act in itself illegal." 3 Chit. Crim. Law, 1139.

Several rules upon the subject seem to be well established, to wit, that the unlawful agreement constitutes the gist of the offence, and therefore that it is not necessary to charge the execution of the unlawful agreement. . . .

Another rule is a necessary consequence of the former, which is, that the crime is consummate and complete by the fact of unlawful combination, and, therefore, that if the execution of the unlawful purpose is averred, it is by way of aggravation, and proof of it is not necessary to conviction; and therefore the jury may find the conspiracy, and negative the execution, and it will be a good conviction.

• • •

From this view of the law respecting conspiracy, we think it an offence which especially demands the application of that wise and humane rule of the common law, that an indictment shall state, with as much certainty as the nature of the case will admit, the facts which constitute the crime intended to be charged. This is required, to enable the defendant to meet the charge and prepare for his defence, and, in case of acquittal or conviction, to show by the record the identity of the charge, so that he may not be indicted a second time for the same offence. It is also necessary, in order that a person, charged by the grand jury for one offence, may not substantially be convicted, on his trial, or another. This fundamental rule is confirmed by the Declaration of Rights, which declares that no subject shall be held to answer for any crime or offence, until the same is fully and plainly, substantially and formally described to him.

From these views of the rules of criminal pleading, it appears to us to follow, as a necessary legal conclusion, that when the criminality of a conspiracy consists in an unlawful agreement of two or more persons to compass or promote some criminal or illegal purpose, that purpose must be fully and clearly stated in the indictment; and if the criminality of the offence, which is intended to be charged, consists in the agreement to compass or promote some purpose, not of itself criminal or unlawful, by the use of fraud, force, falsehood, or other criminal or unlawful means, such intended use of fraud, force, falsehood, or other criminal or unlawful means, must be set out in the indictment. Such, we think, is, on the whole, the result of the English authorities, although they are not quite uniform.

• • •

With these general views of the law, it becomes necessary to consider the circumstances of the present case, as they appear from the indictment itself, and from the bill of exceptions filed and allowed.

One of the exceptions, though not the first in the order of time, yet by far the most important, was this:

The counsel for the defendants contended, and requested the court to instruct the jury, that the indictment did not set forth any agreement to do a criminal act, or to do any lawful act by any specified criminal means, and that the agreements therein set forth did not constitute a conspiracy indictable by any law of this Commonwealth. But the judge refused so to do, and instructed the jury, that the indictment did, in his opinion, describe a confederacy among the defendants to do an unlawful act, and to effect the same by unlawful means; that the society, organized and associated for the purposes described in the indictment, was an unlawful conspiracy, against the laws of this Commonwealth; and that if the jury believed, from the evidence in the case, that the defendants, or any of them, had engaged in such a confederacy, they were bound to find such of them guilty.

We are here carefully to distinguish between the confederacy set forth in the indictment, and the confederacy or association contained in the constitution of the Boston Journeymen Bootmakers' Society, as stated in the little printed book, which was admitted as evidence on the trial. Because, though it was thus admitted as evidence, it would not warrant a conviction for any thing not stated in the indictment. . . .

● ● ●

[Concerning the first count] Now it is to be considered, that the preamble and introductory matter in the indictment—such as unlawfully and deceitfully designing and intending unjustly to extort great sums, &c.—is mere recital, and not traversable, and therefore cannot aid an imperfect averment of the facts constituting the description of the offence. The same may be said of the concluding matter, . . .

Stripped then of these introductory recitals and alleged injurious consequences, and of the qualifying epithets attached to the facts, the averment is this; that the defendants and others formed themselves into a society, and agreed not to work for any person, who should employ any journeyman or other person, not a member of such society, after notice given him to discharge such workman.

The manifest intent of the association is, to induce all those engaged in the same occupation to become members of it. Such a purpose is not unlawful. It would give them a power which might be exerted for useful and honorable purposes, or for dangerous and pernicious ones. If the latter were the real and actual object, and susceptible of proof, it should have been specially charged. Such an association might be used to afford each other assistance in times of poverty, sickness and distress; or to raise their intellectual, moral and social condition; or to make improvement in their art; or for other proper purposes. Or the association might be designed for purposes of oppression and injustice. But in order to charge all those, who become members of an association, with the guilt of a criminal conspiracy, it must be averred and proved that the actual, if not the avowed object of the association, was criminal. An association may be formed, the declared objects of which are innocent and laudable, and yet they may have secret articles, or an agreement communicated only to the members, by which they are banded together for purposes injurious to the peace of society or the rights of its members. Such would undoubtedly be a criminal conspiracy, on proof of the fact, however meritorious and praiseworthy the declared objects might be. The law is not to be hoodwinked by colorable pretences. It looks at truth and reality, through whatever disguise it may assume. . . . In this case, no such secret agreement, varying the objects of the association from those avowed, is set forth in this count of the indictment.

Nor can we perceive that the objects of this association, whatever they may have been, were to be attained by criminal means. The means which they proposed to employ, as averred in this count, and which, as we are now to presume, were established by the proof, were, that they would not work for a person, who, after due notice, should employ a journeyman not a member of their society. Supposing the object of the association to be laudable and lawful, or at least not unlawful, are these means criminal? The case supposes that these persons are not bound by contract, but free to work for whom they please, or not to work, if they so prefer. In this state of things, we cannot perceive, that it is criminal for men to agree together to exercise their own acknowledged rights, in such a manner as best to subserve their own interests. One way to test this is, to consider the effect of such an agreement, where the object of the association is acknowledged on all hands to be a laudable one. Suppose a class of workmen, impressed with the manifold evils of intemperance, should agree with each other not to work in a shop in which ardent spirit was furnished, or not to work in a shop with any one who used it, or not to work for an employer, who should, after notice, employ a journeyman who habitually used it. The consequences might be the same. A workman, who should still persist in the use of ardent spirit, would find it more difficult to get employment; a master employing such an one might, at times, experience inconvenience in his work, in losing the services of a skillful but intemperate workman. Still it seems to us, that as the object would be lawful, and the means not unlawful, such an agreement could not be pronounced a criminal conspiracy.

. . . It is perfectly consistent with every thing stated in this count, that the effect of the agreement was, that when they were free to act, they would not engage with an employer, or continue in his employment, if such employer, when free to act, should engage with a workman, or continue a workman in his employment, not a member of the association. If a large number of men, engaged for a certain time, should combine together to violate their contract, and quit their employment together, it would present a very different question. Suppose a farmer, employing a large number of men, engaged for the year, at fair monthly wages, and suppose that just at the moment that his crops were ready to harvest, they should all combine to quit his service, unless he would advance their wages, at a time when other laborers could not be obtained. It would surely be a conspiracy to do an unlawful act, though of such a character, that if done by an individual, it would lay the foundation of a civil action only, and not of a criminal prosecution. It would be a case very different from that stated in this count.

The second count, . . . alleges that the defendants, did assemble, conspire, confederate and agee together, not to work for any master or person who should employ any workman not being a member of a certain club, society or combination, called the Boston Journeymen Bootmakers' Society, . . . and that by means of said conspiracy they did compel one Isaac B. Wait, a master cordwainer, to turn out of his employ one Jeremiah Horne, a journeyman boot-maker, &c. in evil example, &c. So far as the averment of a conspiracy is concerned, all the remarks made in reference to the first count are equally applicable to this. It is simply an averment of an agreement amongst themselves not to work for a person, who should employ any person not a member of a certain association. It sets forth no illegal or criminal purpose to be accomplished, nor any illegal or criminal means to be adopted for the accomplishment of any purpose. It was an agreement, as to the manner in which they would exercise an acknowledged right to contract with others for their labor. It does not aver a conspiracy or even an intention to raise their wages; and it appears by the bill of exceptions, that the case was not put upon the footing of a conspiracy to raise their wages. . . .

As to the latter part of this count, which avers that by means of said conspiracy, the defendants did compel one Wait to turn out of his employ one Jeremiah Horne, we remark, . . . if no criminal or unlawful conspiracy is stated, it cannot be aided and made good by mere matter of aggravation. If the principal charge falls, the aggravation falls with it.

• • •

The third count, reciting a wicked and unlawful intent to impoverish one Jeremiah Horne, and hinder him from following his trade as a bootmaker, charges the defendants. . . with an unlawful conspiracy, . . .

• • •

If the fact of depriving Jeremiah Horne of the profits of his business, by whatever means it might be done, would be unlawful and criminal, a combination to compass that object would be an unlawful conspiracy, and it would be unnecessary to state the means. . . .

Suppose a baker in a small village had the exclusive custom of his neighborhood, and was making large profits by the sale of his bread. Supposing a number of those neighbors, believing the price of his bread too high, should propose to him to reduce his prices, or if he did not, that they would introduce another baker; and on his refusal, such other baker should, under their encouragement, set up a rival establishment, and sell his bread at lower prices; the effect would be to diminish the profit of the former baker, and to the same extent to impoverish him. And it might be said and proved, that the purpose of the associates was to diminish his profits, and thus impoverish him, though the ultimate and laudable object of the combination was to reduce the cost of bread to themselves and their neighbors. The same thing may be said of all competition in every branch of trade and industry; and yet it is through that competition, that the best interests of trade and industry are promoted. It is scarcely necessary to allude to the familiar instances of opposition lines of conveyance, rival hotels, and the thousand other instances, where each strives to gain custom to himself, by ingenious improvements, by increased industry, and by all the means by which he may lessen the price of commodities, and thereby diminish the profits of others.

We think, therefore, that associations may be entered into, the object of which is to adopt measures that may have a tendency to impoverish another, that is, to diminish his gains and profits, and yet so far from being criminal or unlawful the object may be highly meritorious and public spirited. . . .

The fourth count avers a conspiracy to impoverish Jeremiah Horne, without stating any means; and the fifth alleges a conspiracy to impoverish employers, by preventing and hindering them from employing persons, not members of the Bootmakers' Society; and these require no remarks, which have not been already made in reference to the other counts.

● ● ●

It appears by the bill of exceptions, that it was contended on the part of the defendants, that this indictment did not set forth any agreement to do a criminal act, or to do any lawful act by criminal means, and that the agreement therein set forth did not constitute a conspiracy indictable by the law of this State, and that the court was requested so to instruct the jury. This the court declined doing, but instructed the jury that the indictment did describe a confederacy among the defendants to do an unlawful act, and to effect the same by unlawful means—that the society, organized and associated for the purposes described in the indictment, was an unlawful conspiracy against the laws of this State, and that if the jury believed, from the evidence, that the defendants or any of them had engaged in such confederacy, they were bound to find such of them guilty.

In this opinion of the learned judge, this court, for the reasons stated, cannot concur. Whatever illegal purpose can be found in the constitution of the Bootmakers' Society, it not being clearly set forth in the indictment, cannot be relied upon to support this conviction. . . . But looking solely

at the indictment, disregarding the qualifying epithets, recitals and immaterial allegations, and confining ourselves to facts so averred as to be
capable of being traversed and put in issue, we cannot perceive that it
charges a criminal conspiracy punishable by law. The exceptions must
therefore, be sustained, and the judgment arrested.

3.
American Individualism: Contract and Tort

A "Risking" Bargain: White v.
Flora and Cherry*

The facts of White v. Flora and Cherry *are somewhat complicated. Jesse Flora
was searching for a tract of land in Tennessee that had been given to him by one
Lazarus Flora, deceased, of North Carolina. Flora engaged one White to help him
find the land, and promised to give White, if he found the land, one-half of the tract.
He also promised to sell White the other half "at a price to be fixed by valuers
chosen for that purpose." A contract was entered into between Flora and White
containing the terms of this agreement.*

*White found the land with little effort; it was located within a short distance of
his farm. In the meantime, Flora sold part of the tract of land to Daniel Cherry, in
apparent violation of his agreement with White. The question before the court was
whether the contract should be enforced, in effect requiring Cherry to convey the
land to White. Flora contended that White knew all along where the land was
located but pretended ignorance in order to defraud Flora of his land. The court
ruled in favor of White. Recall the decision of Chancellor Kent in* Seymour v.
Delancey, *discussed in Chapter 4 of the essay. Are the cases similar? Was Flora
foolish? Was White a cunning opportunist? Was the "consideration" equitable? Is
the court concerned with any of these questions?*

*The legal principle behind the Tennessee court ruling gained widespread accep-
tance in the nineteenth century. Does the discussion in Chapters 3 and 4 of the
essay help to explain why? Incidentally, who stands to gain the most from such
law? You may recall from the essay that if this kind of case had been decided a hundred years earlier in a colony, the outcome in all probability would have been different. Can you explain why? Note that there is little discussion of policy in the
court's decision. What, then, is the case about?*

Cooke, J[ustice]., delivered the following opinion of the Court:—[It is

* Supreme Court of Tennesee, 2 (2 Overt.) 426 (1815).

charged] that a grant issued to Lazarus Flora by the State of North Carolina for 274 acres of land, by whom previous to his death the same was devised to the defendant, Jesse Flora; that Jesse Flora, not knowing where the land was situated, applied to [White], and proposed to give him the one-half of the tract if he would find it and be at the expense of investigating the title, and to sell him the other half at a price to be fixed by valuers chosen for that purpose, payable in horses, and that a contract was made and reduced to writing in pursuance of such proposition; that [White] made search in the land office and other places, and found the situation of the land; that afterwards Jesse Flora, with a view to cheat [White], sold and conveyed the whole tract to the defendant, Daniel Cherry, who at the same time had full knowledge of the [agreement with White]. It is also charged that [White] let Flora have a horse, bridle, and saddle at the price of one hundred dollars, and that it was agreed that, should the land be found, it was to stand as so much paid towards the purchase of half of the tract according to the agreement.

The bill prays that the land may be conveyed to [White].

Flora answers, in substance, that the agreement was made [as White claims], but that White was guilty of great fraud and concealment in the transaction; that the land did not lie more than three miles from White's house, and that the situation of it was well known to White at the time the contract was made, although he represented himself to be entirely ignorant upon the subject; and indeed caused Flora to believe it would require great labor and influence to ascertain where the land lay. Flora admits that he sold and conveyed the land to Cherry, believing that White could not compel a performance of the contract, in consequence of the fraud and misrepresentation which he used; that he is willing to pay White the hundred dollars mentioned in the bill upon application, but denies that the horse, bridle, and saddle were received in part payment of the land.

Cherry's answer contains the same allegations as to the fraud practiced by White, of which transaction he admits he was well informed when he took the deed from Flora. . . .

The proof in the cause shows that young Flora and a man by the name of Biggs had been hunting for the land, and, being unsuccessful, came to White's and inquired of him if he knew any thing of the land; he replied that he did not. Flora then pressed him to take a part of the land for finding it and paying the expense of investigating the title, which White at first refused to do; but finally, after much persuasion, the contract was closed as set forth in the bill. The parties then went to an attorney to have writings drawn; and the attorney is particular in stating that he was careful in making Flora understand the nature of the agreement. Flora said he was illiterate, and a stranger in the country, and was willing to make a liberal allowance for finding and securing the land. . . . The agreement was signed on the 18th day of August, 1807, and both parties went on to Nashville, which was only a few miles, to search the register's office. White got a copy of the grant, and the next day, . . . White found where the land was, and that it lay within two or three miles of his own house. The title has not been disputed.

There is no satisfactory proof going to show that White knew where the land was situated, before he made the contract with Flora.

• • •

To the specific execution of the contract sought by the complainant, the defendant's counsel in the argument objected on several grounds.

1st. The fraud alleged to have been practiced by the complainant [White] upon Flora.

2d. The inadequacy of the consideration given by the complainant.

• • •

We shall notice these several objections in their turn.

1st. There is no proof of fraud on the part of White. It is true, when he was first applied to by the defendant Flora, he represented himself as wholly ignorant of the situation of the land, but it is equally true that no proof has been shown to us that this representation was false. If the fact had been with the defendant upon that point, we should have no hesitation in saying the complainant ought not to have a decree. When the complainant was applied to, with a view to ascertain his knowledge upon the subject of this land, if he then knew where it was, a representation on his part that he did not know, would have been a fraud, inasmuch as by means of it Flora would in all probability, have been induced to give a greater price for the trouble and labor of searching, and the expenses incident to an investigation of the title. In all cases of contract any representation of a falsehood or concealment of a truth, which, if correctly known, would probably be a reason for making the terms of the contract different will be a good ground for rescinding the agreement in a court of equity. Equity delights in doing justice, it delights in compelling men, by means of an appeal to the conscience, to do those things which ought to be done. To effect so desirable an object, strict regard must be had that no one is permitted to enjoy property which has been procured through means of an unreal appearance of things, more particularly if that appearance is the result of the fraudulent machinations of the person who seeks to be availed of it.

These remarks do not apply to cases of mutual mistakes and where there is not on either side fraud, concealment, or misrepresentation.

Had White known where to find the land, and apprised Flora of such knowledge, it is more than probable that Flora would not have given so much for the information as if he imagined that White was as ignorant of its situation as himself, and would most likely be put to some considerable trouble and expense in finding it. Therefore the representation on the part of White, that he knew not where the land was, if he did know, was a fraud; but there is no proof that he concealed any fact within his knowledge, or made any suggestion inconsistent with truth.

2d. It is also urged that there is in this case great inadequacy of consideration; and that therefore the Court ought not to decree a specific performance of the contract with Flora.

When a complainant comes into a court for the purpose of having a contract rescinded on the ground of mere inadequacy of consideration, all the books agree that relief can not be afforded. The mere circumstance of the sum paid being greatly inferior in value to the thing contracted to be purchased, will not, of itself, be sufficient to set aside an agreement; but it is in many instances strong evidence of fraud and imposition, and, coupled with other matters, such as the embarrassment of one of the parties, or the like, may frequently occasion the interference of a court of equity. But the situation of a complainant seeking to enforce the execution of an unreasonable and unconscientious bargain is placed on a ground very different. In such cases, the Court has a discretionary power; it will either cause the agreement to be executed or not, depending upon the equity of the whole case.

What cases of mere inadequacy of consideration will authorize the Court to refuse lending its aid to enforce an agreement, is not now necessary to be specified, as we are of opinion this is not one of them.

This sum it really cost White to find this land is, as we conceive, not the proper question; the bargain was clearly a risking one; it might cost only a few dollars to find the land, or it might cost the worth of the land itself. At the time the contract was made, it was utterly unknown to the parties, and impossible to tell which had the advantage; for any thing then known, the result might prove equally valuable, or much more advantageous to one than to the other. Every fact tending to remove uncertainty, was wholly unknown. If White had in the end been put to an expense more than sufficient to absorb the whole value of the land, an event which no man can say was impossible, could a court of equity have relieved him? Could Flora be compelled to pay him for his trouble and expense, and rescind the contract as to land? Clearly not. Why not, then, make the situation of the parties reciprocal? Here, White found this land at a cost much beneath what probably would have been given had the trouble and expense been previously known. But is that any reason why the contract ought not to be specifically executed? When we are asked not to enforce an agreement merely upon the ground of the consideration being inadequate, in a case where that consideration was to be performed in services of an uncertain and dubious value, it is impossible for us not to look at what might have been the amount. When we look at that, we believe there is nothing in it to prevent the interference of this court.

• • •

[White] is therefore entitled to a decree for the balance of the land, . . .

Technology, Private Rights, Public Needs: Hentz v. The Long Island Railroad Company*

The Hentz *case is a good illustration of a legal issue involving legislation (the state chartered the railroad company and authorized it to lay track and run its trains through the city), the interpretation of legislation by a court (the discretion given legislatively to company managers to locate the track route through the city), and the use of a common law doctrine (nuisance) in assessing the legality of "damages" incident to the building and operation of the railroad.*

The facts of this case are similar to those of Lexington and Ohio Railroad Co. v. Applegate, *discussed in Chapter 4 of the essay. Specifically, what is the plaintiff's complaint? Do you believe private property rights have been infringed upon by the railroad? Is he entitled to a "just compensation" for land "taken" to build the railroad? Has the plaintiff's property been damaged, as he claims? How would Sir William Blackstone have ruled in this case? You may recall from the discussion in Chapter 4 that traditional common-law property rights directed that one must use one's property only in ways that do not infringe upon the rights of others. The court recognizes this maxim, and yet it finds nothing inconsistent with this high regard for property rights and its ruling, which favors the railroad. How does the court escape the burden of this rule? Are there instances, according to the court, when the rail-*

---

* 13 Barb. 646 [Supreme Court of New York, 1852].

road might be liable for damages to property owners? What is the economic policy behind the decision? Does the court discuss such policy? Was the decision a "just" and "fair" one? Are there differing considerations of justice and fairness at work in this case?

S. B. STRONG, J[ustice]. The plaintiff alledges in his complaint that he has been for the last five years, and is, lawfully possessed of a lot in the village of Hempstead, in the county of Queens, bounded on the north by the middle of Fulton-street, and on the west by the middle of Main-street, comprising half an acre; on which there are a dwelling house and shop fronting on Main-street, and a barn and other out buildings on Fulton-street. That while he has been so possessed of the said premises, the defendants having previously, and in or about the year 1837, laid down and along Main-street, and upon such premises, certain timbers and iron rails, constituting their railroad track, continued them thereon, running over the same with passenger and freight cars drawn by horses, greatly to his injury, and that such cars were often suffered to stand for an unreasonable time upon his said premises. That about two years ago, and for about one year, the said track was disused, and got "into a ruinous and shattered state," and embarrassed the travel upon the highway, causing the breaking of wagons and other vehicles, and hindering and endangering their passage to and from the premises of the plaintiff. That about the 5th of last August, the defendants took up the old timbers and rails and tore up the soil of his land, and laid down in their place other timbers and iron rails, and have at various times since [violated his land] and run upon the said rails upon and over such [land] with their locomotives, propelled by steam; that "by the coming of the said locomotives upon and running the same over his said [land], the health and lives of his family, tenants and inmates, are prejudiced and endangered, and the value of his property lessened; that an offensive smoke has filled his dwelling house; that the same is a nuisance of the most flagrant character," and that the continuance thereof would be an irreparable injury to his said property and the enjoyment thereof; and that his tenants are likely to abandon the same. That the defendants have since such 5th of August last, run upon and over the said premises certain freight cars loaded with manure and merchandise, propelling the same by means of their steam engine and horses, often without agents to watch and conduct them, and to the danger, nuisance and inconvenience of himself and family; and that from the contiguity of his land to the depot, the locomotives frequently stop opposite to his premises, and he is thus injured more than the rest of mankind.

He therefore claims two thousand dollars damages, and prays for an order of injunction restraining the defendants during the pendency of this suit from running their locomotives or cars of any description upon or over his said premises, and that a judgment may be given him for his said damages, and for a perpetual injunction.

. . . I shall examine with all possible brevity the several points raised and discussed by the counsel for the respective parties on the argument, and shall consider such statements made in the affidavits produced before me as I deem material.

The plaintiff grounds his application on the allegations that the railway has been illegally located; that he has not received any compensation for that part of his land which has been taken by the company; and that the establishment is a public nuisance, peculiarly injurious to him.

The defendants claim the right to construct their road, as it is, under the act authorizing them to construct, maintain and continue a branch railroad from some convenient point on their main railroad, to some proper place or point in or near the village of Hempstead, passed on the 16th of May, 1836. The second section of that act conferred upon them the power which they possessed in reference to their main road, under the second section of their act of incorporation, (*Laws of* 1834, *p.* 231,) to construct the road "on the most practicable route." The company adopted the existing route throughout, and made their road upon it in 1837, and have used it, with but a brief interruption, from that time until the commencement of this suit. No objection is made to the starting point on the main road, but it is contended that the terminus in Hempstead is at an improper place, and that therefore it has been illegally assumed. Much was left by the terms of the act to the discretion of those who might manage the affairs of the company, and unless they *clearly* erred, their selection ought not to be disturbed. If a mere difference of opinion between them and those whose immediate interests might be affected by their acts, should be allowed to annul their proceedings, but few of them could be sustained; particularly when the views of parties are so varied as they usually are relative to the proper location of a railroad. The statute clearly gives to the defendants the right to extend their branch road *into* the village. No *fact* is stated in the plaintiff's papers to show that there is a more appropriate place *in* the village for the terminus of the road than that which has been selected. In any other part of it, the smoke, of which the plaintiff complains, would be equally offensive; there would be the same danger from the fire of the engine, the same exposure of human life, and a similar obstruction to the passage through the streets. If a railroad in, or through a populous village is necessarily a nuisance, that would be a reason for excluding it altogether. But I could not decide that it is, without condemning the action of both the legislative and judicial departments of this state. Many laws have been passed authorizing the construction of railroads through cities and villages. They have been carried into operation, and have been sustained by our courts. . . .

Whether it has been [a nuisance through mismanagement] or, indeed, whether it be a nuisance at all, will be considered in another part of this opinion. If, in considering this question, the opinions of those principally interested are entitled to any weight, a large majority appear to be in favor of the existing location. The plaintiff and one of his counsel and two gentlemen residing near the road, above the village, are opposed to it; and the counsel says that he attented a public meeting in the village of Hempstead, before and in reference to the relaying of the track, where, in all the conversations on the subject, it was expressly understood and declared that the company should on no account go below Fulton-street; it being universally understood and declared that the extension of the road beyond that street would be a nuisance. In this, however, he differs from others who were present at the same meeting. Justice Hendrickson swears that "at such meeting it was neither expressly understood or declared that the railroad company were on no account to run below Fulton-street;" and that the object and business of the meeting were to take measures to raise the necessary funds in money to induce the company to locate a depot and relay their branch railroad track *to its present termination.* Six residents of the village, some of whom are personally known to me to be gentlemen of great respectability and worth, swear that they, together with the counsel, to whom I have alluded, and another person, were a committee appointed by the inhabitants of the village, at a meeting held pursuant to public notice, to confer and agree with the railroad company respecting the relaying of the branch track in the said village; that the said counsel acted and performed his duties as one of such committee; and that it was expressly understood and agreed, by both the committee and the company, that the said company should relay and repair their branch track, entirely through Main-street, to the original termination of the said branch at the brook; and another resident of Hempstead swears that he stated to the said counsel that the understanding was that the railroad track was to be relaid below Fulton-street, for the accommodation of merchants and others, for freighting purposes; . . . Taking all the evidence upon this point together, I cannot think that the company has erred in this particular.

It is also contended that the defendants exceeded their powers in constructing a part of their road on a curved line, until it formed a junction with the highway leading into Main-street, and then laying their track along the highway. When a statute, or a deed, describes a line extending from one designated point to another, without any qualification, it generally calls for a straight course; but in this case there is express authority for a deviation, if it should become necessary or proper in the adoption of "the most practicable route." . . . There is evidence to show very considerable injuries to the highway, when the old track was partially disused; but the statements made in the depositions and memorials, to which I have referred, show very clearly that since the track has been relaid, the condition of the highway, and particularly of the street in the village, has been improved, and is, indeed, better than it was previous to the adoption of either as a part of the route.

• • •

The plaintiff alledges that his land extends to the center of Main-street, and that the company have wrongfully taken a part of it for their railroad. It appears from the diagram accompanying the plaintiff's papers, and from other documents which have been handed to me, that the track has been laid in or near the middle of the street, the rail nearest the plaintiff's dwelling house being about (and upwards of) twenty feet from the outer edge of the side walk on the same side. Whatever interest the plaintiff had in the land thus taken was therefore subject to the public right to use it as a common highway. . . . But have his private rights been impaired or taken, within the meaning of the constitutional provision securing an indemnity for the private property of individuals taken for public purposes?

It does not appear very clearly from the papers what right the plaintiff had in the property taken by the defendants. He alledges in his complaint that on or about the 2d of September, 1852, and for five years prior thereto, he was and now is lawfully *possessed* of the premises described. He does not in that claim any *title* to such premises or any part of them. But he deposes in his affidavit annexed to the order for a temporary injunction, that he owns the property in fee. It is not however competent for a plaintiff to add materially to the causes of action set forth in his complaint, by affidavit. . . .

But if the plaintiff had a full title to the land in question when it was first taken, and if he would then have been entitled to any compensation from the defendants for appropriating it to a species of locomotion different from that for which it had been dedicated or acquired (concerning which it is not necessary that I should give any opinion, nor do I) there is still a serious obstacle in the way of obtaining an injunction. He could have insisted on receiving a compensation when the land was first taken, and could have prevented the company from using it until such compensation had been paid, or at any rate satisfactorily secured; but after the road had been completed and was in full operation, it would not be equitable, it would not be doing justice to the public to allow him to stop the cars until he might coerce the company to pay him an exorbitant amount, or to go through with the dilatory process of having the damages assessed pursuant to the provisions of the statute. . . .

The only remaining question is whether the road where it passes the plaintiff's premises is a nuisance. I have already intimated an opinion that a railroad through a populous village, or a city, is not *per se* a nuisance. The legislature has expressly authorized various companies to lay and use their track through many of our cities and villages, and cars are now drawn by locomotives propelled by steam through Albany, Schenectady, Utica, Syracuse, Rochester, Buffalo, Poughkeepsie, Brooklyn, Jamaica, and many other cities and villages. It was held in the case of *Drake* v. *The Hudson River Railroad Company*, (7 *Barb.* 508,) that a road passing through the streets in the city of New York, and when the cars are drawn by steam-power into a crowded part of the city (although not to the terminus of the road) was not a nuisance. Similar decisions were made in the cases of *Hamilton* v. *The New York and Harlem Railroad Company*, (9 *Paige*, 171;) *The Lexington and Ohio Railroad Company* v. *Applegate*, (8 *Dana*, 289,) and *Chapman* v. *The Albany and Schenectady Railroad Company*, (10 *Barb*. 360.) Is there then any thing peculiar to Main-street, or in the management of the defendants, which makes the railroad where it passes the plaintiff's house a nuisance? It is not averred in the complaint that the railroad constitutes any serious impediment to the travel, along the highway. It no where appears that the rails are badly laid down, so as to create any obstruction on the surface, and it is apparent that the street is of sufficient width for carriages to pass each other without danger or difficulty, on either side of the railway. Besides, a number of respectable inhabitants of the place deposed that the condition of the street as a passway has been considerably improved by the defendants' works upon it.

Is there any thing in the management of the road and its appendages which renders it offensive to the plaintiff, to such an extent as to justify the interposition of this court by way of restraint upon the action of the defendants? One of the causes of complaint is that the steam locomotive passes as far south as Fulton-street, and occasionally below it. It is apparent that many of those who favored the introduction of the road into the village have acted on the supposition that the locomotive was not to proceed below Fulton-street, but there is no evidence of any definite agreement with the defendants to that effect; and as their charter does not restrict them as to the means of transportation on any part of their route, I am not authorized to interfere, but must leave the matter to the good sense of those who may be intrusted with the management of the affairs of the company. It is manifestly for their interest to conduct its operations in such a manner as to gratify the reasonable wishes of that part of the community which gives to the company an efficient support. The plaintiff complains that about two years ago, and for about a year, the track was disused and suffered "to go to ruin," its shattered state embarrassing the travel upon the highway, causing the breaking of vehicles, and hindering their passage to and from his premises. There were no doubt serious grievances at the time, but they resulted from the then impaired condition of the track. The cause has since been removed, . . . The plaintiff complains also of the smoke from the locomotive, on the ground that it is prejudicial to the health and comfort of himself and his family, and he alledges that the establishment as now conducted is a "nuisance of the most flagrant character," and that the lives of his family, tenants and inmates are endangered. The general charge that it is a flagrant nuisance, cannot be taken into consideration, any further than as it may be supported by the facts. In this case there are none except those which I have mentioned. The smoke must undoubtedly be annoying to some extent, but not more disagreeable or prejudicial than what may proceed from many lawful establishments in the village, nor is the inconvenience so constant or continuous. There may be some danger to human life from the rapid passage of a railroad train, but in the opinion of many, not more than what results from the passage of ordinary carriages. . . . It is true that there can be no satisfaction for the loss of life, nor any adequate remuneration for the deprivation of a limb, but the strong probability that the company will encounter a serious loss of property, and that a careless or notoriously incompetent conductor, or engineer, will undergo a disgraceful punishment where serious injuries are inflicted, must necessarily lead to great caution and to consequent security. The evils of which the plaintiff complains are by no means peculiar to himself. They are the necessary concomitants of this species of locomotion, whether in the city or in the country. They cannot be prevented without an entire suspension of one of the greatest improvements of modern times.

Private rights should undoubtedly be effectually guarded, but the courts cannot extend the protection of the interest of any one so far as to restrict the lawful pursuits of another. The maxim [use your property as not to damage another's] is true when correctly construed. It extends to all damages for which the law gives redress, but no further. If it should be applied literally, it would deprive us to a great extent of the legitimate use of our property, and impair, if not destroy its value. A man who sets up a new store or hotel in the vicinity of an old one, or who discovers and makes a new machine which wholly supersedes a prior invention, or who erects a new dwelling house so near that of his neighbor as to endanger it from the cinders which may escape from the chimney, or as to interrupt some fine prospect, or who plants a grove so near the boundary line of another as to shade a valuable garden, or prevent the free circulation of air around a dwelling house, inflicts an injury for which the law gives no redress, and which cannot be averted by the tribunals intrusted with its administration. So too there are some useful employments which endanger the lives of human beings which cannot and ought not be prohibited. Lives are sometimes destroyed by an omnibus, a carman's cart, a stage or a steamboat, but so long as they are not imminently dangerous they cannot be prohibited. We cannot enjoy our private rights nor can we avail ourselves of the many advantages resulting from modern discoveries, without encountering some risk to our lives, or our property, or to some extent endangering the lives or injuring the property of others. The questions in all such cases are, is the business a lawful one, and is the injury or danger to others by or from its legitimate pursuit inevitable? If they are, the law furnishes no remedy by way of indemnity or prevention.

The charges against the company for alledged carelessness and mismanagement are sufficiently answered by the affidavits produced by the defendants. From those papers it appears that the freight cars have at the time designated by the plaintiff been under the management and control of a competent conductor, and that their motion was by no means rapid, nor was any one injured.

Upon the whole I am satisfied that the case presented in behalf of the plaintiff does not call for, or warrant, the interposition of this court by way of restriction upon the future action of the defendants.

The motion for an injunction must therefore be denied, and the order temporarily restraining the defendants must be vacated.

The Workplace: Farwell v. The Boston and Worcester Railroad Corporation*

The use of steam as a motive force in America dates back to the beginning of the century. By 1820 steamboats operated on the Hudson, the Mississippi, and Lakes Erie and Ontario; they also navigated numerous smaller rivers and plied the coastal trade. Not until the late 1820s, following engineering developments in England, did the steam locomotive make headway in America. In 1828 the Baltimore and Ohio became the first chartered railroad corporation in America. By the middle of the 1830s, developments in locomotive technology in the United States (such as the four-wheel truck, which simplified turning maneuvers), combined with the promotion of the railroad as one answer to the national rage for expansion, opened the way for passenger travel. The Boston and Worcester Railroad, the subject of the law suit that appears below, was chartered in 1830 by the Massachusetts state legislature and began business in 1835. The line became an early leader in passenger travel.

We saw in Chapter 3 of the essay that it was a common practice of state government to underwrite expensive and ambitious navigation and transportation projects, and the railroad early received wholehearted state support. As the Hentz *case illustrated, legislators partially subsidized railway expansion, granted rail corporations wide powers of eminent domain, and vested them with certain immunities from cumbersome damage prosecution. However, the future of the railroad was by no means secure. Even in 1840 investors were being asked to take sizable risks. America was still a capital-scarce society (this would not alter for two more decades), and some had judged the railway to be a mere passing fad, pointing to man-made canals such as the Erie (completed in 1825) as a more promising mode of transportation. State and local governments nevertheless continued to back railroad development.*

The railroad created novel problems both of a social and of a legal nature. Not the least was the inherently dangerous nature of the technology. Boilers were apt to explode. Track deteriorated rapidly because of the crude state of iron manufacturing, and derailments were a common occurrence. The explusion of hot cinders through the elongated stacks of the early locomotives posed hazards to passengers and the surrounding countryside. The mechanics alone of building a railroad—charting a route over rough terrain, digging, exploding, and removing tons of earth and rock, grading and laying track—placed workers in a more or less continuous state of peril and inevitably inflicted some damage on contiguous property. Operating the finished line raised additional challenges. A road typically stretched over a wide geographical space and engaged hundreds of employees

---

* 45 Mass. (4 Met.) 49 (1842).

working in separate departments, necessitating a new level of management. Collisions and wrecks inevitably followed when communications broke down, as Farwell *testifies. Thus if the railroad promised to open up the continent and to create new markets, it also brought with it damage, injury, and sometimes death.*

The railroad charters followed the "general incorporation" formulas discussed in Chapter 3 of the essay. This meant, as Hentz *showed, that many of the obligations and responsibilities of the railroad corporation were left for courts to determine. Some of the consequences of building and running the railroad no doubt were unforeseen. And the law provided few precedents for resolving cases involving novel forms of technology.* Shaw *states in his opinion in* Farwell *that the legal issues presented by the case are "of new impression in our courts." He may have been correct regarding the specific facts of the case, but the doctrine of* respondeat superior, *which had existed for some time in common law, arguably could have been extended to apply to* Farwell.

In the passage below, Sir William Blackstone summarizes the responsibilities of "masters" (employers) for the acts of their "servants" (employees).

WILLIAM BLACKSTONE: RESPONSIBILITY OF MASTER*

As for those things which a servant may do on behalf of his master, they seem all to proceed upon this principle, that the master is answerable for the act of his servant, if done by his command, either expressly given, or implied: for he who does a thing by the agency of another, does it himself. Therefore, if the servant commit a trespass by the command or encouragement of his master, the master shall be guilty of it: not that the servant is excused, for he is only to obey his master in matters that are honest and lawful.

If an innkeeper's servants rob his guests, the master is bound to restitution: for as there is a confidence reposed in him, that he will take care to provide honest servants, his negligence is a kind of implied consent to the robbery; for he who does not forbid a crime while he may, sanctions it. So likewise if the drawer at a tavern sells a man bad wine whereby his health is injured, he may bring an action against the master: for although the master did not expressly order the servant to sell it to that person in particular, yet his permitting him to draw and sell it at all is impliedly a general command.

The question put to the court in Farwell *is basic. Is the employer liable to pay damages to his employee who, while performing in a reasonable manner the customary duties of his job, is injured by another employee who has acted negligently? The engineer,* Farwell, *was injured when his locomotive derailed because the switchman,* Whitcomb, *threw the switch improperly.*

Is this case, as Shaw *maintains, one "of new impression"? What does* Shaw

---

* William Blackstone, *Commentaries on the Laws of England*, vol. 1, (1768), p. 431.

have to say about the doctrine of respondeat superior *as described by Blackstone?
How would you have decided this case, and on what basis?*

*Do you think Shaw is being fair to Farwell when Shaw tells him, in essence, that
he had entered into an "implied contract of indemnity" with his employer? What
were the implied terms of the contract? Why does Shaw believe he was acting fairly
to Farwell* and *the railroad? What is the policy of the case, according to Shaw? Is
Shaw acting in concert with the commonwealth theory of legislative activism
discussed in Chapter 3? Is his ruling consistent with the main lines of development
of tort and contract discussed in Chapter 4? Was there a conflict in the policies promoted by legislatures and by courts?*

Shaw's opinion in Farwell *became the foundation of the law of employer liability for injuries sustained by employees through the negligence of their fellow
workmen. Why, do you suppose?*

[Statement of Court reporter] In an action of trespass upon the case,
the plaintiff alleged in his declaration, that he agreed with the defendants
to serve them in the employment of an engineer in the management and care
of their engines and cars running on their rail road between Boston and
Worcester, and entered on said employment, and continued to perform his
duties as engineer till October 30th 1837, when the defendants, at Newton, by
their servants, so carelessly, negligently and unskilfully managed and used,
and put and placed the iron match rail, called the short switch, across the rail
or track of their said rail road, that the engine and cars, upon which the plaintiff was engaged and employed in the discharge of his said duties of engineer,
were thrown from the track of said rail road, and the plaintiff, by means
thereof, was thrown with great violence upon the ground; by means of which
one of the wheels of one of said cars passed over the right hand of the plaintiff, crushing and destroying the same.

● ● ●

C. G. Loring, [attorney] for the plaintiff. The defendants, having
employed the plaintiff to do a specified duty on the road, were bound to
keep the road in such a condition that he might do that duty with safety. If
the plaintiff had been a [non-employee, such as a passenger], the defendants would have been liable; and he contends that the case is not varied
by the fact that both the plaintiff and Whitcomb were the servants of the
defendants; because the plaintiff was not the servant of the defendants in
the duty or service, the neglect of which occasioned the injury sustained
by him. He was employed for a distinct and separate service, and had no
joint agency or power with the other servants whose duty it was to keep

the road in order; and could not be made responsible to the defendants for its not being kept in order. He could not, by any vigilance or any power that he could exercise, have prevented the accident. His duties and those of Whitcomb were as distinct and independent of each other, as if they had been servants of different masters.

The plaintiff does not put his case on the ground of the defendants' liability to passengers, nor upon the general principle which renders principals liable for the acts of their agents; but on the ground, that a master, by the nature of his contract with a servant, stipulates for the safety of the servant's employment, so far as the master can regulate the matter.

The defence rests upon [a] . . . general rule, that a master is not liable to his servant for damage caused by the negligence of a fellow servant. But if that be sound, as a general rule, it does not apply here; for Whitcomb and the plaintiff, as has already been stated, were not fellow servants—that is, were not jointly employed for a common purpose.

• • •

No general rule can be laid down, which will apply to all cases of a master's liability to a servant. But it is submitted that a master is liable to one servant for the negligence of another, when they are engaged in distinct employments, though he is not so liable, where two servants are engaged jointly in the same service; because, in the latter case, each servant has some supervision and control of every other. . . . And unless the servant has a remedy against the master, in such cases, the great fundamental legal rule, that where there is a wrong there is a remedy, is violated or departed from.

• • •

Fletcher & Morey, [attorneys] for the defendants. . . . [N]o rule of policy requires that masters shall be liable to one servant for injuries received by him from a fellow servant. On the contrary, policy requires an entirely different rule, especially in the present case. The aim of all the statutes concerning rail roads is to protect passengers; and if this action is maintained, it will establish a principle which will tend to diminish the caution of rail road servants, and thus increase the risk of passengers.

The defendants have been in no fault, in this case, either in the construction of their road, the use of defective engines, or the employment of careless or untrusty servants. So that the question is, whether they are liable to the plaintiff, on an implied contract of indemnity. The contract between the parties to this suit excludes the notion that the defendants are liable for the injury received by the plaintiff. He agreed to run an engine on their road, knowing the state of the road, and also knowing Whitcomb, his character, and the specific duty intrusted to him. The plaintiff therefore assumed the risks of the service which he undertook to perform; and one of those risks was his liability to injury from the carelessness of others who were employed by the defendants in the same service. As a consideration for the increased risk of this service, he received higher wages than when he was employed in a less hazardous business.

• • •

SHAW, [Chief Justice]. This is an action of new impression in our courts, and involves a principle of great importance. . . The question is, whether, for damages sustained by one of the persons so employed, by means of the carelessness and negligence of another, the party injured has a remedy against the common employer. It is an argument against such an action, though certainly not a decisive one, that no such action has before been maintained.

It is laid down by Blackstone, that if a servant, by his negligence, does any damage to a stranger, the master shall be answerable for his neglect. But the damage must be done while he is actually employed in the master's service; otherwise, the servant shall answer for his own misbehavior. 1Bl. Com. 431. *McManus* v. *Crickett*, 1 East, 106. This rule is obviously founded on the great principle of social duty, that every man, in the management of his own affairs, whether by himself or by his agents or servants, shall so conduct them as not to injure another; and if he does not, and another thereby sustains damage, he shall answer for it. If done by a servant, in the course of his employment, and acting within the scope of his authority, it is considered, in contemplation of law, so far the act of the master, that the latter shall be answerable. But this presupposes that the parties stand to each other in the relation of strangers, between whom there is no privity; and the action, in such case, is an action sounding in tort. The form is trespass on the case, for the consequential damage. The maxim *respondeat superior* is adopted in that case, from general considerations of policy and security.

But this does not apply to the case of a servant bringing his action against his own employer to recover damages for an injury arising in the course of that employment, where all such risks and perils as the employer and the servant respectively intend to assume and bear may be regulated by the express or implied contract between them, and which, in contemplation of law, must be presumed to be thus regulated.

The same view seems to have been taken by the learned counsel for the plaintiff in the argument; and it was conceded, that the claim could not be placed on the principle indicated by the maxim *respondeat superior*, which binds the master to indemnify a stranger for the damage caused by the careless, negligent or unskilful act of his servant in the conduct of his affairs. The claim, therefore, is placed, and must be maintained, if maintained at all, on the ground of contract. As there is no express contract between the parties, applicable to this point, it is placed on the footing of an implied contract of indemnity, arising out of the relation of master and servant. It would be an implied promise, arising from the duty of the master to be responsible to each person employed by him, in the conduct of every branch of business, where two or more persons are employed, to pay for all damage occasioned by the negligence of every other person employed in the same service. If such a duty were established by law—like that of a common carrier, to stand to all losses of goods not caused by the act of God or of a public enemy—or that of an innkeeper, to be responsible, in like manner, for the baggage of his guests; it would be a rule of frequent and familiar occurrence, and its existence and application, with all its qualifications and restrictions, would be settled by judicial precedents. But we are of opinion that no such rule has been established, and the authorities, as far as they go, are opposed to the principle. *Priestley* v. *Fowler*, 3 Mees. & Welsb. 1. *Murray* v. *South Carolina Rail Road Company*, 1 McMullan, 385.

The general rule, resulting from considerations as well of justice as of policy, is, that he who engages in the employment of another for the performance of specified duties and services, for compensation, takes upon himself the natural and ordinary risks and perils incident to the performance of such services, and in legal presumption, the compensation is adjusted accordingly. And we are not aware of any principle which should except the perils arising from the carelessness and negligence of those who are in the same employment. These are perils which the servant is as likely to know, and against which he can as effectually guard, as the master. They are perils incident to the service, and which can be as distinctly foreseen and provided for in the rate of compensation as any others. To say that the master shall be responsible because the damage is caused by his agents, is assuming the very point which remains to be proved. They are his agents to some extent, and for some purposes; but whether he is responsible, in a particular case, for their negligence, is not decided by the single fact that they are, for some purposes, his agents.

• • •

If we look from considerations of justice to those of policy, they will strongly lead to the same conclusion. In considering the rights and obligations arising out of particular relations, it is competent for courts of justice to regard considerations of policy and general convenience, and to draw from them such rules as will, in their practical application, best promote the safety and security of all parties concerned. This is, in truth, the basis on which implied promises are raised, being duties legally inferred from a consideration of what is best adapted to promote the benefit of all persons concerned, under given circumstances. To take the well known and familiar cases already cited; a common carrier, without regard to actual fault or neglect in himself or his servants, is made liable for all losses of goods confided to him for carriage, except those caused by the act of God or of a public enemy, because he can best guard them against all minor dangers, and because, in case of actual loss, it would be extremely difficult for the owner to adduce proof of embezzlement, or other actual fault or neglect on the part of the carrier, although it may have been the real cause of the loss. The risk is therefore thrown upon the carrier, and he receives, in the form of payment for the carriage, a premium for the risk which he thus assumes. So of an innkeeper; he can best secure the attendance of honest and faithful servants, and guard his house against thieves. Whereas, if he were responsible only upon proof of actual negligence, he might connive at the presence of dishonest inmates and retainers, and even participate in the embezzlement of the property of the guest, during the hours of their necessary sleep, and yet it would be difficult, and often impossible, to prove these facts.

The liability of passenger carriers is founded on similar considerations. They are held to the strictest responsibility for care, vigilance and skill, on the part of themselves and all persons employed by them, and they are paid accordingly. The rule is founded on the expediency of throwing the risk upon those who can best guard against it.

We are of opinion that these considerations apply strongly to the case in question. Where several persons are employed in the conduct of one common enterprise or undertaking, and the safety of each depends much on the care and skill with which each other shall perform his appropriate duty, each is an observer of the conduct of the others, can give notice of any misconduct, incapacity or neglect of duty, and leave the service, if the common employer will not take such precautions, and employ such agents as the safety of the whole party may require. By these means, the safety of each will be much more effectually secured, than could be done by a resort to the common employer for indemnity in case of loss by the negligence of each other. Regarding it in this light, it is the ordinary case of one sustaining an injury in the course of his own employment, in which he must bear the loss himself, or seek his remedy, if he have any, against the actual wrong-doer.

In applying these principles to the present case, it appears that the plaintiff was employed by the defendants as an engineer, at the rate of wages usually paid in that employment, being a higher rate than the plaintiff had before received as a machinist. It was a voluntary undertaking on his part, with a full knowledge of the risks incident to the employment; and the loss was sustained by means of an ordinary casualty, caused by the negligence of another servant of the company. Under these circumstances, the loss must be deemed to be the result of a pure accident, like those to which all men, in all employments, and at all times, are more or less exposed; and like similar losses from accidental causes, it must rest where it first fell, unless the plaintiff has a remedy against the person actually in default; of which we give no opinion.

It was strongly pressed in the argument, that although this might be so, where two or more servants are employed in the same department of duty, where each can exert some influence over the conduct of the other, and thus to some extent provide for his own security; yet that it could not apply where two or more are employed in different departments of duty, at a distance from each other, and where one can in no degree control or influence the conduct of another. But we think this is founded upon a supposed distinction, on which it would be extremely difficult to establish a practical rule. When the object to be accomplished is one and the same, and the several persons employed derive their authority and their compensation from the same source, it would be extremely difficult to distinguish, what constitutes one distinct department of duty. It would vary with the circumstances of every case. If it were made to depend upon the nearness or distance of the persons from each other, the question would immediately arise, how near or how distant must they be, to be in the same or different departments. In a blacksmith's shop, persons working in the same building, at different fires, may be quite independent of each other, though only a few feet distant. In a ropewalk, several may be at work on the same piece of cordage, at the same time, at many hundred feet distant from each other, and beyond the reach of sight and voice, and yet acting together.

Besides, it appears to us, that the argument rests upon an assumed principle of responsibility which does not exist. The master, in the case supposed, is not exempt from liability, because the servant has better

means of providing for his safety, when he is employed in immediate connexion with those from whose negligence he might suffer; but because the
implied contract of the master does not extend to indemnify the servant
against the negligence of any one but himself; and he is not liable in tort,
as for the negligence of his servant, because the person suffering does not
stand towards him in the relation of a stranger, but is one whose rights are
regulated by contract express or implied. The exemption of the master,
therefore, from liability for the negligence of a fellow servant, does not
depend exclusively upon the consideration, that the servant has better
means to provide for his own safety, but upon other grounds. Hence the
separation of the employment into different departments cannot create that
liability, when it does not arise from express or implied contract, or from
a responsibility created by law to third persons, and strangers, for the
negligence of a servant.

• • •

. . . It ought, perhaps, to be stated, in justice to the person to whom
this negligence is imputed, that the fact [of Whitcomb's negligent con-
duct] is strenuously denied by the defendants, and has not been tried by
the jury. By consent of the parties, this fact was assumed without trial, in
order to take the opinion of the whole court upon the question of law,
whether, if such was the fact, the defendants, under the circumstances,
were liable. Upon this question, supposing the accident to have occurred,
and the loss to have been caused by the negligence of the person employed
to attend to and change the switch, in his not doing so in the particular
case, the court are of opinion that it is a loss for which the defendants are
not liable, and that the action cannot be maintained.

"Fault" or "Accident"? The New Idea of Negligence: Brown v. Kendall* *(1850)*

Brown v. Kendall *was decided by the same judge who decided* Farwell. *For many
years legal historians believed it was* Brown *that had established the foundation of
modern negligence doctrine. In fact,* Brown *merely restates the doctrine that judges
had been elaborating at least since 1820. The case is significant—and of interest to
us—for its suggestion of the intellectual rationale of negligence doctrine. Up to this
point, negligence doctrine has been described as a legal element with vast*

* (6 Cush.) 292 (1850) [Court reporter's summary].

economic implications for persons engaged in business enterprises. This case involves a dogfight. And as such, it leads us to believe that there may have been much more involved, for the intellectual history of legal doctrine, than the business interests of the parties. What, specifically, was involved in this case? What social assumptions lay behind the decision?

FACTS OF THE CASE

This was an action of trespass for assault and battery, originally commenced against George K. Kendall, the defendant, who died pending the suit, and his executrix was summoned in.

It appeared in evidence, on the trial, which was before *Wells,* C.J., in the court of common pleas, that two dogs, belonging to the plaintiff and the defendant, respectively, were fighting in the presence of their masters; that the defendant took a stick about four feet long, and commenced beating the dogs in order to separate them; that the plaintiff was looking on, at the distance of about a rod, and that he advanced a step or two towards the dogs. In their struggle, the dogs approached the place where the plaintiff was standing. The defendant retreated backwards from before the dogs, striking them as he retreated; and as he approached the plaintiff, with his back towards him, in raising his stick over his shoulder, in order to strike the dogs, he accidentally hit the plaintiff in the eye, inflicting upon him a severe injury.

Whether it was necessary or proper for the defendant to interfere in the fight between the dogs; whether the interference, if called for, was in a proper manner, and what degree of care was exercised by each party on the occasion; were the subject of controversy between the parties, upon all the evidence in the case, of which the foregoing is an outline.

The defendant requested the judge to instruct the jury, that "if both the plaintiff and defendant at the time of the blow were using ordinary care, or if at that time the defendant was using ordinary care and the plaintiff was not, or if at that time both plaintiff and defendant were not using ordinary care, then the plaintiff could not recover."

The defendant further requested the judge to instruct the jury, that, "under the circumstances, if the plaintiff was using ordinary care and the defendant was not, the plaintiff could not recover, and that the burden of proof on all these propositions was on the plaintiff."

The judge declined to give the instructions, as above requested, but left the case to the jury under the following instructions: "If the defendant, in beating the dogs, was doing a necessary act, or one which it was his duty under the circumstances of the case to do, and was doing it in a proper way; then he was not responsible in this action, provided he was using ordinary care at the time of the blow. If it was not a necessary act; if he was not in duty bound to attempt to part the dogs, but might with propriety interfere or not as he chose; the defendant was responsible for the consequences of the blow, unless it appeared that he was in the exercise of extraordinary care, so that the accident was inevitable, using the word inevitable not in a strict but a popular sense."

"If, however, the plaintiff, when he met with the injury, was not in the exercise of ordinary care, he cannot recover, and this rule applies, whether the interference of the defendant in the fight of the dogs was necessary or not. If the jury believe, that it was the duty of the defendant to interfere, then the burden of proving negligence on the part of the defendant, and ordinary care on the part of the plaintiff, is on the plaintiff. If the jury believe, that the act of interference in the fight was unnecessary, then the burden of proving extraordinary care on the part of the defendant, or want of ordinary care on the part of the plaintiff, is on the defendant."

The jury under these instructions returned a verdict for the plaintiff; whereupon the defendant alleged exceptions.

OPINION OF CHIEF JUSTICE SHAW

This is an action of trespass *vi et armis,* brought by George Brown against George K. Kendall, for an assault and battery; and the original defendant having died pending the action, his executrix has been summoned in. The rule of the common law, by which this action would abate by the death of either party, is reversed in this commonwealth by statute, which provides that actions of trespass for assault and battery shall survive. Rev. Sts. *c.* 93, § 7.

The facts set forth in the bill of exceptions preclude the supposition, that the blow, inflicted by the hand of the defendant upon the person of the plaintiff, was intentional. The whole case proceeds on the assumption, that the damage sustained by the plaintiff, from the stick held by the defendant, was inadvertent and unintentional; and the case involves the question how far, and under what qualifications, the party by whose unconscious act the damage was done is responsible for it. We use the term "unintentional" rather than involuntary, because in some of the cases, it is stated, that the act of holding and using a weapon or instrument, the movement of which is the immediate cause of hurt to another, is a voluntary act, although its particular effect in hitting and hurting another is not within the purpose or intention of the party doing the act.

It appears to us, that some of the confusion in the cases on this subject has grown out of the long-vexed question, under the rule of the common law, whether a party's remedy, where he has one, should be sought in an action of the case, or of trespass. This is very distinguishable from the question, whether in a given case, any action will lie. The result of these cases is, that if the damage complained of is the immediate effect of the act of the defendant, trespass *vi et armis* lies; if consequential only, and not immediate, case is the proper remedy. . . .

In these discussions, it is frequently stated by judges, that when one receives injury from the direct act of another, trespass will lie. But we think this is said in reference to the question, whether trespass and not case will lie, assuming that the facts are such, that some action will lie. These *dicta* are no authority, we think, for holding, that damage received by a direct act of force from another will be sufficient to maintain an action of trespass, whether the act was lawful or unlawful, and neither wilful, intentional, or careless. In the principal case cited, *Leame* v. *Bray*, the damage arose from the act of the defendant, in driving on the wrong side of the road, in a dark night, which was clearly negligent if not unlawful. In the course of the argument of that case, (p. 595,) Lawrence, J., said: "There certainly are cases in the books, where, the injury being direct and immediate, trespass has been holden to lie, though the injury was not intentional." The term "injury" implies something more than damage; but, independently of that consideration, the proposition may be true, because though the injury was unintentional, the act may have been unlawful or negligent, and the cases cited by him are perfectly consistent with that supposition. So the same learned judge in the same case says, (p. 597,) "No doubt trespass lies against one who drives a carriage against another, whether done wilfully or not." But he immediately adds, "Suppose one who is driving a carriage is negligently and heedlessly looking about him, without attending to the road when persons are passing, and thereby runs over a child and kills him, is it not manslaughter? and if so, it must be trespass; for every manslaughter includes trespass;" showing what he understood by a case not wilful.

We think, as the result of all the authorities, the rule is correctly stated by Mr. Greenleaf [a contemporary treatise writer on the law of evidence—ed.], that the plaintiff must come prepared with evidence to show either that the *intention* was unlawful, or that the defendant was *in fault;* for if the injury was unavoidable, and the conduct of the defendant was free from blame he will not be liable. 2 Greenl. Ev. §§ 85 to 92; *Wakeman* v. *Robinson,* 1 Bing. 213. If, in the prosecution of a lawful act, a casualty purely accidental arises, no action can be supported for an injury arising therefrom. . . . In applying these rules to the present ease, we can perceive no reason why the instructions asked for by the defendant ought not to have been given; to this effect, that if both plaintiff and defendant at the time of the blow were using ordinary care, or if at that time the defendant was using ordinary care, and the plaintiff was not, or if at that time, both the plaintiff and defendant were not using ordinary care, then the plaintiff could not recover.

In using this term, ordinary care, it may be proper to state, that what constitutes ordinary care will vary with the circumstances of cases. In general, it means that kind and degree of care, which prudent and cautious men would use, such as is required by the exigency of the case, and such as is necessary to guard against probable danger. A man, who should have occasion to discharge a gun, on an open and extensive marsh, or in a forest, would be required to use less circumspection and care, than if he were to do the same thing in an inhabited town, village, or city. To make an accident, or casualty, or as the law sometimes states it, inevitable accident, it must be such an accident as the defendant could not have avoided by the use of the kind and degree of care necessary to the exigency, and in the circumstances in which he was placed.

We are not aware of any circumstances in this case, requiring a distinction between acts which it was lawful and proper to do, and acts of legal duty. There are cases, undoubtedly, in which officers are bound to act under process, for the legality of which they are not responsible, and perhaps some others in which this distinction would be important. We can have no doubt that the act of the defendant in attempting to part the fighting dogs, one of which was his own, and for the injurious acts of which he might be responsible, was a lawful and proper act, which he might do by proper and safe means. If, then, in doing this act, using due care and all proper precautions necessary to the exigency of the case, to avoid hurt to others, in raising his stick for that purpose, he accidentally hit the plaintiff in his eye, and wounded him, this was the result of pure accident, or was involuntary and unavoidable, and therefore the action would not lie. Or if the defendant was chargeable with some negligence, and if the plaintiff was also chargeable with negligence, we think the plaintiff cannot recover without showing that the damage was caused wholly by the act of the defendant, and that the plaintiff's own negligence did not contribute as an efficient cause to produce it.

The court instructed the jury, that if it was not a necessary act, and the defendant was not in duty bound to part the dogs, but might with propriety interfere or not as he chose, the defendant was responsible for the consequences of the blow, unless it appeared that he was in the exercise of extraordinary care, so that the accident was inevitable, using the word not in a strict but a popular sense. This is to be taken in connection with the charge afterwards given, that if the jury believed, that the act of interference in the fight was unnecessary, (that is, as before explained, not a duty incumbent on the defendant,) then the burden of proving extraordinary care on the part of the defendant, or want of ordinary care on the part of plaintiff, was on the defendant.

The court are of opinion that these directions were not conformable to law. If the act of hitting the plaintiff was unintentional, on the part of the defendant, and done in the doing of a lawful act, then the defendant was not liable, unless it was done in the want of exercise of due care, adapted to the exigency of the case, and therefore such want of due care became part of the plaintiff's case, and the burden of proof was on the plaintiff to establish it.

Perhaps the learned judge, by the use of the term extraordinary care, in the above charge, explained as it is by the context, may have intended nothing more than that increased degree of care and diligence, which the exigency of particular circumstances might require, and which men of ordinary care and prudence would use under like circumstances, to guard against danger. If such was the meaning of this part of the charge, then it does not differ from our views, as above explained. But we are of opinion, that the other part of the charge, that the burden of proof was on the defendant, was incorrect. Those facts which are essential to enable the plaintiff to recover, he takes the burden of proving. The evidence may be offered by the plaintiff or by the defendant; the question of due care, or want of care, may be essentially connected with the main facts, and arise from the same proof; but the effect of the rule, as to the burden of proof, is this, that when the proof is all in, and before the jury, from whatever side it comes, and whether directly proved, or inferred from circumstances, if it appears that the defendant was doing a lawful act, and unintentionally hit and hurt the plaintiff, then unless it also appears to the satisfaction of the jury, that the defendant is chargeable with some fault, negligence, carelessness, or want of prudence, the plaintiff fails to sustain the burden of proof, and is not entitled to recover.

4.

Privilege or Competition? The Corporation and Society

Privilege: Dartmouth College ====================
v. Woodward*

Chief Justice Marshall's opinion has already been examined in Chapter 2 of the essay. In your opinion, is this a case about contracts? What is the nature of the "contract" that Marshall rules was impaired by the legislature? On the surface, the decision appears to restrict state legislatures from subsequently modifying their own statutory charters of incorporation. Why would such a decision become so controversial? What does this case have to do with the protection of "privilege" and "vested rights," the archvillains of Jacksonian Democrats?

• • •

The opinion of the court was delivered by MARSHALL, Ch. J.—

This court can be insensible neither to the magnitude nor delicacy of this question. The validity of a legislative act is to be examined; and the opinion of the highest law tribunal of a state is to be revised—an opinion which carries with it intrinsic evidence of the diligence, of the ability, and the integrity, with which it was formed. On more than one occasion, this court has expressed the cautious circumspection with which it approaches the consideration of such questions; and has declared, that in no doubtful case, would it pronounce a legislative act to be contrary to the constitution. But the American people have said, in the constitution of the United States, that "no state shall pass any bill of attainder, *ex post facto* law, or law impairing the obligation of contracts." In the same instrument, they have also said, "that the judicial power shall extend to all cases in law and equity arising under the constitution." On the judges of this court, then, is imposed the high and solemn duty of protecting, from even legislative violation, those contracts which the constitution of our country has placed beyond legislative control; and, however irksome the task may be, this is a duty from which we dare not shrink.

The title of the plaintiffs originates in a charter dated the 13th day of December, in the year 1769, incorporating twelve persons therein men-

---

* 17 U.S. (4 Wheat.) 518 (1819).

tioned, by the name of "The Trustees of Dartmouth College," granting to them and their successors the usual corporate privileges and powers, and authorizing the trustees, who are to govern the college, to fill up all vacancies which may be created in their own body.

The defendant claims under three acts of the legislature of New Hampshire, the most material of which was passed on the 27th of June 1816, and is entitled, "an act to amend the charter, and enlarge and improve the corporation of Dartmouth College." Among other alterations in the charter, this act increases the number of trustees to twenty-one, gives the appointment of the additional members to the executive of the state, and creates a board of overseers, with power to inspect and control the most important acts of the trustees. This board consists of twenty-five persons. The president of the senate, the speaker of the house of representatives, of New Hampshire, and the governor and lieutenant-governor of Vermont, for the time being, are to be members *ex officio.* The board is to be completed by the governor and council of New Hampshire, who are also empowered to fill all vacancies which may occur. The acts of the 18th and 26th of December are supplemental to that of the 27th of June, and are principally intended to carry that act into effect. The majority of the trustees of the college have refused to accept this amended charter, and have brought this suit for the corporate property, which is in possession of a person holding by virtue of the acts which have been stated.

It can require no argument to prove, that the circumstances of this case constitute a contract. An application is made to the crown for a charter to incorporate a religious and literary institution. In the application, it is stated, that large contributions have been made for the object, which will be conferred on the corporation, as soon as it shall be created. The charter is granted, and on its faith the property is conveyed. Surely, in this transaction every ingredient of a complete and legitimate contract is to be found. The points for consideration are, 1. Is this contract protected by the constitution of the United States? 2. Is it impaired by the acts under which the defendant holds?

1. On the first point, it has been argued, that the word "contract," in its broadest sense, would comprehend the political relations between the government and its citizens, would extend to offices held within a state, for state purposes, and to many of those laws concerning civil institutions, which must change with circumstances, and be modified by ordinary legislation; which deeply concern the public, and which, to preserve good government, the public judgment must control. That even marriage is a contract, and its obligations are affected by the laws respecting divorces.

That the clause in the constitution, if construed in its greatest latitude, would prohibit these laws. Taken in its broad, unlimited sense, the clause would be an unprofitable and vexatious interference with the internal concerns of a state, would unnecessarily and unwisely embarrass its legislation, and render immutable those civil institutions, which are established for purposes of internal government, and which, to subserve those purposes, ought to vary with varying circumstances. That as the framers of the constitution could never have intended to insert in that instrument, a provision so unnecessary, so mischievous, and so repugnant to its general spirit, the term "contract" must be understood in a more limited sense. That it must be understood as intended to guard against a power, of at least doubtful utility, the abuse of which had been extensively felt; and to restrain the legislature in future from violating the right to property. That, anterior to the formation of the constitution, a course of legislation had prevailed in many, if not in all, of the states, which weakened the confidence of man in man, and embarrassed all transactions between individuals, by dispensing with a faithful performance of engagements. To correct this mischief, by restraining the power which produced it, the state legislatures were forbidden "to pass any law impairing the obligation of contracts," that is, of contracts respecting property, under which some individual could claim a right to something beneficial to himself; and that, since the clause in the constitution must in construction receive some limitation, it may be confined, and ought to be confined, to cases of this description; to cases within the mischief it was intended to remedy.

The general correctness of these observations cannot be controverted. That the framers of the constitution did not intend to restrain the states in the regulation of their civil institutions, adopted for internal government, and that the instrument they have given us, is not to be so construed, may be admitted. The provision of the constitution never has been understood to embrace other contracts, than those which respect property, or some object of value, and confer rights which may be asserted in a court of justice. . . .

The parties in this case differ less on general principles, less on the true construction of the constitution in the abstract, than on the application of those principles to this case, and on the true construction of the charter of 1769. This is the point on which the cause essentially depends. If the act of incorporation be a grant of political power, if it create a civil institution, to be employed in the administration of the government, or if the funds of the college be public property, or if the state of New Hampshire, as a government, be alone interested in its transactions, the subject is one in which the legislature of the state may act according to its own judgment, unrestrained by any limitation of its power imposed by the constitution of the United States.

But if this be a private eleemosynary institution, endowed with a capacity to take property, for objects unconnected with government, whose funds are bestowed by individuals, on the faith of the charter; if the donors have stipulated for the future disposition and management of those funds, in the manner prescribed by themselves; there may be more difficulty in the case, . . . It becomes then the duty of the court, most seriously to examine this charter, and to ascertain its true character.

From the instrument itself, it appears, that about the year 1754, the Rev. Eleazer Wheelock established, at his own expense, and on his own estate, a charity school for the instruction of Indians in the Christian religion. The success of this institution inspired him with the design of soliciting contributions in England, for carrying on and extending his undertaking. In this pious work, he employed the Rev. Nathaniel Whitaker, who, by virtue of a power of attorney from Dr. Wheelock, appointed the Earl of Dartmouth and others, trustees of the money, which had been, and should be, contributed; which appointment Dr. Wheelock confirmed by a deed of trust, authorizing the trustees to fix on a site for the college. They determined to establish the school on Connecticut river, in the western part of New Hampshire; that situation being supposed favorable for carrying on the original design among the Indians, and also for promoting learning among the English; and the proprietors in the neighborhood having made large offers of land, on condition, that the college should there be placed. Dr. Wheelock then applied to the crown for an act of incorporation; and represented the expediency of appointing those whom he had, by his last will, named as trustees in America, to be members of the proposed corporation. "In consideration of the premises," "for the education and instruction of the youth of the Indian tribes," &c., "and also of English youth, and any others," the charter was granted, and the trustees of Dartmouth College were, by that name, created a body corporate, with power, for the use of the said college, to acquire real and personal property, and to pay the president, tutors and other officers of the college, such salaries as they shall allow.

The charter proceeds to appoint Eleazer Wheelock, "the founder of said college," president thereof, with power, by his last will, to appoint a successor, who is to continue in office, until disapproved by the trustees. In case of vacancy, the trustees may appoint a president, and in case of the ceasing of a president, the senior professor or tutor, being one of the trustees, shall exercise the office, until an appointment shall be made. The trustees have power to appoint and displace professors, tutors and other officers, and to supply any vacancies which may be created in their own body, by death, resignation, removal or disability; and also to make orders, ordinances and laws for the government of the college, the same not being repugnant to the laws of Great Britain, or of New Hampshire, and not excluding any person on account of his speculative sentiments in religion, or his being of a religious profession different from that of the trustees. This charter was accepted, and the property, both real and personal, which had been contributed for the benefit of the college, was conveyed to, and vested in, the corporate body.

From this brief review of the most essential parts of the charter, it is apparent, that the funds of the college consisted entirely of private donations. It is, perhaps, not very important, who were the donors. The probability is, that the Earl of Dartmouth, and the other trustees in England, were, in fact, the largest contributors. . . . But be this as it may, Dartmouth College is really endowed by private individuals, who have bestowed their funds for the propagation of the Christian religion among the Indians, and for the promotion of piety and learning generally. From these funds, the salaries of the tutors are drawn; and these salaries lessen the expense of education to the students. It is then an eleemosynary (1 Bl. Com. 471), and so far as respects its funds, a private corporation.

• • •

Whence, then, can be derived the idea, that Dartmouth College has become a public institution, and its trustees public officers, exercising powers conferred by the public for public objects? Not from the source whence its funds were drawn; for its foundation is purely private and eleemosynary—not from the application of those funds; for money may be given for education, and the persons receiving it do not, by being employed in the education of youth, become members of the civil government. Is it from the act of incorporation? Let this subject be considered.

A corporation is an artificial being, invisible, intangible, and existing only in contemplation of law. Being the mere creature of law, it possesses only those properties which the charter of its creation confers upon it, either expressly, or as incidental to its very existence. These are such as are supposed best calculated to effect the object for which it was created. Among the most important are immortality, and, if the expression may be allowed, individuality; properties, by which a perpetual succession of many persons are considered as the same, and may act as a single individual. They enable a corporation to manage its own affairs, and to hold property, without the perplexing intricacies, the hazardous and endless necessity, of perpetual conveyances for the purpose of transmitting it from hand to hand. It is chiefly for the purpose of clothing bodies of men, in succession, with these qualities and capacities, that corporations were invented, and are in use. By these means, a perpetual succession of individuals are capable of acting for the promotion of the particular object, like one immortal being. But this being does not share in the civil government of the country, unless that be the purpose for which it was created. Its immortality no more confers on it political power, or a political character, than immortality would confer such power or character on a natural person. It is no more a state instrument, than a natural person exercising the same powers would be. If, then, a natural person, employed by individuals in the education of youth, or for the government of a seminary in which youth is educated, would not become a public officer, or be considered as a member of the civil government, how is it, that this artificial being, created by law, for the purpose of being employed by the same individuals, for the same purposes, should become a part of the civil government of the country? Is it because its existence, its capacities, its powers, are given by law? Because the government has given it the power to take and to hold property, in a particular form, and for particular purposes, has the government a consequent right substantially to change that form, or to vary the purposes to which the property is to be applied? This principle has never been asserted or recognised, and is supported by no authority. Can it derive aid from reason?

The objects for which a corporation is created are universally such as the government wishes to promote. They are deemed beneficial to the country; and this benefit constitutes the consideration, and in most cases, the sole consideration of the grant. In most eleemosynary institutions, the object would be difficult, perhaps unattainable, without the aid of a charter of incorporation. Charitable or public-spirited individuals, desirous of making permanent appropriations for charitable or other useful purposes, find it impossible to effect their design securely and certainly, without an incorporating act. They apply to the government, state their beneficent object, and offer to advance the money necessary for its accomplishment, provided the government will confer on the instrument which is to execute their designs the capacity to execute them. The proposition is considered and approved. The benefit to the public is considered as an ample compensation for the faculty it confers, and the corporation is created. If the advantages to the public constitute a full compensation for the faculty it gives, there can be no reason for exacting a further compensation, by claiming a right to exercise over this artificial being, a power which changes its nature, and touches the fund, for the security and application of which it was created. There can be no reason for implying in a charter, given for a valuable consideration, a power which is not only not expressed, but is in direct contradiction to its express stipulations.

From the fact, then, that a charter of incorporation has been granted, nothing can be inferred, which changes the character of the institution, or transfers to the government any new power over it. The character of civil institutions does not grow out of their incorporation, but out of the manner in which they are formed, and the objects for which they are created. The right to change them is not founded on their being incorporated, but on their being the instruments of government, created for its purposes. The same institutions, created for the same objects, though not incorporated, would be public institutions, and, of course, be controllable by the legislature. The incorporating act neither gives nor prevents this control. Neither, in reason, can the incorporating act change the character of a private eleemosynary institution.

We are next led to the inquiry, for whose benefit the property given to Dartmouth College was secured? The counsel for the defendant have insisted, that the beneficial interest is in the people of New Hampshire. The charter, after reciting the preliminary measures which had been taken, and the application for an act of incorporation, proceeds thus: "Know ye, therefore, that we, considering the premises, and being willing to encourage the laudable and charitable design of spreading Christian knowledge among the savages of our American wilderness, and also that the best means of education be established in our province of New Hampshire, for the benefit of said province, do, of our special grace," &c. Do these expressions bestow on New Hampshire any exclusive right to the property of the college, any exclusive interest in the labors of the professors? Or do they merely indicate a willingness that New Hampshire should enjoy those advantages which result to all from the establishment of a seminary of learning in the neighborhood? On this point, we think it impossible to entertain a serious doubt. The words themselves, unexplained by the context, indicate, that the "benefit intended for the province" is that which is derived from "establishing the best means of education therein;" that is, from establishing in the province, Dartmouth College, as constituted by the charter. But, if these words, considered alone, could admit of doubt, that doubt is completely removed, by an inspection of the entire instrument.

The particular interests of New Hampshire never entered into the mind of the donors, never constituted a motive for their donation. The propagation of the Christian religion among the savages, and the dissemination of useful knowledge among the youth of the country, were the avowed and the sole objects of their contributions. In these, New Hampshire would participate; but nothing particular or exclusive was intended for her. Even the site of the college was selected, not for the sake of New Hampshire, but because it was "most subservient to the great ends in view," and because liberal donations of land were offered by the proprietors, on condition that the institution should be there established. . . .

From this review of the charter, it appears, that Dartmouth College is an eleemosynary institution, incorporated for the purpose of perpetuating the application of the bounty of the donors, to the specified objects of that bounty; that its trustees or governors were originally named by the founder, and invested with the power of perpetuating themselves; that they are not public officers, nor is it a civil institution, participating in the administration of government; but a charity school, or a seminary of education, incorporated for the preservation of its property, and the perpetual application of that property to the objects of its creation.

Yet a question remains to be considered, of more real difficulty, on which more doubt has been entertained, than on all that have been discussed. The founders of the college, at least, those whose contributions were in money, have parted with the property bestowed upon it, and their representatives have no interest in that property. The donors of land are equally without interest, so long as the corporation shall exist. Could they be found, they are unaffected by any alteration in its constitution, and probably regardless of its form, or even of its existence. The students are fluctuating, and no individual among our youth has a vested interest in the institution, which can be asserted in a court of justice. Neither the founders of the college, nor the youth for whose benefit it was founded, complain of the alteration made in its charter, or think themselves injured by it. The trustees alone complain, and the trustees have no beneficial interest to be protected. Can this be such a contract, as the constitution intended to withdraw from the power of state legislation? Contracts, the parties to which have a vested beneficial interest, and those only, it has been said, are the objects about which the constitution is solicitous, and to which its protection is extended.

● ● ●

According to the theory of the British constitution, their parliament is omnipotent. To annul corporate rights might give a shock to public opinion, which that government has chosen to avoid; but its power is not questioned. Had parliament, immediately after the emanation of this charter, and the execution of those conveyances which followed it, annulled the instrument, so that the living donors would have witnessed the disappointment of their hopes, the perfidy of the transaction would have been universally acknowledged. Yet, then, as now, the donors would have no interest in the property; then, as now, those who might be students would have had no rights to be violated; then, as now, it might be said, that the trustees, in whom the rights of all were combined, possessed no private, individual, beneficial interests in the property confided to their protection. Yet the contract would, at that time, have been deemed sacred by all. What has since occurred, to strip it of its inviolability? Circumstances have not changed it. In reason, in justice, and in law, it is now, what it was in 1769.

• • •

The opinion of the court, after mature deliberation, is, that this is a contract, the obligation of which cannot be impaired, without violating the constitution of the United States. This opinion appears to us to be equally supported by reason, and by the former decisions of this court.

2. We next proceed to the inquiry, whether its obligation has been impaired by those acts of the legislature of New Hampshire, to which the special verdict refers?

• • •

On the effect of this law, two opinions cannot be entertained. Between acting directly, and acting through the agency of trustees and overseers, no essential difference is perceived. The whole power of governing the college is transferred from trustees, appointed according to the will of the founder, expressed in the charter, to the executive of New Hampshire. The management and application of the funds of this eleemosynary institution, which are placed by the donors in the hands of trustees named in the charter, and empowered to perpetuate themselves, are placed by this act under the control of the government of the state. The will of the state is substituted for the will of the donors, in every essential operation of the college. This is not an immaterial change. The founders of the college contracted, not merely for the perpetual application of the funds which they gave, to the objects for which those funds were given; they contracted also, to secure that application by the constitution of the corporation. They contracted for a system, which should, so far as human foresight can provide, retain for ever the government of the literary institution they had formed, in the hands of persons approved by themselves. This system is totally changed. The charter of 1769 exists no longer. It is re-organized; and re-organized in such a manner, as to convert a literary institution, moulded according to the will of its founders, and placed under the control of private literary men, into a machine entirely subservient to the will of government. This may be for the advantage of this college in particular, and may be for the advantage of literature in general; but it is not according to the will of the donors, and is subversive of that contract, on the faith of which their property was given.

• • •

It results from this opinion, that the acts of the legislature of New Hampshire, which are stated in the special verdict found in this cause, are repugnant to the constitution of the United States; and that the judgment on this special verdict ought to have been for the plaintiffs. The judgment of the state court must, therefore, be reversed.

• • •

John W. Vethake, The Doctrine of Anti-Monopoly*

John W. Vethake was a physician and a lecturer in chemistry at Dickinson College and at the Baltimore medical branch of Washington College in Pennsylvania. The following article presents a popular Jacksonian Democratic view of the evils of monopoly. Note that Vethake is not opposed to corporations per se, but rather to the "special law" that allows corporations to "tyrannize over the weak." More broadly, Vethake is interested in the role of legislation in promoting certain kinds of economic or class interests. What is Vethake's vision of the ideal government? The ideal law? The ideal society? Precisely why, in his view, are "moneyed" incorporations dangerous? What solution does he propose?

To prevent misunderstanding and possible misrepresentations, the anti-monopoly Democrats of the City of New York tender to their brethren of the Democratic family the following *address:* The equal rights of mankind and free competition in all departments of social industry were held by our political fathers to be the primitive element of republican government. Accordingly, these, with all the sub-principles which distinctly

* From the *New York Evening Post* (October 21, 1835); as reprinted in Joseph L. Blau, *Social Theories of Jacksonian Democracy*, (1954), pp. 211–219. Reprinted by permission.

flow from them, as, for example, universal suffrage, a liberal code of naturalization laws, liberty of conscience, of speech, and of the press, purity of elections, right of instruction, limited term of official tenures, and careful avoidance of legal favoritism in any possible form, constitute with us, as they did with our ancestors, the essential ingredients of democratic institutions. By these, as by the beaconlights to social happiness, or monumental signals directing to the *greatest good of the greatest number*, do we propose to be always exclusively guided, in full confidence of the inherent justice of the Democratic cause and the ultimately permanent success of our united exertions.

But however proud of our victorious party and confident of our principles, there are in vogue some grievous perversions thereof which it is our leading object to remedy.

It will not be questioned that the sovereignty of the people is, in theory, an indisputable truth; but in its practical bearing, in its direct operation upon systems of law and public policy, it is not in the power even of universal suffrage, unless exercised with a severe and jealous vigilance, to preserve it from gradually sinking into an empty sound. It has been well said that it is the natural tendency of power "to steal from the many to the few." The selfishness of individual character augmented by the confiding indulgence of the many, is continually encouraging the forwardness of some *spoiled children* in the republican family. It has, therefore, happened that during a just now terminated period of deep repose, when, for a long series of years, all the cardinal interests of society were utterly forgotten in a mere money-making mania, the tacit and thoughtless assent of the people to some one exclusive privilege or to the establishment of a monopoly having a specious outside was greedily seized upon by the aforesaid *forward ones* as a pretext for other and much larger favors, until special grants and charters upon charters have come to constitute nearly the whole mass of legislative enactments; while, by a coordinate procedure, the pert few for whose benefit these things are have usurped all the powers and claim even the name itself to "the party" or "the people." The monopoly principle has thus been artfully and corruptly engrafted upon democratic institutions, and its weedy spread has so entirely covered up the Jeffersonian basis of the Constitution that all distinction has vanished between practical democracy and practical toryism. The common good, the interests of the many, have long been entirely neglected in a confused scramble for personal favors; and instead of leaving one business man to cope with another, on the fair and equitable principles which nature and the Constitution sanction, the Legislature, the *democratic* Legislature of the

State of New York, by means of chartered privileges, has been all along engaged in *siding* with some to the injury of others and in doing all that is possible to make the *unchartered* multitude "poor indeed."

Special charters for particular objects are rarely applied for unless they will contribute to special and particular gain. This is emphatically true of *moneyed* incorporations which are always sought for with a zeal commensurate with the unfair advantages expected to be derived from them. Under the flimsy disguise of some secondary measure of public utility, which but too often is itself a deception, or even a winning and popular title such as the name of some revered patriot or mechanic occupation, personal and evidently exorbitant profit is in every case the real object of the application and the real substance of the grant. The price, or *bonus*, as it is insidiously termed, which is sometimes paid for such privileges, the open and the half-developed bribery to which such legislation is eminently subject, the indefatigable labor bestowed by *lobbying* agents in furthering the acquisition of these abominations, and the ravenous grasp very generally made for a portion of them when granted by law, are glaring and resistless proofs of their wholly artificial character, their injustice, and their evil nature. If the public good, as is often and falsely alleged, were the actual motive for the creation of moneyed incorporations, if mercantile or any other convenience really called for such things, they would come into being, as do all *impartial* enactments, by the spontaneous, unbought, and ordinary action of the legislature. It is, therefore, but too plainly evident that gross selfishness, the most mercenary spirit, and mere private considerations are at the basis of this species of legislation.

But it has been repeatedly said, and with effect upon the thoughtless, that banks, insurance companies, ferry grants, etc., however accompanied with objectionable qualities, are indispensable to "the business wants of the community." That there is gross deception in this claim will be briefly shown by the following remarks and accompanying illustrations.

The wealthy of the land are the strong of the *legal* world, as the athletic are of the *natural*; in haughtiness and in oppressive disposition the analogy is perfect between them. Relatively considered, it is now precisely as if all things were in a state of nature; the *strong* tyrannize over the weak; live, as it were, in a continual victory, and glut themselves on incessant plunder. It is as humiliating now to be poor, as in the state of nature to be feeble of body; and although the ordinary difference between the rich and the poor, as between the athletic and the feeble, is clearly unavoidable and doubtless right, just, proper, and expedient, yet that such difference should be enhanced by legal enactments, that the rich or the strong should be artificially legislated into still greater riches or still greater strength, is not only unnecessary, but decidedly improper and even *cruel*. True it is, civilization, in substituting an artificial mode of relative strength for that which is natural, has brought within control an ungovernable quality of varying man; a control, however, which we think has of late been exercised more for general woe than weal. But let us for an instant suppose that human muscularity, as is human wealth, were manageable by law and that it was proposed to *incorporate*—that is, to give *individuality* and in some cases *immortality* to a considerable number of ordinary men, say one hundred, and thus to constitute a giant being, or some fifty of them, for the City of New York—we are confident that the public voice would exclaim against such a project with extraordinary unanimity. It might be said in vain, and uselessly repeated again and again, that such creatures are well calculated to aid in the erection of massive buildings and the extinction of fires, and *might be* extremely useful in case of a sudden insurrection or invasion. Such reasoning would be futile indeed. The huge arms of the proposed monsters, wielded by a multiplied selfishness, and without fear of immediate death, would be anticipated in fancy as but too likely to be used for other purposes than the public good; and a general conviction would possess the whole community that the aggregate of evils to be reasonably apprehended from such incorporations would render all their positive advantage to society an inconsiderable mite. Nay, we risk nothing in saying that if enacted into being all evil power and social influence would soon come into their exclusive possession and their oppressions know no other bounds than as remotely fixed by their own peculiar and mutual interests.

The above picture, fellow Democrats, is but an allegory of the real state of things. There are now in the midst of us many of the peculiar giants of civilized society. All honor be to the energy of democratic freemen and to the firmness and skill of their venerable chief; the Goliath is slain, but there remain vast numbers of his dangerous kind among the Philistines of wealth. Habit, long endurance, and the bias of early education have indeed rendered these beings familiar to us all and blunted our perception of their more abhorrent characteristics. But it needs not demonstration to show that if *moneyed* incorporations, say *fifty* of them for the City of New York, were to be now for the first time suggested, the proposition would be quite as revolting to an unsophisticated community as the supposed case of incorporated athletes. It would be grievous folly to recommend their creation by asserting that a poor man, if rich in friends, might occasionally borrow a small sum of money from them; it would be at once seen that if they did not exist, did not absorb, so to speak, the *loanable* means of society, aided by a friend, he could borrow of individuals. It would be alike useless to argue that they might work wonders on great public emergencies; it would be distinctly perceived that like as by a monster's touch, wholly destitute of gentleness, their benefits, if benefits they can be called, and injuries would be always at unhealthy extremes: at one time effecting mushroom prosperity; at another unreasonable distress; and it would then be most clearly absurd to attribute to such artificial creations, as is now too often done, the multiplication of valuable capital and the production of indispensable facilities for mercantile business. Such qualities belong not to their nature, but are simply impressed upon them by the neglect of other commercial means.

If incorporated banks were at once suppressed, an event by no means desirable, but contemplated only for the argument's sake, not a cent of money would be lost to the business community. The evolutions of capital and of credit, in all abundance, would be conducted by active and intelligent individuals under a measure of competition and a degree of personal responsibility to society which, when compared with incorporated institutions, would be vastly great and vastly advantageous to the humbler circles of business men. The "indispensable utility" of moneyed incorporations is at best but a common and empty prejudice. Were society equally accustomed to immense giant laborers, solely employed, under a *restraining law*, in the construction of buildings, their sudden and total extinction would doubtless convey to the minds of many an impression that building would, in consequence, cease altogether; they would fear that no contrivances of human ingenuity could enable ordinary men to supply the vacant places. We, wise on this one point, full well know that such a calamitous supposition would be grossly absurd, while, at the same time, some of us are ready to yield assent to a similar absurdity in the case of individual banking.

There is, we admit, an extensively prevalent aversion to private banks, arising out of the impositions which have heretofore been practised upon the public by a few of the kind. An analysis, however, of these cases will invariably point out their true cause to belong, not to their *singleness of direction*, but to certain prejudices and customs attached to the existing banking system at large. The magnificence of incorporated banks, the formal ostentation with which they do business, has long since clothed the simple idea of a *bank* with some sort of mystic right to extra respect. Like as to monarchs among the enthralled nations of Europe, there is a species of imposing dignity belonging to institutions consecrated by special law which effectually repels all inquiry into the details of character and forbids a doubt of their immaculate honor. When, therefore, it has happened that some daring individual, with cunning equal to the task, has assumed the outward guise of a *bank*, as practised by the chartered samples, the same attributes of sanctuary and of honor have been readily imputed to his institution. Taking advantage of this weakness of human nature, or yielding to the temptations involved in the reigning system of business, the vile and mercenary have occasionally robbed the public through facilities *not of their own creation*, but incidental to the general or chartered mode of banking. If to this cause be added the equally dangerous facility of becoming largely indebted to the public by means of *paper money*, a sort of pictured notes of hand which it has become customary rarely to present for redemption, we have abundant explanation of the evils of private banking while charters and paper money are the principal elements of the banking business. Let but this sort of employment be left free to general competition and paper money be forbidden, private bankers will stand in a very different and much safer relation to the community than they, or even chartered banks have ever stood. Banking institutions will lose much of that spurious character upon which their undue credit is based, and the public be effectually protected against the most dangerous, the most insidious of impositions.

For the reasons here assigned, we, as constituent members of an ascendant political party, call for the repeal of the restraining law which forbids private banking, and require that no more moneyed incorporations be henceforth created. We are satisfied that the repeal of the law alluded to will, by opening a wide, unlimited field for competition, sufficiently disarm the incorporated institutions now in being and, in all probability, cause even their premature death in the ordinary progress of business. So far from relatively increasing the money monopolies now existing, by refusing to create more, the repeal of the restraining law will at once destroy much that belongs to them of the monopoly character; and even without such repeal, it may be justly said that the profits and influence of incorporated banks are always at the full, in proportion to their capitals, and therefore cannot be enhanced by the diminution of numbers.

And instead of our plan promoting the social and political power of the few individuals who possess actual capital, we are confident that their power would be greatly abbreviated, inasmuch as, under the present system, it is their private *influence at bank*, much more than the loan of their money, that renders them the objects of servile homage and productive of degrading adulation. The high grandeur of giant incorporations forbids the near approach of but a select few, and through that few all moneyed operations must now be transacted; these are thereby constituted a virtual nobility, not by their own power or wealth, but by the sovereign pleasure of the magisterial monopolies. Again, we desire the repeal of the famous restraining law on the principle of even-handed justice. There is no such protection in existence for the mechanic or producing classes. If solicited, for example, by an association of carpenters, if these were to ask for a restraining law to prevent persons from following their craft unless specially chartered so to do by law, they would be hooted at as presumptuous fools, and thus tacitly informed that *they* are not entitled to so very exclusive a privilege; that such legislative favors belong only to the wealthy and *respectable* among our citizens, and that if such matters were to become general, in accordance with mechanics' ideas of justice, they would cease to be advantageous. The partiality of the obnoxious law constitutes at once its whole value and its gross unfairness.

The above remarks particularly apply to banking institutions, but the principles involved are equally applicable to all species of partial legislation. Charters for objects of mere empty show or fulsome dignity are unworthy of even a passing objection. For the more efficient promotion of literature, science, and the arts, or for the purposes of social benevolence, a law, like that under which libraries may now be instituted without special leave, would meet, we think, with general approbation; for assuredly if any advantages are to be derived to learning or charity from the use of "a corporate seal" with artificial immortality, they ought to be within easy reach of any two or more individuals without selection or favor. And with regard to the subject of internal improvements—ferries, railways, turnpikes, etc.—we hold that like the Great Erie and Champlain Canals they should all be paid for out of the common purse for the common benefit of all. If national in character, these works should be constructed by the general government; if local, by the state, county, or town to which their benefits are more especially confined; for it is as palpably wrong that any partial associations of individuals should possess the privilege of levying and collecting taxes for their own benefit under the specious appellation of tolls, as it is for similar associations to levy the like upon the gross amount of commercial business by means of incorporated banks, or upon the calamities of fire and shipwreck by means of insurance companies, under the equally specious terms of *discounts* and *premiums*.

To save the public from the evils of complicated and excessive legislation, the statute book from ridiculous changeableness, the legislature itself from systematic corruption, . . . and above all to redeem the Constitution and its great predominant principle of equal rights from the wretched degradation into which it has long been plunged by *loose construction*, or, in the language of the justly celebrated Veto, "to restore the government to that simple machine which it was originally designed to be," we are, in addition to the great points of public policy urged above, in favor of a general law of partnerships, and opposed to every species of special legislation. A general law by which any two or more individuals may declare themselves in business partnership, as well for wood-sawing, if they choose, as for manufacturing or banking, and regulated by such provisions as careful inquiry and practical experience may point out, would possess nothing of an exclusive or monopoly character. Without some such law, the suspension of special charters would totally prevent the prosecution of every business which requires a heavy capital, inasmuch as ordinary partnerships are constantly liable to be suddenly dissolved by the death or self will of a member. A limited form of permanent succession and a circumscribed right to transfer an interest in such partnerships seems to us to be perfectly reasonable and requisite. We are confident that a wholesome system of general business on this scheme would grow up gradually amongst us, infinitely more favorable than the present to the small capitalist, on account of the plenitude of semi-incorporated partnerships to which it would give rise and its evident tendency to divide, and not, as the present system, to concentrate patronage. We are sure an unprecedented activity on equitable principles would thereby come to pervade all occupations, and, instead of as now, a few becoming rich at the expense of the many, the advances of society would be comparatively uniform and in mass; and, instead of observing as now nought but rapid and destructive flucuations of prosperity and adversity, with continual commercial alarm, the *money market* would be relatively stable and the public mind settled and serene.

It is scarcely necessary for us to add that we are warmly in favor of the constitutional currency of gold and silver, and therefore opposed to the repeal of the existing law in relation to the smaller bank notes; and in the desired general law of partnerships we believe it will be found expedient to forbid the issue of paper "on demand" except, perhaps, when drawn by one house or firm upon another.

Thus, fellow citizens and fellow members of the Democratic party, we present to you a system of public policy which we confidently believe will stand the test of examination by Jeffersonian principles. The selfish advocates of banks and the armies of abject dependents on the *tender mercies* of moneyed incorporations are endeavoring to deceive you and us into their mercenary purposes; they resort to even the meanest expedients to gain their ends. The laboring and producing classes are scandalously branded as agrarians. You are told that banking is an affair above your feeble comprehension, and a subject that exclusively belongs to the mercantile community—as if you did not know that all social interests, to the minutest ramification, are subject to the baneful control of moneyed power. They indeed predicate much of their plans on the alleged ignorance of the poor, in despite of their professions of democratic principles which, if just, must be based upon the truth of the all-sufficient virtue and intelligence of the people. But, fellow citizens, we entreat you to ponder the subject of monopolies in your minds. Trace, as you easily may, your ill-paid toil and humiliation to unfairness of legislation. Claim your right, your unquestionable right, to equal participation in the one and only justly *chartered company*, viz., the people of the State of New York, and take especial care that those who are elected to the directorship of the general concern deceive you not, but that they, in despite of all self interested motives to the contrary, are in some way obliged to obey your will. Be not deceived by the clamor against *the pledge*; specific instructions of any kind would be precisely the same thing to them and the same thing to us; it is our anti-monopoly principles, our resolute determination to put an end to partial and selfish legislation, that galls them to the quick. The mere *form* of their unwilling obligation to do justice to all is to them, as to us, of little importance. When, therefore, they cry out against the pledge, they covertly cry out against the principles we profess. We beseech you then, fellow citizens, that none but anti-monopoly Democrats obtain your suffrages, and thus doing all in your power to set your house in order, rest confident of that ultimate success which is an attribute of truth.

Privilege v. "Progress": Proprietors of Charles River Bridge v. Proprietors of Warren Bridge*

In 1650, the legislature of Massachusetts granted to Harvard College the "liberty and power" to operate a ferry between Charlestown and Boston. Under that grant, Harvard College had the sole right to maintain the ferry "and to receive the profits of it" until 1785. In that year, the legislature chartered a bridge company (The Proprietors of Charles River Bridge) and empowered it to construct a bridge, and to collect tolls, over the site of the Harvard College ferry. The franchise was to expire in forty years "from the first opening of the bridge for passengers." In 1792,

* 36 U.S. (11 Pet.) 420 (1837).

the legislature amended the charter to extend the franchise for seventy years from the day of opening.

The legislature incorporated another bridge company (The Proprietors of the Warren Bridge) in 1828, authorizing it to construct a bridge that, in effect, would run parallel to the Charles River Bridge. Like the Charles River Bridge, the Warren Bridge would be able to extract tolls from passengers, but only for the first six years from the day of opening. At the end of this period (or before, depending on when the proprietors' initial investment had been recovered), the Warren Bridge "was to be surrendered to the state." Obviously, passengers traveling to and from Charlestown Square ("which receives the travel of many great public roads leading from the country"), the terminus of both bridges, would then use the free Warren Bridge. The free Warren Bridge would thus deprive the Charles River Bridge of its business, "whereby the franchise . . . should be rendered of no value."

Several questions are presented to the court. All parties agree that Harvard College, during the period that it operated the ferry, enjoyed a monopoly right. No ferry could be operated, nor bridge be constructed, if it would compete with the ferry for business. But did this monopoly right die in 1785 with the college's charter? If not, did the right transfer automatically to the Charles River Bridge? If so, the Warren Bridge unconstitutionally infringed upon the Charles River Bridge's "contract" with the state. A second and related question was whether the incorporation of the Charles River Bridge constituted a "contract" with the state, the impairment of which would be unconstitutional. A third issue was whether it was in the power of the legislature to grant an exclusive franchise to a corporation, thereby barring it from making future competing grants.

As you read Chief Justice Taney's opinion, ask yourself if the Court convincingly met each of the three questions posed above. Justice Story dissented from Taney's opinion. Is Story's dissent consistent with Marshall's opinion in Dartmouth College? *Story was said to have been outraged by the Court's decision. Why, do you suppose? Can you link Taney's opinion with the discussion, in Chapters 2 and 3 of the essay, of the Jacksonian attack on "special privileges" and "chartered monopolies," and Vethake's attack on "moneyed incorporations"? What did Vethake have to say about toll bridges and turnpikes? Is Taney's political persuasion evident in the opinion?*

Taney believes that his decision will advance economic growth and protect the public interest. Story makes exactly the opposite point: that the Court's opinion will undermine economic growth by discouraging investors from supporting new forms of enterprise. How can they make such opposing claims?

Review the discussion, in Chapter 4 of the essay, concerning the breakdown of traditional common-law property rights in the nineteenth century. Can you relate the ruling in the Charles River Bridge *case to the changes occurring in property rights under common law? Who, or what interests, do you suppose, would most benefit from Taney's decision? Who, or what interests, stand to lose the most? To help answer these questions, compare the discussion of the Marshall Court, in*

Chapter 2 of the essay, with the discussion of the growth of laissez-faire policy and the rise of the private business corporation after 1840, in Chapter 3.

• • •

Mr. Chief Justice TANEY delivered the opinion of the Court.

The questions involved in this case are of the gravest character, and the Court have given to them the most anxious and deliberate consideration. The value of the right claimed by the plaintiffs is large in amount; and many persons may no doubt be seriously affected in their pecuniary interests by any decision which the Court may pronounce; and the questions which have been raised as to the power of the several states, in relation to the corporations they have chartered, are pregnant with important consequences; not only to the individuals who are concerned in the corporation franchises, but to the communities in which they exist. The Court are fully sensible that it is their duty, in exercising the high powers conferred on them by the constitution of the United States, to deal with these great and extensive interests with the utmost caution; guarding, as far as they have the power to do so, the rights of property, and at the same time carefully abstaining from any encroachment on the rights reserved to the states.

It appears, from the record, that in the year 1650, the legislature of Massachusetts, granted to the president of Harvard college "the liberty and power," to dispose of the ferry from Charlestown to Boston, by lease or otherwise, in the behalf and for the behoof of the college: and that, under that grant, the college continued to hold and keep the ferry by its lessees or agents, and to receive the profits of it until 1785. In the last mentioned year, a petition was presented to the legislature, by Thomas Russell and others, stating the inconvenience of the transportation by ferries, over Charles river, and the public advantages that would result from a bridge; and praying to be incorporated for the purpose of erecting a bridge in the place where the ferry between Boston and Charlestown was then kept. Pursuant to this petition, the legislature, on the 9th of March, 1785, passed an act incorporating a company, by the name of "The Proprietors of the Charles River Bridge," for the purposes mentioned in the petition. Under this charter the company were empowered to erect a bridge, in "the place where the ferry was then kept;" certain tolls were granted, and the charter was limited to forty years, from the first opening of the bridge for passengers; and from the time the toll commenced, until the expiration of this term, the company were to pay two hundred pounds, annually, to Harvard college; and at the expiration of the forty years the bridge was to be the property of the commonwealth; "saving (as the law expresses it) to the said college or university, a reasonable annual compensation, for the annual income of the ferry, which they might have received had not the said bridge been erected."

The bridge was accordingly built, and was opened for passengers on the 17th of June, 1786. In 1792, the charter was extended to seventy years, from the opening of the bridge; and at the expiration of that time it was to belong to the commonwealth. The corporation have regularly paid to the college the annual sum of two hundred pounds, and have performed all of the duties imposed on them by the terms of their charter.

In 1828, the legislature of Massachusetts incorporated a company by the name of "The Proprietors of the Warren Bridge," for the purpose of erecting another bridge over Charles river. This bridge is only sixteen rods, at its commencement, on the Charlestown side, from the commencement of the bridge of the plaintiffs; and they are about fifty rods apart at their termination on the Boston side. The travellers who pass over either bridge, proceed from Charlestown square, which receives the travel of many great public roads leading from the country; and the passengers and travellers who go to and from Boston, used to pass over the Charles River Bridge, from and through this square, before the erection of the Warren Bridge.

The Warren Bridge, by the terms of its charter, was to be surrendered to the state, as soon as the expenses of the proprietors in building and supporting it should be reimbursed; but this period was not, in any event, to exceed six years from the time the company commenced receiving toll.

• • •

The plaintiffs in error insist, mainly, upon two grounds: 1st. That by virtue of the grant of 1650, Harvard college was entitled, in perpetuity, to the right of keeping a ferry between Charlestown and Boston; that this right was exclusive; and that the legislature had not the power to establish another ferry on the same line of travel, because it would infringe the rights of the college; and that these rights, upon the erection of the bridge in the place of the ferry, under the charter of 1785, were transferred to, and became vested in "the proprietors of the Charles River Bridge;" and that under, and by virtue of this transfer of the ferry right, the rights of the bridge company were as exclusive in that line of travel, as the rights of the ferry. 2d. That independently of the ferry right, the acts of the legislature of Massachusetts of 1785, and 1792, by their true construction, necessarily implied that the legislature would not authorize another bridge, and especially a free one, by the side of this, and placed in the same line of travel, whereby the franchise granted to the "proprietors of the Charles River Bridge" should be rendered of no value; and the plaintiffs in error contend, that the grant of the ferry to the college, and of the charter to the proprietors of the bridge, are both contracts on the part of the state; and that the law authorizing the erection of the Warren Bridge in 1828, impairs the obligation of one or both of these contracts.

• • •

[Turning first to the question of whether the ferry right, which was a contractual grant of monopoly, could be interpreted as having transferred to the state:] The nature and extent of the ferry right granted to Harvard college, in 1650, must depend upon the laws of Massachusetts; and the character and extent of this right has been elaborately discussed at the bar. But in the view which the Court take of the case before them, it is not necessary to express any opinion on these questions. For assuming that the grant to Harvard college, and the charter to the Bridge company, were both contracts, and that the ferry right was as extensive and exclusive as the plaintiffs contend for; still they cannot enlarge the privileges granted to the bridge, unless it can be shown, that the rights of Harvard college in this ferry have, by assignment, or in some other way, been transferred to the proprietors of the Charles River Bridge, and still remain in existence, vested in them, to the same extent with that in which they were held and enjoyed by the college before the bridge was built.

It has been strongly pressed upon the Court, by the plaintiffs in error, that these rights are still existing, and are now held by the proprietors of the bridge. If this franchise still exists, there must be somebody possessed of authority to use it, and to keep the ferry. Who could now lawfully set up a ferry where the old one was kept? The bridge was built in the same place, and its abutments occupied the landings of the ferry. The transportation of passengers in boats, from landing to landing, was no longer possible; and the ferry was as effectually destroyed, as if a convulsion of nature had made there a passage of dry land. The ferry then, of necessity, ceased to exist, as soon as the bridge was erected; and when the ferry itself was destroyed, how can rights which were incident to it, be supposed to survive? The exclusive privileges, if they had such, must follow the fate of the ferry, and can have no legal existence without it—and if the ferry right had been assigned by the college, in due and legal form, to the proprietors of the bridge, they themselves extinguished that right, when they erected the bridge in its place. It is not supposed by any one, that the

Bridge company have a right to keep a ferry. No such right is claimed for them, nor can be claimed for them, under their charter to erect a bridge—and it is difficult to imagine how ferry rights can be held by a corporation, or an individual, who have no right to keep a ferry. It is clear, that the incident must follow the fate of the principal, and the privilege connected with property, cannot survive the destruction of the property; and if the ferry right in Harvard college was exclusive, and had been assigned to the proprietors of the bridge, the privilege of exclusion could not remain in the hands of their assignees, if those assignees destroyed the ferry.

● ● ●

[The Court next asks whether there was an implied assignment of rights from the ferry to the Charles River Bridge] This brings us to the act of the legislature of Massachusetts, of 1785, by which the plaintiffs were incorporated by the name of "The Proprietors of the Charles River Bridge;" and it is here, and in the law of 1792, prolonging their charter, that we must look for the extent and nature of the franchise conferred upon the plaintiffs.

Much has been said in the argument of the principles of construction by which this law is to be expounded, and what undertakings, on the part of the state, may be implied. The Court think there can be no serious difficulty on that head. It is the grant of certain franchises by the public to a private corporation, and in a matter where the public interest is concerned. The rule of construction* in such cases is well settled, both in England, and by the decisions of our own tribunals. In 2 Barn. & Adol. 793, in the case of the Proprietors of the Stourbridge Canal against Wheely and others, the court say, "the canal having been made under an act of parliament, the rights of the plaintiffs are derived entirely from that act. This, like many other cases, is a bargain between a company of adventurers and the public, the terms of which are expressed in the statute; and the rule of construction in all such cases, is now fully established to be this; that any ambiguity in the terms of the contract, must operate against the adventurers, and in favour of the public, and the plaintiffs can claim nothing that is not clearly given them by the act."

● ● ●

Borrowing, as we have done, our system of jurisprudence from the

---

* The stipulated manner in which legislation is to be read and understood by the court (author's note).

English law; and having adopted, in every other case, civil and criminal, its rules for the construction of statutes; is there any thing in our local situation, or in the nature of our political institutions, which should lead us to depart from the principle where corporations are concerned? Are we to apply to acts of incorporation, a rule of construction differing from that of the English law, and, by implication, make the terms of a charter in one of the states, more unfavourable to the public, than upon an act of parliament, framed in the same words, would be sanctioned in an English court? . . . We think not; and it would present a singular spectacle, if, while the courts in England are restraining, within the strictest limits, the spirit of monopoly, and exclusive privileges in nature of monopolies, and confining corporations to the privileges plainly given to them in their charter; the courts of this country should be found enlarging these privileges by implication; and construing a statute more unfavourably to the public, and to the rights of the community, than would be done in a like case in an English court of justice.

• • •

[The Court finally turns to the question of whether the very nature of a legislative grant of franchise, absent specific language in the statutes, permanently bars the legislature from taking any action in the future that might weaken the property value of the franchise]. [T]he case most analogous to this, and in which the question came more directly before the Court, is the case of the Providence Bank v. Billings & Pittmann, 4 Pet. 514; and which was decided in 1830. In that case, it appeared that the legislature of Rhode Island had chartered the bank, in the usual form of such acts of incorporation. The charter contained no stipulation on the part of the state, that it would not impose a tax on the bank, nor any reservation of the right to do so. It was silent on this point. Afterwards, a law was passed, imposing a tax on all banks in the state; and the right to impose this tax was resisted by the Providence Bank, upon the ground, that if the state could impose a tax, it might tax so heavily as to render the franchise of no value, and destroy the institution; that the charter was a contract, and that a power which may in effect destroy the charter is inconsistent with it, and is impliedly renounced by granting it. But the Court said that the taxing power was of vital importance, and essential to the existence of government; and that the relinquishment of such a power is never to be assumed. And in delivering the opinion of the Court, the late Chief Justice states the principle in the following clear and emphatic language. Speaking of the taxing power, he says, "as the whole community is interested in retaining it undiminished, that community has a right to insist that its abandonment ought not to be presumed, in a case in which the deliberate purpose of the state to abandon it does not appear." The case now before the Court, is, in principle, precisely the same. It is a charter from a state. The act of incorporation is silent in relation to the contested power. The argument in favour of the proprietors of the Charles River Bridge, is the same, almost in words, with that used by the Providence bank; that is, that the power claimed by the state, if it exists, may be so used as to destroy the value of the franchise they have granted to the corporation. The argument must receive the same answer; and the fact that the power has been already exercised so as to destroy the value of the franchise, cannot in any degree affect the principle. The existence of the power does not, and cannot depend upon the circumstance of its having been exercised or not.

It may, perhaps, be said, that in the case of the Providence Bank, this Court were speaking of the taxing power; which is of vital importance to the very existence of every government. But the object and end of all government is to promote the happiness and prosperity of the community by which it is established; and it can never be assumed, that the government intended to diminish its power of accomplishing the end for which it was created. And in a country like ours, free, active, and enterprising, continually advancing in numbers and wealth; new channels of communication are daily found necessary, both for travel and trade; and are essential to the comfort, convenience, and prosperity of the people. A state ought never to be presumed to surrender this power, because, like the taxing power, the whole community have an interest in preserving it undiminished. And when a corporation alleges that a State has surrendered for seventy years its power of improvement and public accomodation, in a great and important line of travel, along which a vast number of its citizens must daily pass; the community have a right to insist, . . . "that its abandonment ought not to be presumed, in a case in which the deliberate purpose of the State to abandon it does not appear." The continued existence of a government would be of no great value, if by implications and presumptions, it was disarmed of the powers necessary to accomplish the ends of its creation, and the functions it was designed to perform, transferred to the hands of privileged corporations. . . . While the rights of private property are sacredly guarded, we must not forget that the community also have rights, and that the happiness and well being of every citizen depends on their faithful preservation.

Adopting the rule of construction above stated as the settled one, we proceed to apply it to the charter of 1785, to the proprietors of the Charles River Bridge. This act of incorporation is in the usual form, and the privileges such as are commonly given to corporations of that kind. It confers on them the ordinary faculties of a corporation, for the purpose of building the bridge; and establishes certain rates of toll, which the company are authorized to take. This is the whole grant. There is no exclusive privilege given to them over the waters of Charles River, above or below their bridge. No right to erect another bridge themselves, nor to prevent other persons from erecting one. No engagement from the State that another shall not be erected, and no undertaking not to sanction competition, nor to make improvements that may diminish the amount of its income. Upon all these subjects the charter is silent and nothing is said in it about a line of travel, so much insisted on in the argument, in which they are to have exclusive privileges. No words are used from which an intention to grant any of these rights can be inferred. If the plaintiff is entitled to them, it must be implied simply from the nature of the grant, and cannot be inferred from the words by which the grant is made.

The relative position of the Warren Bridge has already been described. It does not interrupt the passage over the Charles River Bridge, nor make the way to it or from it less convenient. None of the faculties or franchises granted to that corporation have been revoked by the Legislature; and its right to take the tolls granted by the charter remains unaltered. In short, all the franchises and rights of property enumerated in the charter, and there mentioned to have been granted to it, remain unimpaired. But its income is destroyed by the Warren Bridge; which, being free, draws off the passengers and property which would have gone over it, and render their franchise of no value. This is the gist of the complaint. For it is not pretended that the erection of the Warren Bridge would have done them any injury, or in any degree affected their right of property, if it had not diminished the amount of their tolls. In order, then, to entitle themselves to relief, it is necessary to soow that the Legislature contracted not to do the act of which they complain; and that they impaired, or in other words violated, that contract, by the erection of the Warren Bridge.

The inquiry then is, does the charter contain such a contract on the part of the State? Is there any such stipulation to be found in that instrument? It must be admitted on all hands, that there is none—no words that even relate to another bridge, or to the diminution of their tolls, or to the line of travel. If a contract on that subject can be gathered from the charter, it must be by implication, and cannot be found in the words used. Can such an agreement be implied? The rule of construction before stated is an answer to the question. In charters of this description, no rights are taken from the public or given to the corporation, beyond those which the words of the charter, by their natural and proper construction, purport to convey. There are no words which import such a contract as the plaintiffs in error contend for, and none can be implied. . . . The whole community are interested in this inquiry, and they have a right to require that the power of promoting their comfort and convenience, and of advancing the public prosperity, by providing safe, convenient, and cheap ways for the transportation of produce, and the purposes of travel, shall not be construed to have been surrendered or diminished by the State, unless it shall appear by plain words that it was intended to be done.

• • •

And what would be the fruits of [the] doctrine of implied contracts on the part of the states, and of property in a line of travel by a corporation, if it should now be sanctioned by this Court? To what results would it lead us? If it is to be found in the charter to this bridge, the same process of reasoning must discover it, in the various acts which have been passed, within the last forty years, for turnpike companies. And what is to be the extent of the privileges of exclusion on the different sides of the road? The counsel who have so ably argued this case, have not attempted to define it by any certain boundaries. How far must the new improvement be distant from the old one? How near may you approach without invading its rights in the privileged line? If this Court should establish the principles now contended for, what is to become of the numerous rail roads established on the same line of travel with turnpike companies; and which have rendered the franchises of the turnpike corporations of no value? Let it once be understood that such charters carry with them these implied contracts, and given this unknown and undefined property in a line of travelling; and you will soon find the old turnpike corporations awakening from their sleep, and calling upon this Court to put down the improvements which have taken their place. The millions of property which have been invested in rail roads and canals, upon lines of travel which had been before occupied by turnpike corporations, will be put in jeopardy. We shall be thrown back to the improvements of the last century, and obliged to stand still, until the claims of the old turnpike corporations shall be satisfied; and they shall consent to permit these states to avail themselves of the lights of modern science, and to partake of the benefit of those improvements which are now adding to the wealth and prosperity, and the convenience and comfort, of every other part of the civilized world. Nor is this all. This Court will find itself compelled to fix, by some arbitrary rule, the width of this new kind of property in a line of travel; for if such a right of property exists, we have no lights to guide us in marking out its extent, unless, indeed, we resort to the old feudal grants, and to the exclusive rights of ferries, by prescription, between towns; and are prepared to decide that when a turnpike road from one town to another, had been made, no rail road or canal, between these two points, could afterwards be established. This Court are not prepared to sanction principles which must lead to such results.

• • •

The judgment of the supreme judicial court of the commonwealth of Massachusetts, dismissing the plaintiffs' bill, must, therefore, be affirmed, with costs.

JUSTICE STORY, DISSENTING

. . . [W]e have been told at the argument, that this very charter is a restriction upon the legislative power; that it is in derogation of the right and interests of the state, and the people; that it tends to promote monopolies, and exclusive privileges; and that it will interpose an insuperable barrier to the progress of improvement.

. . . This charter is not . . . any restriction upon legislative power; unless it be true, that because the legislature cannot grant again, what it has already granted, the legislative power is restricted. If so, then every grant of the public land is a restriction upon that power; a doctrine, that has never yet been established, nor (as far as I know) ever contended for. . . .

Then again, how is it established that this is a grant in derogation of the rights and interests of the people? No individual citizen has any right to build a bridge over navigable waters; and consequently he is deprived of no right, when a grant is made to any other persons for that purpose. . . . If it had been said that the grant of this bridge was in derogation of the common right of navigating the Charles river, by reason of its obstructing a free and open passage, the ground would have been intelligible. . . .

The erection of a bridge may be of the highest utility to the people. It may essentially promote the public convenience, and aid the public interests, and protect the public property. And if no persons can be found willing to undertake such a work, unless they receive in return the exclusive privilege of erecting it, and taking toll; surely it cannot be said, as of course, that such a grant, under such circumstances, is, per se, against the interest of the people. . . .

Again, it is argued that the present grant is a grant of monopoly, and of exclusive privileges; and therefore to be construed by the most narrow mode of interpretation. . . .

There is great virtue in particular phrases; and when it is once suggested, that a grant is of the nature or tendency of a monopoly, the mind almost instantaneously prepares itself to reject every construction which does not pare it down to the narrowest limits. It is an honest prejudice, which grew up in former times from the gross abuses of the royal prerogatives; to which, in America, there are no analogous authorities. But, what is a monopoly, as understood in law? It is an exclusive right granted to a few, of something which was before of common right. . . .

No sound lawyer will, I presume, assert that the grant of a right to erect a bridge over a navigable stream, is a grant of a common right. . . . It was neither a monopoly; nor, in a legal sense, had it any tendency to a monopoly. . . .

But it has been argued, and the argument has been pressed in every form which ingenuity could suggest, that if grants of this nature are to be construed liberally, as conferring any exclusive rights on the grantees, it will interpose an effectual barrier against all general improvements of the country. . . . For my own part, I can conceive of no surer plan to arrest all public improvements, founded on private capital and enterprise, than to make the outlay of that capital uncertain, and questionable both as to security, and as to productiveness. No man will hazard his capital in any enterprise, in which, if there be a loss, it must be borne exclusively by himself; and if there be success, he has not the slightest security of enjoying the rewards of that success for a single moment. If the government means to invite its citizens to enlarge the public comforts and conveniences, to establish bridges, or turnpikes, or canals, or railroads, there must be some pledge, that the property will be safe; that the enjoyment will be co-extensive with the grant: and that success will not be the signal of a general combination to overthrow its rights, and to take away its profits. . . .

But if there were any foundation for the argument itself in a general view, it would totally fail in its application to the present case. Here, the grant, however exclusive, is but for a short and limited period, more than two-thirds of which have already elapsed; and, when it is gone, the whole property and franchise are to revert to the state. The legislature exercised a wholesome foresight on the subject; and within a reasonable period it will have an unrestricted authority to do whatever it may choose, in the appropriation of the bridge and its tolls. There is not, then, under any fair aspect of the case, the slightest reason to presume that public improvements either can, or will, be injuriously retarded by a liberal construction of the present grant. . . .

The argument of the defendants is, that the plaintiffs are to take nothing by implication. Either (say they) the exclusive grant extends only to the local limits of the bridge; or it extends the whole length of the river, or at least up to old Cambridge bridge. The latter construction would be absurd and monstrous; and therefore the former must be the true one. Now, I utterly deny the alternative involved in the dilemma. The right to build a bridge over a river, and to take toll, may well include an exclusive franchise beyond the local limits of the bridge; and yet not extend through the whole course of the river, or even to any considerable distance on the river. There is no difficulty in common sense, or in law, in maintaining such a doctrine. But then, it is asked, what limits can be assigned to such a franchise? The answer is obvious; the grant carries with it an exclusive franchise to a reasonable distance on the river; so that the ordinary travel to the bridge shall not be diverted by any new bridge to the injury or ruin of the franchise. A new bridge, which would be a nuisance to the old bridge, would be within the reach of its exclusive right.

Now, I put it to the common sense of every man, whether if at the moment of granting the charter the legislature had said to the proprietors; you shall build the bridge; you shall bear the burthens; you shall be bound by the charges; and your sole reimbursement shall be from the tolls of forty years: and yet we will not even guaranty you any certainty of receiving any tolls. On the contrary we reserve to ourselves the full power and authority to erect other bridges, toll, or free bridges, according to our own free will and pleasure, contiguous to yours, and having the same termini with yours; and if you are successful we may thus supplant you, divide, destroy your profits, and annihilate your tolls, without annihilating your burthens: if, I say, such had been the language of the legislature, is there a man living of ordinary discretion or prudence, who would have accepted such a charter upon such terms? . . .

But it is said, if this is the law, what then is to become of turnpikes and canals? Is the legislature precluded from authorizing new turnpikes or new canals, simply because they cross the path of the old ones, and incidentally diminish their receipt of tolls? The answer is plain. Every turnpike has its local limits and local termini; its points of beginning and of end. No one ever imagined that the legislature might grant a new turnpike, with exactly the same location and termini. That would be to rescind its first grant. . . .

To the answer already given to the objection, that, unless such a reservation of power exists, there will be a stop put to the progress of all public improvements; I wish, in this connexion, to add that there never can any such consequence follow upon the opposite doctrine. If the public exigencies and interests require that the franchise of Charles river bridge should be taken away, or impaired; it may be lawfully done upon making due compensation to the proprietors. . . .

Upon the whole, my judgment is, that the act of the legislature of Massachusetts granting the charter of Warren bridge, is an act impairing the obligation of the prior contract and grant to the proprietors of Charles river bridge; and, by the constitution of the United States, it is, therefore utterly void. I am for reversing the decree of the state court, and for remanding the cause to the state court, for further proceedings, as to law and justice shall appertain.

5.

Personal Autonomy: The Family

*The Nature of the Matrimonial Contract: Elizabeth Cady Stanton on Divorce**

Until the first half of the nineteenth century, "domestic relations," the law governing relationships within the family, did not exist as a distinct part of English or American jurisprudence. Of course, there was law stipulating legal rights and obligations of persons living in conjugal families, but for the most part that law was interspersed throughout the larger legislative and common law system of rules and principles. The wife's right to own property, for example, was thought of as an element of property law generally and not specifically as one set of rights applicable to married women. The legal capacity of wives and children to enter into contractual relationships was handled in a similar way. The same was true of the law of child custody: guardianship was a property right controlled not by the special interests of the family or the child's needs but by the father's or parent's legal capacity to own, control, or dispose of his or her "property."

* Address of Elizabeth Cady Stanton, on the Divorce Bill, Before the Judiciary Committee of the New York Senate, in the Assembly Chamber, Feb. 8, 1861 (1861). Available in Daniel J. Boorstin (ed.), *An American Primer*, v. 1 (1966), pp. 367–376. Reprinted by permission.

In many respects, the conflicts that erupted over divorce in the nineteenth century were similar to those regarding the law of slavery. The neat, definitional legal categories jarred with social realities. Slaves might technically be defined as property under the law, but slaves possessed a human will and intellect. Marriage might be described as a "contract" between a man and woman, but, as Elizabeth Cady Stanton points out in the passage below, it was not "subject to the restraints and privileges of all other contracts." The woman entered the "contract" as an unequal party, and "no matter how much fraud and deception are practiced . . . the contract cannot be annulled."

Elizabeth Cady Stanton (1815-1902) was one of the foremost social reformers of her day and an early leader in the militant feminist movement. She graduated from Troy Female Seminary in 1832. In 1840, she married Henry Brewster Stanton, a lawyer and well-known abolitionist. Eight years later, Stanton attended a London antislavery convention where she and several other women, including Lucretia Mott, were prevented from officially participating in the proceedings. They were women, and women were to be seen and not heard on such an important occasion. Out of this event came the Seneca Falls Convention of 1848, planned by Stanton and Mott, which adopted a "declaration of sentiments" (modeled after the Declaration of Independence) for women that launched modern feminism. The right of suffrage (denied to women) was at the heart of the movement, but Stanton and the other women also battled against archaic laws of all kinds that kept women in an inferior status.

The New York State legislature gave feminists an important victory when it modified its legislative restrictions on the rights of married women to own their own property and earnings. Traditionally, any property or earnings brought into the marriage by the wife was solely owned by the husband. The New York statute recognized a separate right of ownership and control for the wife. A year later, Stanton presented testimony before a senate legislative committee, again addressing the question of the woman's independence, this time in the context of divorce.

Stanton's testimony is of interest both for what it says about the popular perception of law and about womanhood and the family. Why, exactly, is marriage not like any other contract in law? What sort of contractual relationship does Stanton view as the ideal one? Is marriage, in her opinion, only a legal contract? If Stanton places so much emphasis on the inequity of the marriage contract historically, would it not have been sensible, in the best of all possible worlds, to abandon the contract analogy altogether? Further, can you draw any parallels between the developments in contract law discussed in Chapter 4 of the essay and the matrimonial contract Stanton believes should exist?

We have read elsewhere in the essay and in the documents that Americans tended to view the manipulation of law as desirable, politically and legally legitimate, in order to achieve certain policy outcomes. Does this apply to Stanton and her attack on "archaic laws"? From the standpoint of politics, why was the alteration of some branches of law by the judiciary, such as tort and property law, less objectionable than were Stanton's proposed changes? Ultimately, Stanton won, and she based her arguments for change on the irresistible force of "progress." "We cannot take our gauge of womanhood from the past, but from . . . the higher development of the race." What, in Stanton's view, was that "higher development"? Opponents of a liberalized divorce law believed that the "dilution" of the marriage contract (making the wife the equal of the husband and the dissolution of marriage easier to accomplish) would undermine the family. Stanton, who had seven children of her own, took the opposite position: that the restrictions on divorce made the family less sacred. Can you explain this apparent contradiction? Or, is there no contradiction but only different assumptions about what is a "good" family?

Gentlemen of the Judiciary—In speaking to you, gentlemen, on such delicate subjects as marriage and divorce, in the revision of laws which are found in your statute books, I must use the language I find there.

May I not, without the charge of indelicacy, speak in a mixed assembly of Christian men and women, of wrongs which my daughter may to-morrow suffer in your courts, where there is no woman's heart to pity, and no woman's presence to protect?

I come not before you, gentlemen, at this time, to plead simply the importance of divorce in cases specified in your bill, but the justice of an entire revision of your whole code of laws on marriage and divorce. We claim that here, at least, woman's equality should be recognized. If civilly and politically man must stand supreme, let us at least be equals in our nearest and most sacred relations. . . .

When man suffers from false legislation, he has the remedy in his own hands; but an humble petition, protest or prayer, is all that woman can claim.

The contract of marriage, is by no means equal. From Coke down to Kent, who can cite one law under the marriage contract, where woman has the advantage? The law permits the girl to marry at twelve years of age, while it requires several years more of experience on the part of the boy. In entering this compact, the *man* gives up nothing that he before possessed; he is a *man* still: while the legal existence of the woman is suspended during marriage, and is known but in and through the husband. She is nameless, purseless, childless; though a woman, an heiress, and a mother.

Blackstone says, "the husband and wife are one, and that one is the husband." Kent says, "the legal effects of marriage are generally deducible from the principle of common law by which the husband and wife are regarded as one person, and her legal existence and authority lost or suspended during the continuance of the matrimonial union." . . .

The laws on divorce are quite as unequal as those on marriage; yet, far more so. The advantages seem to be all on one side, and the penalties on the other. In case of divorce, if the husband be the guilty party, he still retains a greater part of the property! If the wife be the guilty party, she goes out of the partnership penniless. . . . In New York, and some other states, the wife of the guilty husband can now sue for a divorce in her own name, and the costs come out of the husband's estate; but in a majority of the states she is still compelled to sue in the name of another, as she has no means of paying costs, even though she may have brought her thousands into the partnership. . . . "Many jurists," says Kent . . . , "are of opinion that the adultery of the husband ought not to be noticed or made subject to the same animadversions as that of the wife, because it is not evidence of such entire depravity, nor equally injurious in its effects upon the morals and good order, and happiness of domestic life." Montesquieu, Pothier, and Dr. Taylor, all insist, that the cases of husband and wife ought to be distinguished, and that the violation of the marriage vow, on the part of the wife, is the most mischievous, and the prosecution ought to be confined to the offense on her part. . . .

Say you, these are but the opinions of men? On what else, I ask, are the hundreds of women depending, who this hour demand in our courts a release from burdensome contracts? Are not these delicate matters left wholly to the discretion of the courts? Are not young women, from our first families, dragged into your public courts—into assemblies of men exclusively? The judges all men, the jurors all men! No true woman there to shield them, by her presence, from gross and impertinent questionings, to pity their misfortunes, or to protest against their wrongs! The administration of justice depends far more on the opinions of eminent jurists, than on law alone, for law is powerless, when at variance with public sentiment.

For years there has been before the legislature of this state, a variety of bills asking for divorce in cases of drunkenness, insanity, desertion, and cruel and brutal treatment, endangering life. My attention was called to this question very early in life, by the sufferings of a friend of my girlhood—a victim of one of those unfortunate unions, called marriage. What my great love for that young girl, and my holy intuitions, then decided to be right, has not been changed by years of experience, observation and reason. I have pondered well these things in my heart, and ever felt the deepest interest in all that has been written and said on this subject; and the most profound respect and loving sympathy for those heroic women, who, in the face of law and public sentiment, have dared to sunder the unholy ties of a joyless, loveless union.

If marriage is a human institution, about which man may legislate, it seems but just that he should treat this branch of his legislation with the same common sense that he applies to all others. If it is a mere legal contract, then should it be subject to the restraints and privileges of all other contracts. A contract, to be valid in law, must be formed between parties of mature age, with an honest intention in said parties to do what they agree. The least concealment, fraud, or intention to deceive, if proved, annuls the contract. A boy cannot contract for an acre of land, or a horse, until he is twenty-one, but he may contract for a wife at fourteen. If a man sell a horse, and the purchaser find in him "great incompatibility of temper"—a disposition to stand still, when the owner is in haste to go—the sale is null and void; the man and his horse part company. But in marriage, no matter how much fraud and deception are practised, nor how cruelly one or both parties have been misled; no matter how young or inexperienced or thoughtless the parties, nor how unequal their condition and position in life, the contract cannot be annulled. . . .

Marriage, as it now exists, must seem to all of you a mere human institution. Look through the universe of matter and mind—all God's arrangements are perfect, harmonious and complete; there is no discord, friction or failure in His eternal plans. Immutability, perfection, beauty, are stamped on all His laws. Love is the vital essence that pervades and permeates from center to circumference—the graduating circle of all thought and action; Love is the talisman of human weal and woe—the "open sesame" to every human soul. Where two human beings are drawn together by the natural laws of likeness and affinity, union and happiness are the result. Such marriages might be divine. But how is it now? You all know our marriage is, in many cases, a mere outward tie, impelled by custom, policy, interest, necessity; founded not even in friendship, to say nothing of love; with every possible inequality of condition and development. In these heterogeneous unions, we find youth and old age, beauty and deformity, refinement and vulgarity, virtue and vice, the educated and the ignorant, angels of grace and goodness with devils of malice and malignity; and the sum of all this is human wretchedness and despair—cold fathers, sad mothers and hapless children, who shiver at the hearth-stone, where the fires of love have all gone out. The wide world and the stranger's unsympathizing gaze are not more to be dreaded for young hearts than homes like these. Now, who shall say that it is right to take two beings so unlike, and anchor them right side by side—fast bound—to stay all time, until God, in mercy shall summon one away?

Do wise Christian legislators need any arguments to convince them, that the sacredness of the family relation should be protected at all hazards? The family—that great conservator of national virtue and strength—how can you hope to build it up in the midst of violence, debauchery and excess. Can there be anything sacred, at that family altar, where the chief priest who ministers, makes sacrifice of human beings— of the weak and innocent? where the incense offered up is not to a God of justice and mercy, but those heathen divinities, who best may represent the lost man, in all his grossness and deformity? Call that sacred, where woman, the mother of the race—of a Jesus of Nazareth—unconscious of the true dignity of her nature, of her high and holy destiny, consents to live in legalized prostitution! her whole soul revolting at such gross association! her flesh shivering at the cold contamination of that embrace! held there by no tie but the iron chain of the law, and a false and most unnatural public sentiment? Call that sacred, where innocent children, trembling with fear, fly to the corners and dark places of the house, to hide from the wrath of drunken, brutal fathers, but forgetting their past sufferings, rush out again at their mother's frantic screams, "Help! oh, help!" Behold the agonies of those young hearts, as they see the only being on earth they love, dragged about the room by the hair of her head, kicked and pounded, and left half dead and bleeding on the floor! Call that sacred, where fathers like these have the power and legal right to hand down their natures to other beings, to curse other generations with such moral deformity and death!

Men and brethren! look into your asylums for the blind, the deaf and dumb, the idiot, the imbecile, the deformed, the insane; go out into the by-lanes and dens of your cities, and contemplate the reeking mass of depravity; pause before the terrible revelations, made by statistics, of the rapid increase of all this moral and physical impotency, and learn how fearful a thing it is, to violate the immutable laws of the beneficent Ruler of the Universe; and there behold the sorrowful retributions of your violence on woman. Learn how false and cruel are those institutions, which, with a coarse materialism, set aside the holy instincts of the woman, to seek no union but one of love.

Fathers! do you say, let your daughters pay a lifelong penalty for one unfortunate step? How could they, on the threshold of life, full of joy and hope, believing all things to be as they seemed on the surface, judge of the dark windings of the human soul? How could they foresee that the young man, to-day, so noble, so generous, would, in a few short years, be transformed into a cowardly, mean tyrant, or a foul-mouthed, bloated drunkard? What father could rest at his home by night, knowing that his lovely daughter was at the mercy of a strong man, drunk with wine and passion, and that, do what he might, he was backed up by law and public sentiment? The best interests of the individual, the family, the state, the nation, cry out against these legalized marriages of force and endurance.

There can be no heaven without love; and nothing is sacred in the family and home, but just so far, as it is built up and anchored in purity and peace. Our newspapers teem with startling accounts of husbands and wives having shot or poisoned each other, or committed suicide, choosing death rather than the indissoluble tie, and still worse, the living death of faithless men and women, from the first families in the land, dragged from the privacy of home into the public prints and courts, with all the painful details of sad, false lives.

Now, do you believe, honorable gentlemen, that all these wretched matches were made in heaven? that all these sad, miserable people are bound together by God? But, say you, does not separation cover all these difficulties? No one objects to separation, when the parties are so disposed. To separation, there are two serious objections: first, so long as you insist on marriage as a divine institution, as an indissoluble tie, so long as you maintain your present laws against divorce, you make separation, even, so odious, that the most noble, virtuous and sensitive men and women, choose a life of concealed misery, rather than a partial, disgraceful release. Secondly, those who, in their impetuosity and despair, do, in spite of public sentiment, separate, find themselves, in their new position, beset with many temptations to lead a false, unreal life. This isolation bears especially hard on woman. Marriage is not all of life to a man. His resources for amusement and occupation are boundless. He has the whole world for his home. His business, his politics, his club, his friendships, with either sex, can help to fill up the void, made by an unfortunate union, or separation. But to woman, as she is now educated, marriage is all and everything—her sole object in life—that for which she is taught to live—the all-engrossing subject of all her sleeping and her waking dreams. Now, if a noble girl of seventeen marries, and is unfortunate in her choice, because the cruelty of her husband compels separation, in her dreary isolation, would you drive her to a nunnery, and shall she be a nun indeed? She, innocent child, perchance the victim of a father's pride, or a mother's ambition, betrayed into a worldy union for wealth, or family, or fame, shall the penalty be all visited on the heart of the only guiltless one in the transaction? Henceforth, do you doom this fair young being, just on the threshold of womanhood, to a joyless, loveless solitude? By your present laws you say, though separated, she is married still; indissolubly bound to one she never loved; by whom she was never wooed or won; but by false guardians sold. And now, no matter though in the coming time her soul should, for the first time, wake to love, and one of God's own noblemen, should echo back her choice, the gushing fountains of her young affections must all be stayed. Because some man still lives, who once called her wife, no other man may give to her his love; and if she love not the tyrant to whom she is legally bound, she shall not love at all.

Think you that human law can set bounds to love? Alas! like faith, it comes upon us unawares. It is not by an act of a will, we believe new doctrines, nor love what is true and noble in mankind. If you think it wise to legislate on human affections, pray make your laws with reference to what our natures are; let them harmonize in some measure with the immutable laws of God. A very wise father once remarked, that in the government of his children he forbid as few things as possible: a wise legislation would do the same. It is folly to make laws on subjects beyond human prerogative, knowing that in the very nature of things they must be set aside. To make laws that man cannot, and will not obey, serves to bring all law into contempt. It is all important in a republican government that the people should respect the laws: for if we throw law to the winds, what becomes of civil government?

What do our present divorce laws amount to? Those who wish to evade them have only to go into another state to accomplish what they desire. If any of our citizens cannot secure their inalienable rights in New York state, they may, in Connecticut and Indiana.

Why is it that all contracts, covenants, agreements and partnerships are left wholly at the discretion of the parties, except that which, of all others, is considered most holy and important, both for the individual and the race?

But, say you, what a condition we should soon have in social life, with no restrictive laws. I ask you, what have we now? Separation and divorce cases in all your courts; men disposing of their wives in every possible way; by neglect, cruelty, tyranny, excess, poison, and imprisonment in insane asylums. We would give the parties greater latitude, rather than drive either to extreme measures, or crime. If you would make laws for our protection, give us the power to release from legal conjugal obligations, all husbands who are unfit for that relation. Woman loses infinitely more than she gains, by the kind of protection you now impose; for, much as we love and honor true and noble men, life and liberty are far dearer to us, than even the legalized slavery of an indissoluble tie. In this state, are over forty thousand drunkards' wives, earnestly imploring you to grant them deliverance from their fearful bondage. Thousands of sad mothers, too, with helpless children, deserted by faithless husbands, some in California, some in insane asylums, and some in the gutter, all pleading to be released. They ask nothing, but a quit-claim deed to themselves.

Thus far, we have had the man-marriage, and nothing more. From the beginning, man has had the whole and sole regulation of the matter. He has spoken in Scripture, and he has spoken in law. As an individual, he has decided the time and cause for putting away a wife; and as a judge and legislator, he still holds the entire control. In all history, sacred and profane, woman is regarded and spoken of, simply, as the toy of man. She is taken or put away, given or received, bought or sold, just as the interests of the parties might dictate. But the woman has been no more recognized in all these transactions through all the different periods and conditions of the race, than if she had had no part or lot in the whole matter. The right of woman to put away a husband, be he ever so impure, is never hinted at in sacred history.

We cannot take our gauge of womanhood from the past, but from the solemn convictions of our own souls, in the higher development of the race. No parchments, however venerable with the mould of ages, no human institutions, can bound the immortal wants of the royal sons and daughters of the great I Am.

I place man above all governments, all institutions, ecclesiastical and civil, all constitutions and laws. It is a mistaken idea that the same law that oppresses the individual can promote the highest good of society. The best interests of a community never can require the sacrifice of one innocent being, of one sacred right.

In the settlement, then, of any question, we must simply consider the highest good of the individual. It is the inalienable right of all to be happy. It is the highest duty of all to seek those conditions in life, those surroundings, which may develop what is noblest and best, remembering that the lessons of these passing hours are not for time alone, but for the ages of eternity. They tell us, in that future home, the heavenly paradise, that the human family shall be sifted out, and the good and pure shall dwell together in peace. If that be the heavenly order, is it not our duty to render earth as near like heaven as we may? Inasmuch as the greater includes the less, let me repeat, that I come not before you to plead simply the importance of divorce in cases proposed in your bill, but the justice of an entire revision of your whole code of laws on marriage and divorce. In our common law, in our whole system of jurisprudence, we find man's highest idea of right. The object of law is to secure justice. But inasmuch as fallible man is the maker, administrator and adjudicator of law, we must look for many and gross blunders in the application of its general principles to individual cases. The science of theology, of civil, political, moral and social life, all teach the common idea that man ever has been, and ever must be, sacrificed to the highest good of society—the one to the many—the poor to the rich—the weak to the powerful—and all to the institutions of his own creation. Look, what thunderbolts of power man has forged in the ages for his own destruction! at the organizations to enslave himself! And through those times of darkness, those generations of superstition, behold, all along, the relics of his power and ˙skill, that stand like milestones, here and there, to show how far back man was great and glorious. Who can stand in those vast cathedrals of the old world, as the deep-toned organ reverberates from arch to arch, and not feel the grandeur of immortality. Here is the incarnated thought of man, beneath whose stately dome, the man himself, now bows in fear and doubt—knows not himself—and knows not God, a mere slave to symbols—and with holy water signs the cross, while he who died thereon, declared man, God.

In closing, let me submit for your consideration the following propositions:

1st. In the language (slightly varied) of John Milton, "Those who marry intend as little to conspire their own ruin, as those who swear allegiance, and as a whole people is *to an ill government,* so is one man or woman to *an ill marriage.* If a whole people against any authority, covenant or statute, may, by the sovereign edict of charity, save not only their lives, but honest liberties, from unworthy bondage, as well may a married party, against any private covenant, which he or she never entered *to his or her mischief,* be redeemed from unsupportable disturbances to honest peace and just contentment."

2nd. Any constitution, compact or covenant between human beings, that failed to produce or promote human happiness, could not, in the nature of things. be of any force or authority; and it would be not only a right, but a duty to abolish it.

3rd. Though marriage be in itself divinely founded, and is fortified as an institution by innumerable analogies in the whole kingdom of universal nature, still, a true marriage is only known by its results; and like the fountain, if pure, will reveal only pure manifestations. Nor need it ever be said, "What God hath joined together, let not man put asunder," for man could not puṭ it asunder; nor can he any more unite what God and nature have not joined together.

4th. Of all insulting mockeries of heavenly truth and holy law, none can be greater than that *physical impotency* is cause sufficient for divorce, while no amount of mental or moral or spiritual imbecility is ever to be pleaded in support of such a demand.

5th. Such a law was worthy those dark periods when marriage was held by the greatest doctors and priests of the Church to be a *work of the flesh only,* and almost, if not altogether, a defilement; denied wholly to the clergy, and a second time, forbidden to all.

6th. An unfortunate or ill-assorted marriage is ever a calamity, but not ever, perhaps never, a crime; and when society or government, by its laws or customs, compels its continuance, always to the grief of one of the parties, and the actual loss or damage of both, it usurps an authority never delegated to man, nor exercised by God himself.

7th. Observation and experience daily show how incompetent are men, as individuals, or as governments, to select partners in business, teachers for their children, ministers of their religion, or makers, adjudicators or administrators of their laws; and as the same weakness and blindness must attend in the selection of matrimonial partners, the dictates of humanity and common sense alike show that the latter and most important contract should no more be perpetual than either or all of the former.

8th. Children born in these unhappy and unhallowed connections, are in the most solumn sense of *unlawful birth*—the fruit of lust, but not of love; and so not of God, divinely descended, but from beneath, whence proceed all manner of evil and uncleanness.

9th. Next to the calamity of such a birth to the child, is the misfortune of being trained in the atmosphere of a household where love is not the law but where discord and bitterness abound; stamping their demoniac features on the moral nature, with all their odious peculiarities; thus continuing the race in a weakness and depravity that must be a sure precursor of its ruin, as a just penalty of a long violated law.

Power in the Family: The Nickerson *Case**

At the conclusion of her statement, Stanton argued that a wise divorce law was not only in the interest of "matrimonial partners" but also in the interests of the children of the marriage.

Traditional English law customarily viewed children as marital property—but, like all marital property, "owned" by the husband. The citation of English cases as leading precedent in an American court decision was always a sensitive matter. But American courts showed an uncharacteristic lack of reticence about doing so when

* 19 Wend. 16 (New York, 1837).

it came to family law. The Nickerson *case is noteworthy for its heavy reliance on English precedent. The court, after reviewing the case law (citing only English cases), decides to place the care and custody of the child with the father, against the wishes of the mother, who is separated from her husband. While this case technically involves a question of custody, it is essentially about the status of wives who separate from their husbands. Did courts in fact, as Stanton implies, apply a double standard to the marriage relationship? Under this case, when would the mother have been entitled to custody? What is the court's view of the family? Does the court discuss the child's needs? In your opinion, does the case rest on "good" law? The decision cites a New York statute that apparently had voided the common-law rule that made custodial rights of the father absolute. Given the legislation, how do you explain this case?*

Habeas corpus in the case of a *minor child*, on the question of its custody, as between the parents. The mother in this case had withdrawn herself from the protection of her husband and went to reside in the house of her father, and took with her an infant child; to obtain the custody of which the father sued out a *habeas corpus*. On the return of the writ numerous affidavits were produced on both sides, and after hearing counsel, the following opinion was delivered:

By the Court, NELSON, Ch. J. The father is the natural guardian of his infant children, and in the absence of good and sufficient reasons shown to the court, such as ill usage, grossly immoral principles or habits, want of ability, &c. is entitled to their custody, care and education. All the authorities concur on this point. . . .

Many of the cases are very strong and decisive in vindication of this paternal authority. In *The King* v. *De Manneville*, 5 East, 221, the child was only eight months old, and had been forcibly taken from the mother, and there was some ground of apprehension that the father intended to carry it out of the kingdom. But the court refused to interfere. Lord Ellenborough observed, that the father was the person entitled by law to the custody of his child: that if he abused the right to the detriment of the child, the court would protect it. Having the legal right, and not having abused it in that case, he was entitled to have it restored to him. The case of Mr. *Lytton* and *Sir W. Murray*, referred to by Lawrence, J. in the same case, were equally decisive upon the point. In the case of De Manneville, the mother had separated from her husband on an allegation of ill usage, and taken the child with her. This same case afterwards came before Lord Eldon, 10 Vesey, 51, who also refused the mother the custody of the child, as she had withdrawn herself from the protection of her husband; but restrained him from removing the child out of the kingdom. In the case *Ex parte Skinner*, J. B. Moore, 278, the infant was six years old, and the court refused to take it from the custody of the father and deliver it over to the mother, and placed the refusal upon the authorities above cited. In *Ball* v. *Ball,* 2 Simon, 35, it was decided by the vice chancellor, that the court had no jurisdiction to deprive the father of his common law right to the care and custody of his infant children, even though he was living in a state of adultery, unless he brings the child in contact with the woman. All the cases on the subject, he said, proceeded upon that distinction, and which appears to have been conceded by the counsel for the mother. In the great case of *Wellesley* v. *The Duke of Beaufort,* 2 Russell, 9, Lord Eldon, in vindicating the power of the court of chancery to control the authority of the father over his infant children, concedes that "the law makes the father the guardian of his children by nature and by nurture;" and places the right of the court to interfere upon the abuse of the trust, or special interest of the child. The same ground is stated in *Lyons* v. *Blenkin*, Jacob, 245, 4 Cond. Ch. R. 120. So fully does the law recognize the authority of the father on this subject, that he is permitted to perpetuate it beyond his own life; for he may by deed, or will duly executed, "dispose of the custody and tuition of such (his) child, during his minority or for any less time to any person or persons in possession or remainder." 2 R. S. 150, § 1. And by the following section, such a disposition is declared "valid and effectual against every person claiming the custody or tuition of such minor as guardian in socage, or otherwise."

In one specified case, the revised statutes have enlarged the power of this court over the subject beyond that which it appears from the authorities above referred to existed at common law; and provide, that on the application of the mother, being an inhabitant of this state, in case the husband and wife live in a state of separation without being divorced, "the court on due consideration may award the charge and custody of the child so brought before it (on *habeas corpus*) to the mother, for such time, under such regulations and restrictions, and with such provisions and directions as the case may require." 2 R. S. 148, 9, § 1, 2. It may also annul or modify the order at any time after it is made. § 3. It may be well doubted, I think, whether this statute was intended to apply where the wife withdraws from the protection of the husband and lives separate from him without any reasonable excuse; because then the separation would be unauthorized, and in violation of the law of the land. It was probably designed to remove the difficulty that existed at common law in denying or restraining the authority of the father in the case of an authorized separation, such as for ill usage, or by consent, where no ground existed for impeaching that authority upon common law principles. The legislature could not have intended that the court should ever award to the mother the care and education of her minor children, when she had wilfully and without pretence of excuse, abandoned her family and the protection of her husband, if he was in a situation to take care of them, and no well founded objection existed in the case.

The interference of the court with the relation of father and child, by withdrawing the latter from the natural affection, kindness and obligations of the former, is a delicate and strong measure; and the power should never be exerted except for the most sound and solid reasons. In this country, the hopes of the child in respect to its education and future advancement, is mainly dependent upon the father; for this he struggles and toils through life; the desire of its accomplishment operating as one of the most powerful incentives to industry and thrift. The violent abruption of this relation would not only tend to wither these motives to action, but necessarily in time, alienate the father's natural affections; and if property should be accumulated, the child under such circumstances could hardly expect to inherit it.

In view of the foregoing rights of the father, and duty of the court, I have diligently and carefully examined the facts disclosed in the affidavits, and feel myself bound to say that upon the whole, nothing appears that can justify the conclusion that the father is not a fit and proper person to have the care and education of his child, or that it would be for the interest of the child pecuniarily or otherwise, to commit its custody to the mother, according to the principles of the common law, and the numerous adjudged cases already referred to. I must also say, that unless the case can be materially varied, Mrs. Nickerson has greatly mistaken the obligations and duties which devolved upon her by the marriage vow; and that she is now living in a state unauthorized by the law of the land. The statute, 2 R. S. 145, 6, 7, art. 3, 4, enumerates the cases in which a separation may be legalized, either by a dissolution of the marriage contract or by a divorce from bed and board. The course of the decisions of the court of chancery clearly show that no divorce or separation could be decreed upon the facts before me.

It is, no doubt, possible that the home of the wife may be made intolerable without any actual violence committed upon her person; harsh and cruel usage that would justify a separation, may be practised towards her short of this by an unkind husband, and this is what seems intended to be *intimated* in the affidavits opposing this motion. Upon questions, however, involving such solemn considerations, and so deeply affecting the future condition and character of the parties we cannot act upon *insin-uations*. We regard only the facts. The character of the [husband] in this case, is very strongly supported by his neighbors and acquaintances who have known him from infancy. They declared upon oath that he is a young man of sober, moral and industrious habits, and express the belief that he has ever conducted towards his wife with kindness and affection. Many of them have been on intimate terms with the family, and in a situation to have known or heard of harsh or unkind treatment of the wife if such had existed. They not only discredit such allegations, but are led to the belief that she was well provided for, contented and happy, and appear surprised at allegations to the contrary. The [husband] himself has denied in the most express terms all unkind conduct, and any desire or intention to in-jure the person, or wound the feelings of his wife, and expresses a strong and becoming anxiety that she would return to his protection and home. Under all this weight of evidence, it is difficult for us to conclude that he has meanly and secretly outraged her affections, or sought the privacy of the conjugal relations to torture her feelings and thus render her life wret-ched and insupportable with him, at the same time concealing from his neighbors and even intimate friends any apparent unkindness or want of affection.

[An order was accordingly entered that the child be delivered to the father, and that the care and custody of her be committed to him.]

Natural Rights and State Power—What Can a Court Do?
Mercein v. The People ex. rel. Barry*

The court's decision in the Mercein *case overruled the precedent established in the* Nickerson *case. As in* Nickerson, *the child's parents were living separately, and apparently lacked grounds for divorce. The child in* Mercein *is an infant, "under three years of age," and is "delicate and sickly." This case is extraordinary, how-ever, for the reasoning the court used. What is the relevance of the American Rev-olution (which the court mentions) to a case involving a child's custody? How could the same kind of case, in the same state, involving the same lines of precedent, result in what appears to be an opposite conclusion of law? Is this a case about law at all? (Take special note of the court's discussion of the "law of nature" and the obligation of parents.) What did Stanton mean when she referred to natural law*

---

* Wend. 65 (New York, 1840).

("the immutable laws of the beneficent Ruler of the Universe")? How important are the child's interests and needs? How important is judicial discretion in this case? How is the court's action like that of other courts in nonfamily law cases, discussed in Chapter 4 of the essay? Compare, for example, the reasoning and policy of Mercein *with* Taney's *opinion in the* Charles River Bridge *case.*

By Senator Paige. . . .

. . . The father's right to his child is not absolute and inalienable. In those American cases which uphold to the greatest extent the right of the father, it is conceded that it may be lost by his ill usage, immoral principles or habits, or by his inability to provide for his children. But the great principle which runs through nearly all the American and the earlier English cases, is that which is stated by *Thompson, Ch. J. in the matter of Waldron,* 13 *Johns.* 418, when speaking of the custody of the infant, in the case of the claim made by the father, to such custody, viz: "It is the benefit and welfare of the infant to which the attention of the court ought principally to be directed." As a necessary result of this principle, it follows that the custody of infant children must always be regulated by judicial discretion, exercised in reference to their best interests. Where an infant is brought up on habeas corpus, the court will not decide upon the right of guardianship, and if there is no improper restraint, the court will not deliver over the infant to the custody of another. If the infant is competent to form a judgment and declare his election, the court will after examination allow him to go where he pleases, otherwise will exercise its judgment for him; and this judgment is to be exercised (being in lieu of the judgment of the infant) with reference to the interest and welfare of the infant. *Matter of Wollstonecraft,* 4 *Johns, Ch. R.* 80; *Matter of McDowell's,* 8 *Johns.* 328; *Matter of Waldron,* 13 *Johns,* 418. The interest of the infant is deemed paramount to the claims of both parents. This is the predominant question which is to be considered by the court or tribunal before whom the infant is brought. The rights of the parents must in all cases yield to the interests and welfare of the infant. These principles were recognized and adjudged as a part of the law of this state, in the cases last referred to. And if the cases of *The People* v. *Chegaray,* 18 *Wen.* 640, and of *Nickerson,* 19 *Wen.* 16, conflict with these authorities, they are in my judgment, to the extent of such conflict, a departure from the law as established in the state. But even in the case of *Nickerson,* relied on by the relator, *Nelson, Ch. J.,* admits the general rule above stated. He says, "Nothing appears to show that the father is not a fit and proper person to have the care and education of his child, or that it would be for the interest of the child pecuniarily or otherwise, to commit its custody to the mother.'' It will be found that in a great variety of cases, courts have, in the exercise of a judicial discretion as to the custody of infant children, committed them to the custody of the mother, or of some third person notwithstanding, and in opposition to the claims of the father to such custody.

By the law of nature, the father has no paramount right to the custody of his child. By that law the wife and child are equal to the husband and father; but inferior and subject to their sovereign. The head of a family, in his character of husband and father, has no authority over his wife and children; but in his character of sovereign he has. On the establishment of civil societies, the power of the chief of a family as sovereign, passes to the chief or government of the nation. And the chief or magistrate of the nation not possessing the requisite knowledge necessary to a judicious discharge of the duties of guardianship and education of children, such portion of the sovereign power as relates to the discharge of their duties, is transferred to the parents, subject to such restrictions and limitations as the sovereign power of the nation think proper to prescribe. There is no parental authority independent of the supreme power of the state. But the former is derived altogether from the latter. In the civil state there is no inequality between the father and mother. Ordinarily a child, during infancy, is entirely under the discipline of its mother; and very frequently wives discharge the duty of education of their children better than the husbands. *De Felice, Lectures on Natural Rights—Lecture* 30. It seems then, that by the law of nature, the father has no paramount inalienable right to the custody of his child. And the civil or municipal law in setting bounds to his parental authority, and in entirely or partially depriving him of it in cases where the interests and welfare of his child require it, does not come in conflict with or subvert any of the principles of the natural law. The moment a child is born, it owes allegiance to the government of the country of its birth, and is entitled to the protection of that government. And such government is obligated by its duty of protection, to consult the welfare, comfort and interests of such child in regulating its custody during the period of its minority. By the civil code of *Austria*, where husband and wife are separated, and cannot agree which shall have the charge of the education of the children, the mother has the custody of *males* until they arrive at the full age of *four years*, and of *females* until the full age of *seven years*.

The law of England at the time of the American revolution and even until after the year 1800, in relation to the custody of infant children, was the same as I understand it to be in this state. In *Rex.* vs. *Smith* 2 *Strange* 982. (1735,) a boy of thirteen or sixteen years old, in the custody of his aunt, was brought up on a *habeas corpus* sued out by his father. It was held by the court, that they could only deliver the boy out of the custody of his aunt, and inform him he was at liberty to go where he pleased; and the boy chose to remain with his aunt. In the case of *Rex.* vs. *Delavel,* 3 *Burr.* 1434, decided in 1763, Lord Mansfield held "that in cases of writs of habeas corpus directed to bring up infants, the court is bound *ex debito justitiæ,* to set the infant free from an improper restraint; but they are not bound to deliver them over to anybody, nor to give them any privilege. This must be left to their discretion, according to the circumstances that shall appear before them." And in *Blisset's case, Loft's Rep.* 748, (1774,) Lord Mansfield says: "If the parties disagree, the court will do what shall appear best for the child." It was not until 1804, in the case of *The King* vs. *De Manneville, 5 East,* 221, that the decisions in England took a direction in favor of establishing the paramount right of the father to the custody of his infant, in cases where the interest and welfare of the infant called upon the court to commit it to the custody of the mother. . . . I refer to the speech of *Lord Lyndhurst* in the house of lords on the 30th July, 1838, on the bill in relation to the custody of infants, 44 *vol. Parl. Debates,* 3 *Series, p.* 771, he says: "As the law now stood, the father of a child born in lawful wedlock was entitled to the entire and absolute control and custody of that child, and to exclude from any share in that control and custody the mother of that child. The mother might be the most virtuous woman that ever lived, amiable in her manners, fond and attached to her children; the father, on the other hand, might be profligate in character, brutal in manner, living in adultery, and yet would have the right, under the existing law, to the custody of the children of his marriage, to the exclusion of even access to them of his wife, their mother." *Lord Denman,* the chief justice of the queen's bench, in a speech on the same subject in the house of lords, on the 18th July, 1839, 49 *vol. Parl. Debates, p.* 494, says: "In the case of *The King* vs. *Greenhill,* which had been decided in 1836, before himself and the other judges of the king's bench, he believed that there was not one judge who had not felt ashamed of the state of the law, and that it was such as to render it odious in the eyes of the country. The effect in that case was to enable the father to take his children from his young and blameless wife, and place them in the charge of a woman with whom he then cohabited."

If such was the state of the English law, Lord Denman might well say he was ashamed of it, and that it was odious in the eyes of the country.

This state has never been disgraced by laws so subversive of the welfare of infant children, of the rights of mothers, and of the morals of the people. In 1839, through the untiring xnd praiseworthy exertions of Serjeant *Talfourd*, the British parliament modified the relation to the custody of infants, by an act which authorizes the lord chancellor and master of the rolls, to make an order for the access of the mother to her infant children, and if the infant be within the age of seven years, to make an order that it be delivered to and remain in the custody of the mother until attaining such age.

Upon a review of all the authorities binding upon the courts of this state, I have come to the undoubting conclusion, that the right of the father to the custody of his child is not absolute, and that such custody is referrable to its interest and welfare, and is to be selected by the court in the exercise of a sound judicial discretion, irrespective of the claims of either parent. This conclusion I believe is warranted by the law of this state, as well as by the law of nature. A sense of parental duty ought ever to withhold a parent from pressing his or her claims to the custody of a child, whenever the true interests of such child forbid it; and whenever this parental obligation fails to influence the conduct of the parent, it is fortunate that the enlightened principles of our law authorize our courts to interpose in behalf of the child.

If then a judicial discretion is to be exercised in relation to the welfare, comfort and interest of the infant, as connected with her custody, was this discretion improperly exercised in this case by Judge Inglis?* The infant was under three years of age; was delicate and sickly, requiring peculiarly a mother's care and attention. The mother possessed every qualification to bestow this care and attention. Ought the judge to have delivered this infant, under such circumstances, over to the father, or to have allowed it to remain in the custody of the mother? I confess I have no hesitation in saying that I entirely concur in the position of the chancellor, viz: that all other things being equal, the mother is the most proper person to be entrusted with the custody of a child of this tender age. He says, "the law of nature has given to her an attachment for her infant offspring which no other relative will be likely to possess in an equal degree. And where no sufficient reasons exist for depriving her of the care and nurture of her child, it would not be a proper exercise of discretion in any court to violate the law of nature in this respect." I am, therefore, in favor of reversing the judgment of the supreme court.

* The trial court judge.

[Judgment of the Court]

On the question being put, *shall this judgment be reversed?* nineteen members of the court answered in the *affirmative*, and *three* in the *negative*. The members answering in the negative, were The President of the Senate, and Senators Root and Skinner.

The Child's Needs v. Parent's Right: Gilkeson v. Gilkeson*

The previous two cases involved custodiat rights of parents. Nickerson *acknowledged that under some circumstances a wife living apart from her husband would be entitled to the custody of their child;* Mercein *abandoned Nickerson's focus on marital behavior (in which the award of custody became entangled in the assessment of each parent's conformity with a prescribed marital role), examining instead the nature of motherhood, the child's needs, and the discretionary powers of the court. Custody of a child is also the subject of the* Gilkeson *case, but the parties to the case are not the two parents. This case pitted the weighty right of a father against the child's aunt, with whom the child lived. The mother and father of the child "by contract under seal transferred the custody of her to her uncle and aunt, who, by the same writing, agreed to adopt her as their same child."*

Several points are noteworthy. First, Pennsylvania did not have a general adoption statute. Second, prior to 1851, no appellate court had issued a ruling or decision on a case involving the legality of a private contract of adoption. Third, while an American court reviewing family-law cases could dismiss, and with relative ease, much of the English case law as inapplicable to American values and principles (as the court did in Mercein*), the parents' custodial right as opposed to the "right" of a "stranger" was another matter. Here, all American courts and legislatures agreed with the English principle of law that the parental right was superior, even in most cases by this date, to the "right" of the state.*

It should now be clear that the two previous cases concerned not only the "rights" of the wife and child but also the power of the court to balance rights—and thereby create new ones—of persons living in legally constituted families. This was accomplished by means of courts exercising discretion to, in effect, overlook (but not necessarily overrule) the "presumptive" superior right of the father-husband. Courts steadfastly insisted that they were not creating new rights adverse to those of the father-husband. Yet their discretion increasingly was governed by reference to the "well established principles" that the child's needs should be taken into consideration by the court before issuing a ruling, and that mothers were endowed by "natural law" with a special nurturing ability uniquely suited to the needs of young children and older females. The problem of state power (on what known authority could a court act to overlook a father's or parent's

---

* Wall. Phila. Rep. 194 (Allegheny County District Court, 1851).

superior claim) is at the heart of Gilkeson. What is remarkable about the case is
how quickly the court dispatches this question.

The use of a contract is also of interest in this case. The contract analogy in
marriage was the subject of Stanton's testimony. Stanton called on the legislature to
apply private-contract principles to matrimony. Opponents of a liberalized divorce
law acknowledged the applicability of contract to marriage, but they defined con-
tract in such a way as to make its enforcement by courts difficult, if not impossible.
If matrimonial union was a contract, it was a most bizarre one in the legal sense: a
spiritual seal that once entered into could not or should not be altered by courts.
Transferring custody of a child by contract raised a similar issue. What are the im-
plications for parental rights, and the rights of the child, if parents may "contract
out" of their obligations and legally endowed authority? What are the implications
for the power of the state? English courts routinely refused to enforce adoption con-
tracts that were subsequently contested and brought before them. To do so, they
urged, would belittle the "sacred obligations" of parents toward children. They
believed such a position was in the interest of all parents and their children. What
did they base this position on? Do you agree? What would have been the
result—with regard to the child's interests—in this case? Does the court address
this English concern in Gilkeson? *Based on the discussion in Chapter 4 of the*
essay, can you explain why American courts abandoned English law in such areas
as adoption contracts?

About six years ago, the father and mother of the complainant, by contract under seal transferred the custody of her to her uncle and aunt, who,
by the same writing, agreed to adopt her as their child. The contract,
though of such a character as could not be enforced against the child, was
performed by the uncle and aunt and sanctioned by the father, until the
child has grown up from nine to fifteen years of age. Her mother and her
uncle are now both dead; and her father has recently obtained possession
of her, and insists on retaining the custody of her, though she prefers remaining with her aunt.

This writ was made returnable in open Court, and the case was heard
before both the Judges.

Lowrie, J. Though both the Judges of this Court have heretofore,
severally, decided other cases in the same way in which we have determined to decide this, yet the earnestness with which this case has been
presented, furnishes a reason why we should give it more than ordinary
consideration.

The power entrusted to the judges of the Courts in this State without a
jury, under the writ of habeas corpus, is very great; and the fact that it has
been so long exercised by them, unaltered and unrestrained, and that it
has almost superseded and rendered obsolete the old forms of proceeding

by the writ *homine replegiando* and *de custodia rapta*, shows that as a remedial process it has been well administered and is highly approved.

We have never, in this State, held that the Courts are bound to a strict adherence to the old common law rules as to the right to the custody of children; and this writ, being used as a remedy for the improper interference with that right, we must treat it as a Pennsylvania remedy, governed by the principles of the common law of Pennsylvania, of which equitable principles constitute an illustrious part. And so, I am happy to say it has always been treated in this State.

We do not look upon the wife and the children as mere servants of the husband and father, and as therefore held subject to his will so long as he does not transcend the power of an absolute master. We do not hold that, though a husband drive a wife away from his house by his crimes or his cruelty, still he is entitled to take away from her the custody of her children. We do not look upon the parental authority as one to be exercised merely for the profit of the parent, though it may be so abused; but for the advantage of the child. And though we do still speak of the parental right of property in the services of the child, yet it is chiefly because the duty of service by the child is necessary to the proper exercise of parental authority for the good of the child; and the substantial reality of the old common law right has faded almost to fiction under the ameliorating influence of the modern common law.

In America we have never adopted the stringency of the old English principles, under which the father was held entitled to the custody of his children under all circumstances, however improper his own conduct, more especially when his claim was against the mother of the children. He was her lord and theirs, and her claims to the custody of her children seem to have been much less regarded as against his, than were those of third persons. So far has this principle been carried, especially by the common law judges, that Lord C. J. Denman was compelled to acknowledge in the House of Lords, that the judges and the profession were ashamed of the state of the law; and it is now altered by statute.

With us it has not been so. We have always, in disputes between parents, acted upon much the same principles as a Court of Chancery acts when a *petition* is presented for the custody of a child. And as the Chancellor, for the King, acts as parens patriæ in such cases, so our Courts have considered it their duty to act, looking to the good of the child so far as they can, and restraining the absoluteness of the paternal right, when exercised inconsistently with this end. The case of the *Commonwealth* vs. *Addicks,* 5 Binn. 520, fully illustrates this position, and it is, in fact, the leading American case on the subject, giving tone to all the decisions of other states.

I have taken some pains to examine our American decisions on this subject, and regret that I have not time to refer to them in this opinion.

But the result of them is that in a dispute between the parents for the custody of the children, the Court will exercise a sound discretion for the good of the child, and not gratify the whim, caprice, or malice of either parent. They regard the superior right of the father, as the head of the family; but they do not forget that the mother, too, has rights, and that the rights of both parents as against the children are a means, more of enabling them to perform their parental duties, than to enforce any claims for service on behalf of themselves.

If parents on separation have made an arrangement among themselves as to the custody of the children, they will be held to it, unless the good of the children requires an alteration. And I have failed to find a single case in the books wherein a child of the age of the one now in Court has been forced, by means of a habeas corpus, to submit to parental authority; and especially is it refused where that authority has been so long disclaimed and so solemnly transferred to another. And I do not believe that, in this State, it can be enforced under any form of writ.

In a somewhat similar case in Maine, the Court refused to enforce the father's right as against the mother. State *vs.* Smith, 6 Greenl. 462. See, also, the King *vs.* Delaval, 1 W. Bl. Rep. 410. In the King *vs.* Smith, 2 Stra. 982, a boy had long lived with his aunt, and the father claimed to have him back. He was fourteen years old, and the Court suffered him to go where he pleased, and he returned to his aunt. So in Massachusetts, a girl eleven and a half years old was bound by the *mother* by verbal arrangement, and was afterward claimed by her guardian; but the Court suffered her to elect. Commonwealth *vs.* Hammond, 10 Pick. 274; Commonwealth *vs.* Hamilton, 6 Mass. 273, is a very similar case, the child being fourteen years old.

But in New York we have a case almost exactly similar to this, in relation to two boys, eight and eleven years old, bound by their father by indentures, to which they were not parties. He afterwards claimed them on habeas corpus, alleging that the indentures were void; but the boys wished to remain with their master, and the Court permitted them to elect. In the matter of McDowles, 8 Johns. 328.

A parent may assign and relinquish his right to the services of his child—he may do it by contract; he may do it by refusing to support him, by turning him out of his house, by suffering him to go upon his own resources; he may give or sell him his time, and such arrangements will be enforced as against the parent, even though the child, being a minor, would not be bound by them, and though the public may still claim to enforce the duty of support. Holdship *vs.* Patterson, 7 Watts 549; 6 Conn. R. 550; 7 Cow. R. 92; 3 Pick. 202; 15 Mass. 275; 12 id. 378; 2 id. 115; 5 Wend. 206.

In this case the parental authority has been solemnly renounced for six years, and the child has grown to the age of fifteen years. She has been estranged from the customs and government of her father's house. She has formed new habits and views, and become accustomed to different associations and modes of living. And now the father, disregarding his own contract, and the wishes and comfort of his child, seeks to re-establish the parental authority. We should be glad he could effect it by the influence of parental kindness, and consistently with honesty. We dislike to see the parental and filial relation severed, and should love to see the broken bond re-united. But it cannot be well done by the enforcement of it as a legal right. The father himself broke the bond, and the law will not help him now to mend it. He emancipated his daughter by his own solemn act, and all restraint upon her by him is now improper. We must, therefore, discharge her from restraint, and leave her to elect with whom she will remain.

Legislative Intervention: An Act Concerning the Custody of Infants*

What is the purpose of this statute? Why would a statute even be necessary, given the developments in the case law already read?

Be it enacted *by the Senate and General Assembly of the State of New Jersey,* That when any husband and wife who shall live in a state of separation, without being divorced, and who shall have any minor child or children of the marriage, the chancellor, the supreme court of this state, or any justice of the said supreme court, upon the said child or children being brought before them upon habeas corpus, shall make an order for the access of the mother to her infant child or children at certain times and under such circumstances as they may direct; and if the said child or children be within the age of seven years shall make an order that the said child or children be referred to and remain in the custody of the mother

* Chapter CLXVII, *Laws of New Jersey,* March 20, 1860, p. 437 (session laws).

until said child or children shall attain such age, unless said mother shall be of such character and habits as to render her an improper guardian for said child or children.

And be it enacted, That this act shall take effect immediately.

Family as Contract: An Act to Provide for the Adoption of Children*

Compare the Massachusetts adoption law with the facts in the Gilkeson *case. What is the purpose of the legislation? The Massachusetts act is viewed by many as the first general American adoption statute (and also the first such statute in the modern world). Is this legislation radical? Is it concerned with child welfare? Is adoption, under the legislation, similar to a contract? In light of the discussion in Chapter 4 of the essay, what significance would you apply to this law? Can you relate this legislation to Stanton's statement about the marriage relationship? Can you relate it to the private-law developments discussed elsewhere in the essay? Stanton stated that "if you [the legislature] think it wise to legislate on human affections, pray make your laws with reference to what our natures are; let them harmonize in some measure with the immutable laws of God. A very wise father once remarked, that in the government of his children he forbid as few things as possible: a wise legislation would do the same." What did Stanton mean? Is this the same sentiment expressed by Walt Whitman, quoted in the essay: that man was becoming "a law, a series of laws, unto himself, surrounding and providing for, not only his own personal control, but all his relations to other individuals, and to the State"? Does this statement make sense to you in light of what courts and legislatures were doing in areas of custody and adoption? Are these questions of "law" and "legal process"? Are they questions of social values or politics?*

Any inhabitant of this Commonwealth may petition the judge of probate, in the county wherein he or she may reside, for leave to adopt a child not his or her own by birth.

If both or either of the parents of such child shall be living, they or the survivor of them, as the case may be, shall consent in writing to such adoption; if neither parent be living, such consent may be given by the legal guardian of such child; if there be no legal guardian, no father nor mother, the next of kin of such child within the State may give such con-

* Chapter 324, *Massachusetts Acts and Resolves*, May 24, 1851, p. 815 (session laws).

sent; and if there be no such next of kin, the judge of probate may appoint some discreet and suitable person to act in the proceedings as the next friend of such child, and give or withhold such consent.

If the child be of the age of fourteen years or upwards, the adoption shall not be made without his or her consent.

No petition by a person having a lawful wife shall be allowed unless such wife shall join therein, and no woman having a lawful husband shall be competent to present and prosecute such petition.

If, upon such petition, so presented and consented to as aforesaid, the judge of probate shall be satisfied of the identity and relations of the persons, and that the petitioner, or, in case of husband and wife, the petitioners, are of sufficient ability to bring up the child, and furnish suitable nurture and education, having reference to the degree and condition of its parents, and that it is fit and proper that such adoption should take effect, he shall make a decree setting forth the said facts, and ordering that, from and after the date of the decree, such child should be deemed and taken, to all legal intents and purposes, the child of the petitioner or petitioners.

A child so adopted, as aforesaid, shall be deemed, for the purposes of inheritance and succession by such child, custody of the person and right of obedience by such parent or parents by adoption, and all other legal consequences and incidents of the natural relation of parents and children, the same to all intents and purposes as if such child had been born in lawful wedlock of such parents or parent by adoption, saving only that such child shall not be deemed capable of taking property expressly limited to the heirs of the body or bodies of such petitioner or petitioners.

The natural parent or parents of such child shall be deprived, by such decree of adoption, of all legal rights whatsoever as respects such child; and such child shall be freed from all legal obligations of maintenance and obedience, as respects such natural parent or parents.

Any petitioner, or any child which is the subject of such a petition, by any next friend, may claim and prosecute an appeal to the supreme judicial court from such decree of the judge of probate, in like manner and with the like effect as such appeals may now be claimed and prosecuted in cases of wills, saving only that in no case shall any bond be required of, nor any costs awarded against, such child or its next friend so appealing.

Bibliographic Essay

In the last decade, several overviews of American legal history have appeared in print. The most important of these is Lawrence M. Friedman, *A History of American Law* (1973). Friedman's analysis blends private law, jurisprudence, politics, and economic growth into an insightful and always intelligent portrait of the role of law in American society. Also useful as a summary of the literature is Bernard Schwartz, *The Law in America: A History* (1974). A highly personal account is Grant Gilmore, *Ages of American Law* (1977). J. Willard Hurst is a towering figure in the field of legal history. He has published widely on the nineteenth and twentieth centuries. A valuable though difficult compendium of major institutional developments within the legal system is Hurst, *The Growth of American Law: The Law Makers* (1950). Hurst's more recent effort, *Law and the Social Order in the United States* (1977), contains the reflections of a major historian on the nature and meaning of law in America. Francis R. Aumann, *The Changing American Legal System: Some Selected Phases* (1940), is dated but fills important gaps in our knowledge of the nineteenth-century legal system. An important collection of essays covering a broad topical and chronological range is Lawrence M. Friedman and Harry N. Scheiber, *Law and the Constitutional Order* (1978). An excellent collection of documents on antebellum law and the legal system is Charles M. Haar (ed.), *The Golden Age of American Law* (1965). Haar's volume is distinguished for its lucid introductory essays and its reliance on narrative materials: speeches, contemporary journal articles, excerpts from books and literature, and nontechnical statements from cases. The major "casebook" in legal history, covering the colonial period to the present, is Stephen B. Presser and Jamil S. Zainaldin, *The Law and American History: Cases and Materials* (1980).

There are several valuable introductions to the common-law process and the nature of judicial decision making. The best short work, highly readable and widely

236

used in first-year law courses, is Edward Levi, *Introduction to Legal Reasoning* (1949). Also illuminating is Benjamin Cardozo, *The Nature of the Judicial Process* (1922). Karl N. Llewellyn was a witty and often trenchant critic of "formalism" in judicial reasoning. He wrote from the perspective of a legal realist highly skeptical about the importance of logic and reasoning in the decisions of courts. His two best-known works are *The Bramble Bush* (1930) and *The Common Law Tradition: Deciding Appeals* (1960). Daniel Boorstin's legal biography of Sir William Blackstone (an eighteenth-century English judge and treatise writer), *The Mysterious Science of the Law* (1973 ed.), as the title implies, is a foray not only into the mind of one man but also into the mentality of a profession.

While the focus of legal historical studies has begun to shift from constitutional law to private law at the state level, the history of the U.S. Supreme Court obviously remains of central importance. The essay has devoted relatively less attention to the Supreme Court because the subject is usually well covered in introductory American history texts. The standard histories of the Constitution and the Court are Alfred H. Kelly and Winfred A. Harbison, *The American Constitution: Its Origins and Development*, recently revised by Herman Belz (1982 ed.); Archibald Cox, *The Role of the Supreme Court in American Government* (1976); and Charles Warren, *The Supreme Court in United States History* (1947 ed.). W. W. Crosskey's classic *Politics and the Constitution* is a superb if highly controversial political analysis of the Supreme Court. G. Edward White, *The American Judicial Tradition* (1976), adopts a biographical approach. White's study also contains important chapters on two nineteenth-century state judges of great influence, Lemuel Shaw of Massachusetts and James Kent of New York. The tensions between democratic theory and the Supreme Court's judicial powers of review is aptly displayed in the profoundly critical work of Fred Rodell, *Nine Men: A Political History of the Supreme Court from 1790 to 1955* (1955). For the nineteenth-century Court, see the two important studies: R. Kent Newmyer, *The Supreme Court Under Marshall and Taney* (1968), and Carl B. Swisher, *History of the Supreme Court of the United States;* vol. 5: *The Taney Period 1836–64* (1974). An important recent overview of the period is Harold M. Hyman, *Equal Justice Under Law: Constitutional Development, 1835–1875* (1981).

Most of the "new" legal history produced in the last fifteen to twenty years concerns the nineteenth century. It was in the nineteenth century that the outlines of the modern American legal system came into existence. The law of tort, contract, property, corporations, and domestic relations underwent a transformation during this era in response to changes in American culture, politics, and social values. One of the earliest and still most influential studies is J. Willard Hurst, *Law and the Conditions of Freedom in the Nineteenth Century United States* (1956). Hurst's special talent is an ability to assimilate massive quantities of legal detail and then to link developments among branches of private law to a larger conception of politics and society. His overriding concern is "the public good" and the obstacles to rational planning inherent in the American legal and political systems. A superb assessment of Hurst's contribution and jurisprudence appears in Robert Gordon, "J. Willard Hurst and the Common Law Tradition in American Legal Historiography," *Law and Society Reviews,* 10 (1975) 9, a major contribution in its own right.

Another major contribution to our knowledge of nineteenth-century law is Morton J. Horwitz, *The Transformation of American Law: 1790–1860* (1976). Unlike Hurst, Horwitz emphasizes developments in the classical fields of common law—torts, property, and contracts, at the expense of other areas of private and public law. However, like Hurst, Horwitz never loses sight of the legal historian's broader mission: to explain the interrelationships between law, the exercise of power, and the political process. Much of Horwitz's work is staunchly revisionist and highly critical of the class bias that he believes pervades much of the courts' approach to deciding cases. An example of the kinds of criticism made of his work is Alan Simpson, "The Horwitz Thesis and the History of Contracts," *University of Chicago Law Review,* 46 (1979) 533. Another critique of the manipulative character that Horwitz and others attribute to antebellum decision making can be found in Harry N. Scheiber, "Instrumentalism and Property Rights: A Review of 'Styles of Judicial Reasoning' in the Nineteenth Century," *Wisconsin Law Review* 1 (1975).

A more traditional interpretative approach appears in the superb articles and books of William Nelson. Nelson's most influential publication yet is *The Americanization of the Common Law* (1976). While this study is limited to the law of one state for the sixty years after the Revolution (Massachusetts, 1760–1820), in many respects it is without parallel in the literature. Nelson undertook the extraordinary task of examining thousands of case files of appellate *and* trial courts. He discusses a wide variety of issues, such as the relationship between church and state, freedom of speech, the status of blacks, the law of master and servant, and domestic relations, in addition to the more traditional topics such as torts, contracts, and property law. One of the weak points of the book is the push to relate virtually all legal developments to a few thematic issues. However, this is also the strength of a book that deals so splendidly with such an awesome body of legal detail.

For many years, the literature of bench and bar (biography of famous judges and lawyers) embodied little more than a litany of the important decisions and arguments at the bar of distinguished legal personages. More recently, historians have begun to analyze the legal profession as a political component of society. The possibilities for wide-ranging interpretation, when such a perspective is adopted, are manifold. Morton Horwitz, for example, in "The Conservative Tradition in the Writing of American Legal History," *American Journal of Legal History,* 17 (1973) 275, argues that the historical scholarship of lawyers in the field of law operates as a "disguise" that shields from the public the degree to which judicial decision making is motivated by antidemocratic and class-based values. As the title suggests, John T. Noonan, Jr., *Persons and Masks of the Law* (1976), offers a fascinating exploration (through a series of minibiographies of Thomas Jefferson, George Wythe, Benjamin Cardozo, and others) of the psychology of neutrality and self-consciousness in judging. An equally wideranging and valuable analysis of lawyers and judges appears in Maxwell Bloomfield's elegantly written *American Lawyers in a Changing Society: 1776-1876* (1976). Through a series of deftly crafted miniature biographies of lawyers, Bloomfield demonstrates how the legal profession operates as a moderating influence between conservative and radical elements of society. Implicit in Bloomfield's study is the argument that the power and influence of the legal profession are as great outside as inside the courtroom. This theme is developed in a study by Gerald Gawalt, *The Promise of Power: The Emergence of the Legal Profession in Massachusetts, 1760-1840* (1979).

The biography of Lemuel Shaw by Leonard Levy, *The Law of the Commonwealth and Chief Justice Shaw* (1967), is a model study of a major state judge. Levy provides insight into the nature of judicial decision making in an important industrializing state, Massachusetts, and surveys as well the development of major branches of law. Perhaps most significant, Levy illuminates the crucial role of courts in moderating conflict among competing social groups, and in transforming law to meet the needs of the new republican society. Other biographies of significant judges include: John Horton, *James Kent: A Study in Conservatism, 1763-1847* (1939), Gerald Dunne, *Justice Joseph Story and the Rise of the Supreme Court* (1970), and John P. Reid, *Chief Justice: The Judicial World of Charles Doe (1967)*.

Closely related to the study of lawyers and the judiciary are the studies of legal education. Prior to the nineteenth century, the most common avenue into the legal profession—and the principal means for training aspiring lawyers—was apprenticeship. The method of educating lawyers, as with the nature of legal advocacy itself, is intimately related to the exercise of power by, and the autonomy of, the legal profession. Perhaps the greatest gap in our knowledge of law is the nature of nineteenth-century legal education. We have few reliable studies of the bar prior to the Civil War. Still, studies of the post-Civil War profession and the rise of the law school in the 1870s have important implications for antebellum practice. Jerold Auerbach, for example, in *Unequal Justice: Lawyers and Social Change in Modern America* (1976), suggests that the creation of the law school politicized the legal profession and ultimately destroyed the democratic foundation of professional practice. The adoption of the Socratic method of instruction at Harvard Law School, and its eventual spread, dehumanized the profession of law by blurring the distinctions between logic and morality, the representation of clients and the representation of interests. The time-worn practice of apprenticeship, Auerbach implies, ensured that the bar would remain open and contributed further to the formation of a community of lawyers that drew few distinctions between the public and private interest, or between the needs of rich or poor clients. The rise of the modern law school is well examined in Robert Stevens, "Two Cheers for 1870: The American Law School," *Perspectives in American History*, 5 (1970) 414.

Topical studies of nineteenth-century law abound. The relationship between law and politics is the subject of Richard E. Ellis's masterful work, *The Jeffersonian Crisis: Courts and Politics in the New Republic* (1971). Other studies that explore the political background of law include C.P. McGrath, *Yazoo: Law and Politics in the New Republic: Fletcher v. Peck* (1966); George Dargo, *Jefferson's Louisiana: Politics and the Clash of Legal Traditions* (1975); Mary Bonsteel Tachau, *Federal Courts in the Early Republic: Kentucky, 1789–1816* (1978); and D. O. Dewey, *Marshall Versus Jefferson: The Political Background of Marbury v. Madison* (1970).

The importance of law in the development of the American economy prior to the Civil War is generally undisputed. Some writers have examined the relationship between legal and economic change through analysis of major cases. Two model studies in this tradition are Stanley N. Kutler, *Privilege and Creative Destruction: The Charles River Bridge Case* (1971), and Francis N. Stites, *Private Interest and Public Gain: The Dartmouth College Case, 1819* (1972). Other studies focus on specific branches of law. Lawrence M. Friedman, for example, in *Contract Law in America* (1965), traces the impact of nineteenth-century free-market thought on traditional contract doctrine. J. Willard Hurst, already discussed, is as much an economic as a legal historian; see Harry N. Scheiber, "At the Borderland of Law and Economic History: The Contribution of J. Willard Hurst," *American Historical Review,* 75 (1970) 744.

Closely related to studies of law and economy is the "Commonwealth School" of scholarship produced in the 1950s. Largely unreplicated in recent years, these studies constitute the core of our knowledge about the critical role of state governments during the antebellum period in creating a legal environment conducive to economic growth. For a review of this literature, see Harry N. Scheiber, "Government and the Economy: Studies of the 'Commonwealth' Policy in Nineteenth-Century America," *Journal of Interdisciplinary History,* 3 (1972) 135. The two outstanding monographs are Oscar Handlin and Mary Handlin, *Commonwealth: A Study of the Role of Government in the American Economy: Massachusetts, 1774–1861* (1969 ed.), and Louis Hartz, *Economic Policy and Democratic Thought: Pennsylvania, 1776–1860* (1948). The study by the Handlins emphasizes state regulation of the manufacture and sale of commodities and the growing power of private business corporations; the Hartz study details the political implications of the "marriage" between the legislature and corporate enterprise, and the collapse of the partnership after 1835.

Perhaps the most important historian writing on law and the economy today is Harry N. Scheiber. In addition to the works cited above, he is also author of "Law and Political Institutions," *Encyclopedia of American Economic History,* vol. 2 (1980), pp. 487–508; "Regulation, Property Rights, and 'the Market': Law and the American Economy," *Journal of Economic History,* 41 (1981), 103–109; "Public Economic Policy and the American Legal System: Historical Perspectives," *Wisconsin Law Review* (1980) 1159–1189; *Ohio Canal Era: A Case Study of Government and the Economy, 1820–1861* (1969); "The Road to Munn: Eminent Domain and the Concept of Public Purpose in State Courts," *Perspectives in American History*, 5 (1971) 327; and "Property Law, Expropriation, and Resource Allocation by Government: The United States, 1789–1910," *Journal of Economic History*, 33 (1973) 232.

For other works on aspects of law and the economy that are of general importance, see Gerald Nash, "State and Local Governments," *Encyclopedia of American Economic History*, vol. 2 (1980), pp. 509–523; Stephen Salsbury, *The State, the Investor, and the Railroad: The Boston and Albany, 1825–1867* (1967); Bray Hammond's classic, and still indispensable work, *Banks and Politics in America from the Revolution to the Civil War* (1957); Edward C. Kirkland, *Men, Cities and Transportation: A Study in New England History, 1820–1900* (1948); Tony Freyer, *Forums of Order: The Federal Courts and Business in American History* (1979). Morton Keller's sweeping and highly original interpretation of late nineteenth-century law, society, and public order, *Affairs of State: Public Life in Late Nineteenth Century America* (1977), traces the subsequent development of many of the issues discussed in the essay.

The classic study of the legal status of the slave appears in Kenneth Stampp, *The Peculiar Institution* (1956). Since the publication of Stampp's book, numerous historians, legal and otherwise, have reexamined the institution of slavery, law, and political power. A reassessment of slavery law from a Marxist perspective is Eugene Genovese, *Roll, Jordan, Roll* (1974), pp. 99–120. The sophistication of recent study is also evident in Mark Tushnet's controversial *The American Law of Slavery, 1810–1860* (1981). Don Fehrenbacher, *The Dred Scott Case* (1978), sheds much light on the evolution of the law of slavery in the three decades before the Civil War. Other studies of aspects of slavery and the law are: Paul Finkelman, *An Imperfect Union* (1981); Robert Cover, *Justice Accused: Anti-Slavery and the Judicial Process* (1975); William Wiecek, *The Sources of Antislavery Constitutionalism in America, 1760–1848* (1977); and David Brion Davis, *The Problem of Slavery in Western Culture* (1966).

In many ways, criminal law has changed little in the last two hundred years. The reconceptualization of law that occurred in such areas as contract and property in the nineteenth century is much less evident in the law of crimes. But the movement to abolish capital punishment succeeded in some states, and the procedural protections for defendants in criminal trials were strengthened. A grand attempt at sketching an overview of criminal justice in American history is Lawrence M. Friedman, "Notes Toward a History of American Justice," *Buffalo Law Review*, 24 (1974) 111. David J. Rothman, *The Discovery of the Asylum: Social Order and Disorder in the New Republic* (1971), links the growth of the penitentiary during the antebellum era to conservative fears of democratization. Patterns in criminal prosecution have been studied by William Nelson, *The Americanization of the Common Law*, cited above. Nelson sampled the criminal case files of all the major counties in Massachusetts from the decade before the Revolution through 1820.

Foremost among his numerous findings is a decline in prosecution for crimes of "sin" (predominantly "moral" crimes) during this period and a commensurate rise in prosecution for crimes against property. Nelson concludes that this shift in prosecution reflects a fundamental transition in community values, from a concern with protecting moral values to a concern with protecting private property. Michael Hindus, *Prison and Plantation* (1980), provides a valuable comparative study of crime and prosecution by investigating two states, Massachusetts and South Carolina. Hindus's study is especially valuable for indicating how criminal law and prosecution enforce the dominant values of a social system. Hindus's findings suggest that law *must* function as an ideological appendage of society, and that American law may yet vary radically from state to state, or from region to region.

Perhaps the most difficult of legal-historical subjects is jurisprudence. The leading student of the "life of the mind," both in American history and in legal history, remains Perry Miller. In *The Life of the Mind in America: From the Revolution to the Civil War* (1965), Miller links the philosophy of law with antebellum intellectual currents. However, his work has been criticized as reflecting mainly the ideas and ideals of a few distinguished legal commentators who wrote and spoke publicly about law. Also important is Arthur Sutherland, *The Law at Harvard: A History of Ideas and Men, 1817–1967* (1967). The reflections of Grant Gilmore, a modern commentator and philosopher of sorts, appear in the early chapters of *Ages of American Law,* cited above.

Index

243

About the Author

JAMIL S. ZAINALDIN received his B.A. and M.A. from the University of Virginia, and in 1976 his Ph.D. from the University of Chicago. From 1973 to 1975 he held a Russell Sage Foundation law and social science research residency. In 1978 he received a grant from the National Endowment for the Humanities, the result of which is *Law in Antebellum Society*. He is the author of articles in American history and law, and coauthor, with Stephen B. Presser, of *Law and American History: Cases and Materials* (1980). He has taught at Northwestern University and Case Western Reserve University. He is currently assistant executive director of the American Historical Association and adjunct professor of law at Georgetown University Law Center.

A Note on the Type

The text of this book was set in a computer version of Times Roman, designed by Stanley Morison for *The Times* (London) and first introduced by that newspaper in 1932.

Among typographers and designers of the twentieth century, Stanley Morison has been a strong forming influence as typographical adviser to the English Monotype Corporation, as a director of two distinguished English publishing houses, and as a writer of sensibility, erudition, and keen practical sense.

Typography by Barbara Sturman. Cover design by Maria Epes. Printed and bound by Banta Company, Menasha, Wisconsin.

BORZOI BOOKS
IN LAW AND AMERICAN SOCIETY

Law and American History

EARLY AMERICAN LAW AND SOCIETY
Stephen Botein, *Michigan State University*

This volume consists of an essay dealing with the nature of law and early American socioeconomic development from the first settlements to 1776. The author shows how many legal traditions sprang both from English experience and from the influence of the New World. He explores the development of transatlantic legal structures in order to show how they helped rationalize intercolonial affairs. Mr. Botein also emphasizes the relationship between law and religion. The volume includes a pertinent group of documents for classroom discussion, and a bibliographic essay.

LAW IN THE NEW REPUBLIC: *Private Law and the Public Estate*
George Dargo, *Brookline, Massachusetts*

Though the American Revolution had an immediate and abiding impact on American public law (e.g., the formation of the federal and state constitutions), its effect on private law (e.g., the law of contracts, tort law) was less direct but of equal importance. Through essay and documents, Mr. Dargo examines post-Revolutionary public and private reform impulses and finds a shifting emphasis from public to private law which he terms "privatization." To further illustrate the tension between public and private law, the author develops a case study (the Batture land controversy in New Orleans) in early nineteenth century legal, economic, and political history. The volume includes a wide selection of documents and a bibliographic essay.

LAW IN ANTEBELLUM SOCIETY: *Legal Change and Economic Expansion*
Jamil Zainaldin, *Washington, D.C.*

This book examines legal change and economic expansion in the first half of the nineteenth century, integrating major themes in the development of law with key historical themes. Through a series of topical essays and the use of primary source materials, it describes how political, social, and economic interests and values influence law making. The book's focus is on legislation and the common law.

LAW AND THE NATION, 1865–1912
Jonathan Lurie, *Rutgers University*

Using the Fourteenth Amendment as the starting point for his essay, Mr. Lurie examines the ramifications of this landmark constitutional provision on the economic and social development of America in the years following the Civil War. He also explores important late nineteenth-century developments in legal education, and concludes his narrative with some insights on law and social change in the first decade of the twentieth century. The volume is highlighted by a documents section containing statutes, judicial opinions, and legal briefs, with appropriate questions for classroom discussion. Mr. Lurie's bibliographic essay provides information to stimulate further investigation of this period.

ORDERED LIBERTY: *Legal Reform in the Twentieth Century*
Gerald L. Fetner, *University of Chicago*

In an interpretive essay, the author examines the relationship between several major twentieth-century reform movements (e.g., Progressivism, New Deal, and the Great Society) and the law. He shows how policy makers turned increasingly to the legal community for assistance in accommodating economic and social conflict, and how the legal profession responded by formulating statutes, administrative agencies, and private arrangements. Mr. Fetner also discusses how the organization and character of the legal profession were affected by these social changes. Excerpts from relevant documents illustrate issues discussed in the essay. A bibliographic essay is included.

Law and Philosophy

DISCRIMINATION AND REVERSE DISCRIMINATION
Kent Greenawalt, *Columbia Law School*

Using discrimination and reverse discrimination as a model, Mr. Greenawalt examines the relationship between law and ethics. He finds that the proper role of law cannot be limited to grand theory concerning individual liberty and social restraint, but must address what law can effectively discover and accomplish. Such concepts as distributive and compensatory justice and utility are examined in the context of preferential treatment for blacks and other minorities. The analysis draws heavily on the Supreme Court's Bakke decision. The essay is followed by related documents, primarily judicial opinions, with notes and questions, and a bibliography.

THE LEGAL ENFORCEMENT OF MORALITY
Thomas Grey, *Stanford Law School*

This book deals with the traditional issue of whether morality can be legislated and enforced. It consists of an introductory essay and legal texts on three issues: the enforcement of sexual morality, the treatment of human remains, and the duties of potential rescuers. The author shows how philosophical problems differ from classroom hypotheticals when they are confronted in a legal setting. He illustrates this point using material from statutes, regulations, judicial opinions, and law review commentaries. Mr. Grey reviews the celebrated Hart-Devlin debate over the legitimacy of prohibiting homosexual acts. He places the challenging problem of how to treat dead bodies, arising out of developments in the technology of organ transplantation, in the context of the debate over morals enforcement, and discusses the Good Samaritan as an issue concerning the propriety of the legal enforcement of moral duties.

LEGAL REASONING
Martin Golding, *Duke University*

This volume is a blend of text and readings. The author explores the many sides to legal reasoning—as a study in judicial psychology and, in a more narrow sense, as an inquiry into the "logic" of judicial decision making. He shows how judges justify their rulings, and gives examples of the kinds of arguments they use. He challenges the notion that judicial reasoning is rationalization; instead, he argues that judges are guided by a deep concern for consistency and by a strong need to have their decisions stand as a measure for the future conduct of individuals. *(Forthcoming in 1984)*

Law and American Literature

LAW AND AMERICAN LITERATURE
A one-volume collection of the following three essays:

Law as Form and Theme in American Letters
Carl S. Smith, *Northwestern University*

The author explores the interrelationships between law aned literature generally and between American law and American literature in particular. He explores first the literary qualities of legal writing and then the attitudes of major American writers toward the law. Throughout, he studies the links between the legal and literary imaginations. He finds that legal writing has many literary qualities that are essential to its function, and he points out that American writers have long been wary of the power of the law and its special language, speaking out as a compensating voice for the ideal of justice.

Innocent Criminal or Criminal Innocence: The Trial in American Fiction
John McWilliams, *Middlebury College*

Mr. McWilliams explores how law functions as a standard for conduct in a number of major works of American literature, including Cooper's *The Pioneers,* Melville's *Billy Budd,* Dreiser's *An American Tragedy,* and Wright's *Native Son.* Each of these books ends in a criminal trial, in which the reader is asked to choose between his emotional sympathy for the victim and his rational understanding of society's need for criminal sanctions. The author compares these books with James Gould Cozzens' *The Just and the Unjust,* a study of a small town legal system, in which the people's sense of justice contravenes traditional authority.

Law and Lawyers in American Popular Culture
Maxwell Bloomfield, *Catholic University of America*

Melding law, literature, and the American historical experience into a single essay, Mr. Bloomfield discusses popular images of the lawyer. The author shows how contemporary values and attitudes toward the law are reflected in fiction. He concentrates on two historical periods: antebellum America and the Progressive era. He examines fictional works which were not always literary classics, but which exposed particular legal mores. An example of such a book is Winston Churchill's *A Far Country* (1915), a story of a successful corporation lawyer who abandons his practice to dedicate his life to what he believes are more socially desirable objectives.